Great Bales of Fire

More Tales of a Country Fireman

MALCOLM CASTLE

First published in Great Britain in 2013 by Orion Books
An imprint of the Orion Publishing Group Ltd
Orion House, 5 Upper St Martin's Lane,
London, WC2H 9EA
An Hachette Livre Company

1 3 5 7 9 10 8 6 4 2

A CIP catalogue record for this book
is available from the British Library.

ISBN-13   978 1 4091 3439 8

Typeset by Input Data Services Ltd, Bridgwater Somerset

Printed and bound by CPI Group (UK) Ltd, Croydon, CR0 4YY

The Orion Publishing Group's policy is to use papers
that are natural, renewable and recyclable products and
made from wood grown in sustainable forests. The logging
and manufacturing processes are expected to conform to
the environmental regulations of the country of origin.

www.orionbooks.co.uk

*Thanks to whoever came up with the phrase,
'If you're gonna be a bear, be a grizzly!'*

1

'**Y**ou've missed a bit, Jockey.'

I had my head under the driver's side of the fire engine and I was trying to twist myself around so I could clean the last of the mud and horse manure off the wheel arch.

'Where? I swear you could eat your blinkin' dinner off this engine already. You find me one thing I've missed and I'll give you twenty pence,' I shouted up at my old friend Caddie, who was looming over me the way he almost always did. Mike Cadwallader was a quiet, capable man in his late forties with a mop of wild greying hair and a tough, much-broken nose. It hadn't been easy getting to know him when I'd joined the Fire Brigade four years earlier. Earning his grudging respect had been one of the hardest things I'd ever done. It was also one of the best. He'd long since become a father figure to me, as well as a friend. I didn't even mind that to him, I'd always be the new boy on the watch – the jockey.

'Right there. There's a bloomin' great thumb print on the door panel,' Caddie said, licking his thumb and planting it just below the shiny silver handle. 'You owe me twenty pence, Jockey. But the bar's open upstairs – you can buy me a pint instead.'

I considered throwing a wet sponge at the back of Caddie's head as he left the appliance room but thought better of it. Instead I finished off the wheel arch and wiped away his big fat thumb print. I emptied my water bucket, cleaned it out and lined it up with the rest of the cleaning kit in the boot-wash next door. Then I came back and gazed at the two fire engines. Both of them were loaded up with different types of kit and technically speaking the first was called the water tender and the second was the water-tender ladder. To most people, though, they were fire engines. I walked round them and couldn't stop myself from smiling. I was a fireman. I was being paid to live out every boy's fantasy. And that night I was in an even better mood than normal. Because three hours ago I'd been given some terrific news.

Our Station Officer, John, had called me over shortly before we'd begun our evening's drills on the parade ground.

'You all right? You enjoying your job, Windsor?' he'd asked me. Windsor was the nickname the watch had given me when they'd found out my surname was Castle.

'Yes, sir, I love it,' I'd said, nervous all of a sudden. John was a gruff, fierce-looking man of my dad's age. He didn't exactly go in for pep talks or heart-to-heart chats. No one did in the Fire Brigade. I don't think anyone had asked me if I was all right before. You could probably turn up for work with the bubonic plague and no one would say a word. The basic routine was to get on with things and keep your mouth shut. Feelings were for girls. Firemen didn't need them. So what was all this about? The whole country was on strike in the early eighties. People were losing their jobs left right and centre over at Rolls-Royce and everywhere else in Shropshire. Was I being sacked as well? I could hear a horrible ringing in my ears. I'd never felt as sick.

John didn't rush to put me out of my misery. He looked right at me for what felt like for ever. 'You're young,' he said at last, in his low, slow south-Shropshire drawl. I waited in front of him in silence. I didn't know what my age could have to do with anything. I wasn't sure if he was stating a fact or asking a question. Either way I kept my mouth shut and waited for the boss to continue. 'I want you to keep this under your hat for now, but an opportunity is coming up. You might be interested,' John said at last. He'd been given the nod about a vacancy on a driver training course. The courses were normally filled every November for the following year. When November came and went without me being allocated a place, I'd resigned myself to another year in the back of the wagons.

'It will be two weeks of full-time training. It's tough and there's no guarantee you'll get offered the place. Do you want me to put your name on the list?' John asked. Did I want my name on the list? Did I breathe air? Did bears sort themselves out in the woods? I'd just turned twenty-two. I was being offered the chance to drive a fire engine. I'd never wanted anything that badly in my entire life.

After a final check for sticky fingerprints I clicked out the lights and plunged the appliance room into darkness. It was just after ten o'clock on a fresh, dry night in late June. I wanted to run up to the phone box on the top floor to tell my parents and my girlfriend about the driver training. But the boss wanted me to keep quiet. That was going to be murder.

Up in the mess room a typical night shift was well under way. The station bar had long since filled up with noise and a whole lot of cigarette smoke. Over in the corner by the dartboard John was lighting one cigarette from the stub of another. Beside him by the pool table his deputy, our Sub-O, Joe was drawing on his pipe. As well as smoking almost everyone in the room had a pint in their hand. The exceptions were George and Howard. They were two of the real old-timers on the watch who had both been firemen for longer than I'd been alive. They were already on the whisky.

'I took the liberty of ordering myself that drink, jockey. It's been chalked up on your tab,' Caddie called out from the bar in the corner. He held up his pint as he spoke. He could barely have got upstairs more than a few minutes ahead of me but he'd already sunk almost all of it.

'Here's a pint for you as well, son. If you managed to get all that muck off the engine wheels then you deserve it,' said Pete from behind the bar as I approached. Pete was a lean, sharp-faced, sharp-eyed whippet of a man who ran the bar and managed the money for all our food. To our left my other best pals on the watch, Charlie and Woody, were coming out of the station kitchen. They were closer to my age than anyone else on the watch, and they liked a joke almost as much as I did. We always had a great fireman's dinner on night shifts. That night's feast had been liver and bacon, creamy mash, fried onions and boiled veg. All of it cooked that night by a fierce, burly fireman called Ben, who was ex-army, had armfuls of tattoos, a huge handlebar moustache and ran a plumbing company on his days off. He was probably the best, and least likely, master chef you would ever expect to meet.

'Here's to a quiet night. I really don't want a call-out. I'm cream crackered and I could use a good night's kip,' I said as I settled on a bar stool alongside Caddie and tried to grab the *Daily Mirror* from in front of him.

'If we're quiet then I'll be needing that paper for the cross-word, laddie, so hands off. And I don't know why you'd be needing sleep at your age. I could go days without sleep when I was a youngster. Your new lady friend tiring you out, is she?'

Was it my imagination or was everyone suddenly paying attention? I couldn't stop myself from smiling. Alice and I had been going out for about a month; she was a student at Nottingham University. She had perfect skin, soft, sexy brown eyes, long, chestnut hair and a figure that could – and probably did – stop traffic. She'd popped by to see me in the station a few times and the entire watch fancied her. I knew I'd earned a lot of useful brownie points for being the one to take her home.

'She's visiting friends over in Stafford for the rest of the week, more's the pity. But I'll be seeing her next weekend when we finish our day shifts.'

'You'll be wanting to keep your strength up then, son,' said

Pete, lining me up a second pint. 'That'll be thirty-two pence when you're ready.'

We started talking about anything and nothing for a while. Woody and Charlie joined us at the bar and jokily accused Pete of putting pesetas in everyone's change. Then Arfer turned up. He was a spare-looking, wolf-like cockney in his forties with greased-back hair and a tough smoker's face who had become another great pal of mine. He piled in and accused Pete of watering down the beer, selling out-of-date crisps and fiddling the books. Pete fought back by taking the mickey out of one of the drives Arfer had done on our last set of day shifts. 'I thought you were going to take off when you hit that mini-roundabout. I swear all four wheels left the road. We could have been the first firemen in space.'

'Backin' cheek. That roundabout was only painted on last time I went round it. No one told me they'd concreted it over and built it up into some kind of backin' mountain. At least I kept us on the road, though. There's no driving down the pavements knocking off pub signs when I'm behind the wheel.'

Charlie let out a few choice swear words. 'I've said it a million times. Going on the pavement was the only way I could get us through the traffic. Anyway, it's the worst pub in Shrewsbury, so it doesn't deserve a fancy sign. Their pints cost more than yours, Pete. Their bitter is even worse.'

Pete shrugged off the latest attacks. 'You reckon getting on the pavement was the only way to get through the gap in the traffic?' he asked. 'I could have got a bus through that gap.'

'Well, I could've got a bus through that gap sideways,' boasted Arfer.

The insults carried on flying for a while and the conversation moved back to the state of Pete's bar and the quality of his beer. I joined in but I was distracted. I wanted to drag the conversation back to driving fire engines. That had become my new favourite subject.

'You've gone quiet, jockey. Dreaming of the lovely Alice?' Caddie asked.

'A little bit,' I admitted, 'but I'm also thinking about that old guy Arfer yelled at the other week.' It turned out to be the perfect bait.

'He had it backin' coming!' Arfer protested.

'What, yelling: "I hope it's not your backin' house that's on fire!" out of the window because some poor old codger can't get his car out of the way quick enough for you?' Charlie asked. 'You nearly made an old man cry. The poor sod was doing his best.'

'Well, he should have been doing better. If you can't get your car over to the side of the road without stalling half a dozen times then you shouldn't be driving in the first backin' place.'

The whole group laughed and Caddie slapped Arfer on the back so hard he almost came off his stool. And Arfer's fightback continued. 'Anyway, it's a backin' sight better to yell at some crap driver than to flatten his car altogether,' he said. 'Remember that time George killed the Mini?'

I didn't, to be honest. But the others were happy to fill me in. It seemed that the latches hadn't been shut on all the equipment before leaving the station. The light portable pump, which was neither light nor particularly portable, had swung out of its moorings as the engine left the station yard and turned on to the main road. It had fallen off the back of the engine altogether as George had accelerated up St Michael's Street. Worse still, it had landed on the roof of a brand-new Mini. The Mini had not come out of the situation particularly well – so thank God there'd not been anyone in it at the time. We dragged George over from the dartboard to try and explain why none of it had been his fault. As expected the jokes and insults kept on coming for the rest of the night.

'Thirsty work all this conversation, Jockey,' Caddie said as the mood calmed down and our little group finally broke up. He was holding up another empty glass. I gave Pete the nod and had it filled on my tab. I spotted something else as I passed the drink down the bar. Caddie caught my eye for a fraction of a second as he tackled his latest pint. Was that a hint of a twinkle? It was. I realised that I might have fooled all the others by dragging the conversation back to the way everyone drove the fire engines. But I'd not fooled old Caddie. I might have known he'd cotton on that something was up.

I headed into the dormitory shortly after midnight. That was a good three or four hours earlier than the old-timers and the hard-core canasta players back in the bar would probably manage. I'd long since grown out of my belief that I had to stay up later than everyone else to try and prove myself. Plus those jokes about needing extra rest now I had a new girl-friend gave me all the cover I needed for an early night. The main dorm was on the first floor, separated from the noise of the bar by a set of flimsy folding doors we opened out for the occasional party.

'Sorry, mate,' I mumbled after tripping over Ben's boots as I made my way to bed.

'Put 'em right back where they were,' he growled, more asleep than awake. I did so. Back then, if we had a shout in the middle of the night we had precisely fifty-three seconds to get dressed, down the pole and on to the fire engines. Nowadays we've got a bit longer because we have seat belts in the fire engines and we're supposed to use them. It means today's firefighters have to pull on their full kit before climbing aboard and strapping in. In my day we just leapt on board and got rigged and ready while we were thundering down the road. Either way, you still need to move fast when the call-out comes in. That's why everyone leaves their clothes and boots in a slightly different position, but in a position that's somehow imprinted on their own subconscious. We need to be able to reach for everything before our eyes have fully woken up, so we need to know exactly where it will be. I returned Ben's kit to its former state and continued to weave my way through the maze of twelve metal-framed beds. Sleep didn't come easily when I reached my own berth, and not just because only a thin piece of plywood separated it from the pool table next door where Joe and George had interrupted their game with a ridiculously long and loud discussion about the relative merits of Ron Greenwood and Bobby Robson as England manager. Less than four feet from them I lay awake and thought about the fire engine in the appliance room below us. I tried to imagine what it would feel like to be up front, behind the wheel and in charge of it. When I did finally nod off I was dead to the world. I might be wrong, but I bet I had the biggest, most stupid grin on my face all night. I'd never expected to drive one of our fire engines so soon. Even though John had only said there was a possibility I'd get a place on a course, I was convinced it was going to come up. This summer was going to be the best ever. That night I don't think there could have been a happier man in all of Shropshire.

It stayed all quiet on the western front that night. I was up brushing my teeth in the row of sinks near the lockers on the ground floor just before seven. We rarely showered on duty, not least because you don't want to be wet, and naked as the day you were born if there's an emergency call. Caddie had been up for twenty minutes or so and had already made a pot of tea so I got a stewed brew out of that and sat by an open window upstairs. Our morning papers had arrived. They were delivered by a surprisingly mouthy fourteen-year-old lad called Kevin who always stopped for a while to tell us some tall story about his latest get-rich-quick idea. The couple who ran the frozen-food store opposite us on the main road were also up early. Mr Thom was having a chat with Caddie after dropping off a box of broken biscuits he and his wife hadn't been able to sell. Kevin, the Thoms and a few others were all part of the tapestry that made fire station life feel less like a job and more like a bunch of mates or even a family. I looked at my watch. The others would all be up in twenty minutes or so. We'd be having our usual full English at around seven thirty – with the offer of toast and cereal for any lightweights. Ben was still on kitchen duty so I knew it would be a good spread. With him in charge we wouldn't have a repeat of the morning George threw his bacon against the mess-room wall, roared that it was as hard as shrapnel and told the fireman who'd cooked it to start all over again.

We didn't get a call-out over breakfast, or while we had the usual water fight in the kitchen doing the dishes before our early morning cleaners arrived. Babs and Maggie were hilarious. Babs was skinny as a rake, always smoking and loved making suggestive jokes. Maggie, who'd only joined a few months earlier, was twice Babs' size and about twice as much fun. 'How's the fireman's pole this morning?' was the first question she asked us every day. Every day she all but collapsed in a fit of giggles as we came up with increasingly lewd replies.

All told we had a good hour of backchat and banter with the girls as we got our other chores done, got in their way and drank a lot more tea. Shortly before nine the car park began to fill up as Blue Watch arrived to take over the station. We headed downstairs to get into our dress uniform, formal black trousers, pale blue shirts, black ties and epaulettes. Then we headed into the muster bay next to the appliance room. The two watches lined up facing each other. We stood at attention. The bosses said their stuff. Then it was over. 'Off-going watch – dismiss!' John barked.

I quick-changed into jeans and a T-shirt, shut my locker door on my dress uniform and ran over to my car on the edge of the parade ground. I drove a yellow-and-black Ford Cortina GXL, but I was hoping to have enough cash to upgrade pretty soon. Learning to drive a fire engine wasn't going to be my only challenge that year. I was going to defy the recession, follow everyone else's example and get what we called a spiv job – a second job to make some extra money in my time off. And I'd picked one that I had no qualifications for whatsoever.

2

My dad had set it all in motion at the start of the year. One of his fellow teachers was a builder on the side and despite the grim economy he had too much work to do all on his own.

'Does your lad know anything about building?' he'd asked.

'He's a bit handy, is Malcolm,' my dad had said.

So off I went.

'You ever done any slate repair work?' my new boss Paul Rogers asked me when I first met him. I didn't have a clue what he was on about.

'Yes I have,' I lied.

So off I went. I dashed into W H Smith's on Shrewsbury High Street and bought a copy of the *Reader's Digest Concise Repair Manual*. I read it like a maniac. A few days later it turned out that not only could I do slate repair work but I could actually do it pretty well.

'Mal, you ever pointed a wall?' Paul asked the following week. Of course I hadn't.

'Yeah, loads of them,' I said. Flick, flick, flick through my new manual, and I got the gist of it. Six parts sand to one part cement, mix in water and plasticiser, and Bob's your uncle.

'Mal, I need you to sort out the flashing on this roof. You've done it before, right?'

'Course I have.'

And so it went on. By the end of spring I was earning money hand over fist. The newspapers were full of doom and gloom but I was twenty-two. I was cocky enough to think I could branch out on my own. Paul had given me a weekend's work on his holiday cottage just over the Welsh border. Instead of paying me cash he gave me a load of his old building equipment. As he was giving up the building work to concentrate on his teaching career, I decided to put the kit to use and set up my own business. I'd put the word out with the men on the watch to see if they'd recommend me for anything. Between us we had fingers in a lot of useful pies. Charlie and Woody were painters and decorators in their time off. Arfer and George, his fellow cockney, ran a furniture removals business. We had plumbers, mechanics, electricians and furniture restorers among us. Even the Station Officer was a busy man. John had his own building firm and occasionally used to do some of his invoices, send out quotes and order any materials he needed from the station office on the ground floor. Like all the others he was always ready to shake his head disapprovingly and criticise when I told any building stories round the mess-room table. But once I'd been put straight I was regularly offered jobs helping one or other of them out. Everyone was always looking for extra help so I got a lot of experience fast. I got a lot of recommendations from satisfied customers as well.

On this particular day I was due at a house in Upton Magna to give a quote for building a greenhouse and repairing a garden wall that looked to be several miles long. As if that wasn't good enough, summer had arrived. I'd be working my usual two days, two nights, and four days off as a fireman. Then I'd be spending the rest of my time out in the open air getting a tan in some rich family's garden. There was only one way life could get better – if I got a definite spot on the driver training course. But would I?

John was the first person I saw when I clocked on for my next tour of duty at the fire station the following Tuesday. We were back on days and I was twenty minutes early as usual.

'Is there any news on the driving?' I asked quickly.

'Funny you should ask, jockey. I'm expecting to get a call from them later on in the morning. But don't get your hopes up too high, son. They give priority to the watches that are short of drivers – that means someone on Blue Watch and probably even White Watch will get it before you do. But we'll find out soon enough. Patience, Castle. It's a virtue, remember.'

It was also a blinkin' pain in the neck. I'd never been good at waiting for things to happen. I was always the one tearing off the corner of Christmas presents under the tree at midnight because I wanted to know what I was getting the next morning. I tried to think of other things as the rest of Red Watch ambled in and we got on with our day. We drank tea straight after parading and munched our way through a mountain of hot, buttery toast. Ten minutes later we hit the yard in our overalls and trainers for our usual morning's game of volleyball. We were doing well in a local league and the following week we had a game in a sports centre over in Sundorne. So we were even more psychotic and competitive than usual.

'Got ants in your pants?' Caddie said to me later on as we loitered waiting for the call to lunch. 'It's only ten seconds past the last time you looked at your watch, jockey. What you waiting for?'

I couldn't tell him I was trying to gauge exactly what John might have meant by 'later in the morning'. I couldn't say I was desperate to know exactly when he might be making the phone call.

'It's nothing,' I said unconvincingly. 'I'm just—'

To be honest I had no idea what I planned to say next. Fortunately, I didn't have to say anything at all, because at that exact moment we got our first emergency call of the week. The single word: 'Attention!' boomed out of the station's tannoy system. It was followed by the three warning tones that got us all ready to listen. Every one of us started moving quickly but quietly as the sounds played out. Every other noise was stilled. Whatever you were doing you stopped when those sounds came on. You had to be paying attention when the bare bones of the shout were read out. You needed to know what was ahead of you. Joe's voice from our control room was next on the PA system: 'Both appliances to fire in the open, on the Lyth road out of Stapleton, one mile past village.' That was all we needed to hear. The moment the last word had been uttered more than a dozen men started shouting where we were going and what we were going to, as if to make sure we were all clear what the message had said. We zipped down the pole, we slammed through the doors and we blasted into the appliance room from all directions.

Where we went next depended on where we were listed on the board each day. Each position on each fire engine has a number. Each number has a different, specific and important responsibility. Number one is the officer in charge and number two is the appliance driver, for example. That day the board had me down as number five. I was the general dogsbody on the first of our fire engines, the water tender. To my left was Woody at number three while Charlie was on my right as number four. Simon was driving and John was up front next to him as our Officer in charge. Caddie, Arfer and a couple of the others were in the second appliance that would be right on our tail for the journey out. We'd all got into position in a matter of seconds. The appliance-room doors were pulled up. We were ready for action.

Simon swung the big beast out of the station and took a hard right on to St Michael's Street. The camber was tough at that point; we all held on to the cab roof to stop us shifting off our slippery plastic seats. 'Bugger,' I heard Simon mutter as we approached the first tall, red-brick buildings on the outskirts of Shrewsbury. I didn't need to look round. We must have hit traffic already.

'I'm going to get us through this,' John yelled. It was our signal that the sirens and the lights were going on. You can't protect yourself from the ear-splitting two-tone nee-naw of the siren. But it does help to know when it's coming.

John clicked the siren off as we hit a nice clear patch of road going under the railway bridge and past Shrewsbury station. From my perch at the back I could see us shoot past Shrewsbury Castle and then approach the town library, which at one time had been the school that Charles Darwin attended. We were going at a cracking pace for a built-up area. Or at least we had been.

'Get out of the buggering way!' Simon swore as he slammed on the brakes. I looked to see what was going on. A delivery van had parked in a bus stop – and a bus seemed to have got stuck trying to edge on to the other side of the road and pull around it. Simon let out a near continuous stream of wildly imaginative swear words till the various drivers got their acts together and we could finally sweep by and head on through town.

The good news was that we didn't have that far to go. The village of Stapleton was less than six miles out to the south of Shrewsbury itself. The bad news for me was that we still had to go through a fair few windy country roads to get there. I would never admit it to the lads, but I was crippled by travel sickness – a bit of a disaster for a working fireman. That day I felt my usual wave of nausea wash over me as Simon pulled us roughly round the first of many sharp bends. Would I ever grow out of this? At least in these new Renault fire engines the back seats faced forward – not that it seemed to make much difference. Would it be any better if I was driving the engine rather than bouncing around on the middle seat at the back? I had to hope that it would, not least because I'd never live it down if the others found out how close I came to being sick in my helmet on almost every shout.

'Just breathe properly, look out to the distance and focus on the job,' I told myself, the way I always did. And for all the urgency of our departure this job did sound like it should be fun. It was a field fire. So as we weren't heading into a house, shop, factory or other building, Woody and Charlie didn't need to get kitted up in their breathing apparatus sets as we lurched through the countryside. I didn't need to get a tabard on or to man the BA board when we arrived. Instead we pulled on our plastic gloves and leggings and got ready for some fun in the great outdoors.

'That looks like the smoke. I'm guessing that's where we're headed,' Simon said as we approached Stapleton. He took us through the village and out to the other side. The fire itself was easy to find. A huge pile of straw bales were alight in the corner of a field. It was like the biggest and best bonfire night in the county – but at the wrong time of year and the wrong time of day. The flames were intense, darting a dozen or more feet into the air and throwing out sparks in all directions. A sizeable crowd was already gathered on the edge of the field and a good half-dozen cars were parked up on the roadside. As the officer in charge, John was first off the engine as soon as Simon had found us somewhere to park. A tall, angry-looking man with small, sharp eyes and a bald head as brown as a nut marched right up to him.

'This is my farm. It was a pack of kids. Stupid, idiot kids without a brain cell between them. They come over from the houses down the hill when they should be in school. They smoke and play their cassette tapes and leave crisp packets all over the shop. Today they decided that wasn't enough, the little weasels. God only knows why, but they thought it was a good idea to roll about ten bales of my best straw right down the field to that bottom corner. Then they decided to set them alight.'

'They're right up against one of the telegraph poles,' said

a younger man with an equally brown, well-weathered face. 'If you don't get the fire put out soon it'll come down. That's the electricity line the pole is carrying. If that goes down, the whole village will lose power. You need to do something straight away.'

All of us were off the engine and taking in the surroundings by then. The heat from the fire was intense, even from a distance. And it looked as if the telegraph pole wasn't the only hazard. The fire was right up against a hedgerow. This was already burning merrily on each side of the straw bales. There was dry vegetation all over the place. The flames looked set to spread in every direction.

'How long has the fire been burning?' John asked.

'About half an hour. I called you fifteen minutes ago when my wife saw it from the farmhouse windows. It'd probably been burning a while before that. The buggers who did it were nowhere to be seen. Cowardly, rat-faced little buggers. If I find out who they are, I swear I'll have 'em. And the police would thank me for it, I'll tell you that for free.'

John cut him short. He was looking worried. Telegraph poles are designed to last, but half an hour of intense fire was still going to be a problem. We looked up and followed the direction of the electricity cable. It passed right over the heads of the rent-a-crowd on the edge of the field.

'OK, this is what we're going to do.' As usual John came up with a decisive plan in the shortest possible time. 'First, I want all those people moved to the other side of the field. I don't want anyone within thirty yards of the power line – and if they don't want to move then tell them to look above their heads and grow themselves a brain. Castle and Woody, grab a drag hook each then get two hose-reels out to the fire. We'll hit it at full pressure till the flames are knocked right back. Then I want you to run in, drag as much of the straw as you can away from the edge of the fire. Get back in position then hit the whole thing with another burst of water. Then get in there and pull more of the bales apart. We'll keep going till it's under control. Got it?'

'Yes, sir!' I said. I didn't just get it, I loved it! Storming the fire with the hoses then doing a commando raid on it with drag hooks sounded the best fun I'd had in months. I was over the moon at the prospect. It would be a bit like being Rambo.

Woody and I got the kit we needed and lugged the hose-reels across the field while our audience was shepherded into a new position over to our left. Simon had got the pump ready so the water was set to flow.

'On the count of three!' commanded John.

When the word came, Woody and I leapt into action. We doused as much of the flames as possible, dropped the hose-reels then did our first commando raid. We ran headlong towards the fire, roaring like Royal Marines in the process. When we reached it, we slammed the hooks into the straw and pulled back hard. It wasn't easy. Straw's heavier than it looks, even when it's not been drenched in water. Then there was something else. By hacking into it and dragging the bales apart we were allowing precious oxygen to get to the rest of the fire. We had only the briefest window of opportunity before the flames burst up again even more furious than before. The fire was shockingly hot, even before the second wave of water hit. This would not be a good time to stumble.

'Hit it, now!' John gave the command again and Woody and I took aim with the hoses. Then it was back in with the drag hooks. We roared like lions every time we ran at the fire – and in the distance I could hear the crowd roar along in unison. They cheered every time the water hit the flames. They cheered every time we ran towards the bales. They cheered even louder as we attacked the straw with the hooks. What we were doing must have looked like a mix of boy's own, gung-ho bravery and utter stupidity. We were turning one single fire into a mass of mini-fireballs. And we were trying to extinguish each and every one of them. The longer we worked, the more smoke there was in the air and the harder it became to breathe. I was boiling hot, sweating, filthy, and physically exhausted by the time John yelled out for us to stop. But I could have carried on for hours. I loved this job!

We doused the remaining flashes of fire with water and turned our attention to the telegraph pole, dousing it with one more hit of water. Steam and smoke poured off it from top to bottom. It was heavily charred and black as night, but it looked to be in pretty good shape. The flames had barely eaten away more than the very outer layer. The electricity board would have to come and look at it properly. But for now Stapleton's power supply looked to be secure.

John had a chat with the farmer while Arfer, Charlie, Des and I set off to patrol the far side of the field. We were all carrying beaters, basic but effective tools that hadn't changed much in decades. They were like broom handles, around three foot long, with another three foot of rough-cut, flattened-out hose bolted on to the end. We used them to bash out flames and dying embers on heath fires as well as field fires. Out near Stapleton the trick was to make sure the hedgerow wasn't going to catch light again and to stamp out any lively-looking piles of ash. We were doing just that when a black vole shot out of a pile of straw. It ran right past us, straight towards the embers of the main fire. 'Blimey, he's got a death wish, that critter,' Charlie said. But the vole spotted the new danger almost immediately. He skidded to a halt, turned tail and zipped past us again, heading towards pastures safe and new.

'At least he's going in the right direction now. He won't end up toasted or roasted on the fire,' I said as we watched him disappear.

Charlie and Arfer both let out a loud guffaw of laughter. I practically kicked myself for mentioning the animal's lucky escape. For I had a horrible feeling I knew what was coming.

'Castle's good at being a hero when it comes to small animals,' Arfer said to Des with a huge smile on his face. 'Bet you never knew you had a mixture of James Herriot and Doctor backin' Doolittle working next to you on the watch.'

Des was one of the most recent recruits to Red Watch. He and another lad, Dodger, had joined almost a year ago, so they were still on probation. They were both wiry, tough local lads. The good news was that their arrival meant I was no longer the absolute new boy – though I'd long since realised that the jokers on my watch referred to newcomers as 'jockey' and treated them like six-year-olds for at least twenty years. The bad news was that Des and Dodger were a ready-made audience for any tales the others wanted to tell about my early days in the brigade. Every mistake I'd ever made and every stupid thing I'd ever done would be offered up for general amusement. And I'd walked right into this one.

'Tell Des what a hero you were last summer,' Charlie giggled.

'I don't know what you mean.'

'Don't try and get out of it. Tell him about your big, brave moment. The day you risked everything to save a life.'

'Who did you save?' asked Des with interest.

'It's not who, it's what!' Charlie exploded. 'The big man here went to a house fire out in Bayston Hill and he came running out the front door having saved – a hamster!'

'I didn't run out the front door,' I protested.

'You saved a hamster?' Des laughed.

'It nearly died! The poor little sod needed help! Someone had to save it.'

'So what happened?'

I decided that as the story was going to be told anyway I might as well get my side out there first. 'A tumble drier had caught alight. The woman had never emptied the fluff out of it. It was the middle of the morning, over on Lythwood Road, I was number three, Woody was number four. We had our sets on and went in there. It was acrid. There was a hell of a lot of smoke, you couldn't see the hand in front of your face at first. Anyway we got the job done. We put the fire out, got the electrics off and started to ventilate the property. Woody got the drier out the back door and into the garden to make sure it wouldn't cause any more problems and I went back inside to check we'd not missed anything and to start on the clean-up. That was when I spotted him.'

'Spotted who?'

'The hamster.'

'Hogan, the hamster, if memory serves. Windsor even asked his name.'

'I wanted to know his name! It was an excuse to talk to the housewife. She looked a bit like Debbie Harry. So, yeah, Hogan had been on top of the drier. Woody had carried the cage over to the other side of the room and put it on a worktop where he'd forgotten all about it. When I spotted him a bit later he was like no other hamster I'd ever seen. One of my mates at school had owned one years ago. All it ever seemed to do was sleep, suck water from its drinking thing or run around in its wheel. This one thought he was Michael Jackson. He was doing this crazy dance. And he was looking at me.'

'Looking at you?'

'I swear that he was. He had beady black eyes. They were locked on mine from the moment I got into the kitchen. It was like he was trying to tell me something. And he was doing a dance routine like he was in the video.'

'Hallucinating, you were. You should take more water with it, Windsor,' Arfer chipped in.

'It was real,' I protested. 'And I remembered a TV show I'd seen from years ago. It was about lizards in the deserts of Mexico. They'd hopped from one foot to another, lifting each one up for as long as they could to cool it before putting it back down on the hot sand and repeating the process with another one. That was what the hamster was doing.'

'Hogan the hamster,' Charlie added helpfully.

'Yes, Hogan the blinkin' hamster! Anyway, I got my gloves off and checked the bottom of his cage. It was made of metal and it was hot as heck. So no wonder the poor little sod was dancing. His feet had been burning up from underneath him. And he didn't have anywhere to go.'

'So what did you do?'

'I got an old ice-cream carton out of one of the kitchen cupboards. I put an inch of cold water in it. I needed a cloth to open the fiddly door to the thing's cage – it was still burning hot. Then I grabbed him, held him over the water in the ice-cream container, dipped his feet into it and held him there.'

We were still laughing as we returned to the main field and headed over towards John and the others. Thinking back, I was still pretty glad I'd looked after Hogan the hamster. If it had been a Tom and Jerry cartoon you'd have seen steam rise up from the pads of the little fellow's feet when he went into the water. As it was, I swear you really could have seen a happy hamster smile break out on his sooty face.

'So that's the kind of bravery you've got to live up to if you're going to survive on this watch,' Arfer told our newcomer. 'You need to join Windsor and talk to the backin' animals. That's how you get a commendation from the Chief Fire Officer.'

'Which seems to have got lost in the post, to be honest.'

I was unsuccessfully trying to think of some way to embarrass Arfer or Charlie when the farmer called the three of us over to his Land Rover. He'd got few cans of drink in there for us – and that turned out to be only the start. The locals were over the moon that we'd saved their electricity supply and were doing their best to show it. About six young mums trekked over from the houses on the edge of the village bringing trays of tea, coffee, biscuits and even booze. It was the start of the school holidays so there were loads of kids around and they were having a high old time. They loved having jobs to do. We were soon sending them off to the village to refill the teapots, collect family-sized bags of crisps and as many cans of Coke as they could carry. One lad even asked us all to sign his autograph book, like we were famous. The whole thing was great. The sun was shining and someone opened up their car doors so we could all listen to Radio One as we kicked back and enjoyed the hospitality. It was a bit like the Queen's jubilee all over again. It was as if we were having a giant street party in the middle of a straw field.

In a perfect world I reckon we could happily have stayed there all day. But after forty-five minutes and a few final patrols of the field it was clear that the fire was well and truly out.

'Right, lads. That's enough lazing around – there's work to be done back at the station,' John said after downing his last drink.

A variety of mugs and glasses had been brought out by the neighbours and it took a while to make sure they'd all been returned to their rightful owners. The cheekiest of us crammed a few more crisps and biscuits into our mouths, then we waved everyone goodbye and climbed back on board the fire trucks. It was almost exactly half past twelve. We'd had plenty of excitement and fresh air. We'd played at being commandos and chatted to loads of pretty women. Oh, and we were going to be back at the station bang on time for lunch. Days didn't get much better than that.

If we weren't out on a shout then lunch was served in the mess room every weekday at one o'clock on the nose. While we took turns cooking the evening meal on night shifts, we had two wonderful old ladies who came in every morning to cook the food when we were on days. Mabel and Betty had long since become Shrewsbury institutions. They were around twenty years older than Babs and Maggie – and as I was about to discover yet again, they gave every impression of ruling the roost.

Mabel locked eyes with me the moment I turned the corner at the top of the station stairs and walked through the mess room to the serving hatch. She was a stout, grey-haired lady in her late sixties. She was wearing a crisp green-and-white apron, standing by the kitchen door, hands on her hips, looking up at me through fierce blue eyes. 'Young man, I want a word with you,' she began. I stepped towards her, standing aside from all the others and feeling like a ten-year-old. Mabel had a big thing about us all washing our hands before we came up for lunch. She almost always asked if we'd remembered, and we almost always lied and said we had. Today, as usual, I hadn't. Did she know? Was I going to be made an example of yet again by someone old enough to be my gran?

'A little birdie has told us you're going to be the next one of my boys to drive the fire engine,' Mabel pronounced. 'About time too, if you ask me. Though no one does ever ask me, more's the pity.'

I took a couple of steps back. Part of me was pleased I wasn't in trouble. No one on the watch ever wanted to be on the wrong end of Mabel's temper. But most of me was in shock. 'How do you know about the driving? It's supposed to be a secret. And I've not been given a course for certain. I'm still waiting to find out,' I mumbled.

A big smile broke over Mabel's face and she clasped her hands together in delight. 'You should know by now that there are no secrets in this station. At least, no secrets from me and Betty. If something is happening on any of the watches then we expect to be told at the earliest possible opportunity.'

I saw her eyes flick towards John. Had he told her the news? Or had she found out through some other jungle drum? I smiled suddenly. If she'd got the news from elsewhere then John was in trouble, not me. I loved the fact that dozens of tough firemen turned to mush in front of our two elderly cooks. They could tell us to take our hands out of our pockets, to watch our language, to stand up straight instead of slouching – whatever they liked. 'Stop smirking, young man, and tell me if it's true,' Mabel barked, bringing me back to reality with a bump. I had to prevent myself clicking to attention as I focused on her again.

'It's true that a slot's opened up for a training course. I'm definitely hoping to be offered it. I'd give anything to drive the fire engine. I'm the only qualified fireman on Red Watch who's not a driver. I really want to do it.'

Mabel pursed her lips and looked me up and down, the way she often did. 'How old are you now, son, twelve?' she asked, a glint of humour in her pale, heavily lidded eyes. 'You know, I still remember the day you first arrived at this station. You looked like a string bean inside your uniform. You reminded me of a scared rabbit trapped in the headlights, trying to make sense of it all. But what is it, four or so years on, and you're still here, aren't you, lad? So happen you really are ready for this next big adventure of yours. Just don't go letting it get to your head.'

'You won't be getting bigger portions or extra seconds because you're a driver,' Betty called out from the other side of the serving hatch, proving that whatever other aches and pains she complained about, her hearing was as good as ever.

'And if you leave this kitchen a mess after a night shift you'll still feel the back of my hand, driver or no driver,' Mabel followed up before turning on her heels and disappearing into the kitchen. Not entirely sure whether or not I had been dismissed, I grabbed my plate and sloped off towards my seat at the table.

'So, you're going to be a driver. That's what all the questions were about the other night,' said Caddie, who had already demolished at least half of his huge, Desperate Dan pork chop and almost all of his mash and peas.

'I've not had it confirmed yet. John's still waiting to hear if they're putting me on the course or not,' I said. 'But I want it more than anything. I'll be over the moon if I get a shot at driving. It will be the best news ever.'

'Best news? What, you think it's good news, do you?' George chipped in from across the table. 'You're a fool and I think you're out of your mind, Windsor. Trust me, you don't want to become a driver. If you get offered a course you should turn it down. Driving the engine is the worst possible thing you could do.'

I did an instant double take. I'd not expected a reaction like that from anyone. What the heck was George talking about? What possible reason was there to turn this opportunity down? Acutely aware that the entire watch was paying attention, I asked George what he meant. He was only too happy to tell me.

'For starters, you want to steer clear because once you start driving the appliances you put your own personal licence up for grabs. An accident going through a red light on a shout because you want to save someone's life – the police will have you for it. Hit something at any time and you'll get the blame. Go the wrong way down a one-way street because it's the only way to a fire and they can prosecute you. Cross an unbroken white line and cause a smash – they can have you for that too. They can take your licence away as fast as anything. And think about what that means, Windsor. Lose your licence and it'll be goodbye to that Cortina you've got parked out on the parade ground. Goodbye to all your fancy girlfriends as well, just as likely. Trust me, son, you'd be better off staying the way you are. You do not want to become a driver.'

I can't remember who said what after that. Talk about having the wind taken out of your sails. I'd not expected much enthusiasm from the rest of the watch, no back slapping or good luck cards. But I'd thought the men would at least support me in their own quiet way. To get the exact opposite reaction from someone like George was a real blow. Forget slap on the back – it was a short, sharp slap in the face. Still, like a dog with a bone, I wouldn't let it go. When we'd finished a hot, sweaty and typically fierce volleyball game I tracked George down. He was sitting in a sunny corner of the yard cleaning his boots.

'You really think I should say no to the driving course?' I began.

He shrugged and put down his cloth. 'It's up to you, but trust me, no one will thank you for taking it on. You don't get a single penny extra in your pay packet for driving. So what's the sodding point? It's just a mountain of extra hassle and no extra reward.' He repeated all his earlier warnings about losing our personal driving licences if we cause any accidents getting to a shout and went on about colleagues on Blue and Green Watch who reckoned becoming a driver was the worst thing they'd ever done. Ten minutes later when everyone was called up to tea I slunk over to the corner by the window and threw myself down on a chair. I threw myself down so hard I nearly broke the thing. A few minutes later Caddie came across to join me.

'Knocked you back, hasn't he? Well, you remember what Davie on Blue Watch said when you told him you were going to buy your house?' he asked softly.

I thought back. I did a weak parody of Davie's thick Welsh accent. 'Don't do it, laddo. You'd be mad to sink your money into a house at your age. You should be spending your money down the pub, on girls and on a decent pair of wheels.'

'Exactly. And you went on and bought the place anyway,' Caddie said.

I started to brighten up a bit. Eighteen months earlier my dad had lent me £1,200 to use as a deposit and I'd bought myself a two-bedroom house on Bynner Street for £15,000. It was an ex-railway worker's house. There was a pub right opposite, a corner shop at one end of the terrace and a post box at the other. It was a five-minute walk into town. I had plenty of room for my sports kit in the back bedroom, a thriving home-brew production line in my front room and I could play my guitar as late as

I liked at night. I'd always been happy at my mum and dad's, but nothing could beat having a place of my own.

'I don't care what George says. If I get the chance, I'm going to be a driver,' I told Caddie.

It was his turn to smile. 'I never doubted that for a moment, jockey.'

3

It took two more days for John to get word from headquarters. I was out in the yard when he tracked me down and gave me the good news. I cheered so loud you could have heard me in Welshpool. He and the leading firemen then juggled the rosters and managed to release me for the training in the middle two weeks of July. As the date drew nearer I was practically counting the days. In fact I think I really did count the days, especially towards the end. But as the last of them got ticked off my list I was given two final reminders – as if I needed them – of exactly how unpredictable life can be on country roads.

Our first gruesome roadside shout came after lunch on a cool early July day. Two cars had apparently had a near miss on a lane just outside of Halfway House. A man and woman in an Austin Allegro had slammed on the brakes and screeched to a halt in the middle of the road. A girl about my age in a Ford Fiesta had done something different. She'd meant to slam on the brakes only she'd put her foot on the accelerator by mistake. By the time she realised what she'd done, she'd flown across a ditch, broken through a low hedge and ended up in the middle of a wet, muddy field. The woman from the Allegro had run to her side while the man had driven on to find a phone and call for help. He was back at the scene by the time we arrived.

'She's OK, she's not badly hurt, but she can't get out of the car. It's her leg. It's trapped,' he said as we jumped off the engine and began to tramp across the field.

'At least there's nothing wrong with her lungs,' Caddie commented as we approached.

The girl was screaming like Kate blinkin' Bush. You could have heard her over in Telford. You could probably have heard her underwater.

'Her name's Barbara. She's twenty. She can't get out,' the lady from the Allegro said breathlessly when we got to the car.

It wasn't hard to spot the problem. But Barbara was happy to point it out just in case we missed it. 'Got to get me out. Got to help me. My leg. Can't look. Something in my leg. Got to get me out,' she said between screams.

'That's what we're here for, love. Now, lean back and let the dog see the rabbit,' Caddie said in his kindliest manner. We all leaned in to look. The girl's right leg was almost entirely hidden by a mangle of twisted bodywork. Closer examination and a strong torch revealed something else. A thick shard of metal from the bulkhead of the car wasn't merely surrounding her leg – it had pierced it, halfway down her shin. It looked to have gone right through to the other side. So no wonder she was still in her seat. She was impaled there. And no wonder she was screaming. It must have hurt like hell.

'Barbara, love, we'll have you out of there in no time. There's an ambulance on its way as well. Between us, we'll get you sorted before you know it,' Caddie said optimistically. He turned to us once we'd stepped back towards the engine. 'Looks like we're finally going to get to use our shiny new kit,' he said with a smile. Until recently we'd have relied on the hideously noisy Cengar saw or a Stihl circular saw to cut through metal, always hoping that the sparks that flew from the latter wouldn't react badly to all the petrol splashed around your typical car accident. If we weren't all blown to kingdom come we'd then use a set of hand-pump-operated spreaders to pull the car apart. Now, however, we were loaded up with brand-new hydraulic tools. We'd already had hours of fun using them on the training ground. Using them for real would be even better. We knew the cutters would easily slice through any part of a car. And the powered spreaders could do all sorts of tricks. We could use them to open things up, push them apart or crush things together. Oh, and we'd have around twelve tonnes of pressure to play with. Best of all, the new hydraulic kit was spark free and comparatively quiet.

'We're going to take the door off to give us a bit more room to work,' Barbara was told. She didn't take the news very well.

'It's my dad's car. He doesn't know I've taken it. He's gonna kill me. Can't take the door off,' she said between screams.

'Would you rather stay where you are?'

'He's gonna kill me. But get me out. Can't look at my leg,' she said, flashing her eyes in all directions and gulping in air like it was going out of fashion. She'd clearly taken a couple of mental steps closer to hysteria, so we had to act. The ambulance had arrived and we told the Allegro drivers to wait alongside it while we got going. Our fantastic new kit worked brilliantly and it only took a matter of seconds to slice through the hinges of the driver's door. Woody lifted the door free and threw it into the mud behind us.

'Dad's gonna kill me,' Barbara moaned.

And we weren't going to get her free. Her right leg was too far away from us and we couldn't begin to tackle all the metal that was trapping it. So a couple of minutes later the passenger door was off and lying in a puddle next to the driver's. For all our efforts we still couldn't get close enough to the problem. Next to go was the Fiesta's roof. 'I'm dead. You can't do this to me. Dad's gonna kill me,' Barbara repeated again and again. Then we cut out the passenger seat. Then the driver's side wheel arch. If you stood back and looked, the more of the car we cut away, the more bizarre the scene appeared to be. The girl wasn't in a car any more. What was left of the car was in a pile slowly sinking into the mud. To all intents and purposes, Barbara was in the middle of a field sitting on a seat on a small metal platform. But after forty-five minutes' work we still couldn't get her free. We'd got as close as we dared to the shard of metal that had stabbed into her, but how on earth were we supposed to pull it out of her shin?

'Dodger, we're off to have a chat in the cab. Stay with her and look busy for a moment,' Caddie instructed in a quiet voice as he led the rest of us back to the roadside. Dodger stretched out under what was left of the car's dashboard with a spanner. There was nothing practical he could do, but Caddie wanted him there so the poor girl at least got the impression that we had a plan. Despite Dodger's best efforts at calming her down she was still screeching like a banshee and going on about all the different ways her dad would kill her for destroying his car.

The rest of us walked out of the girl's eye- and earshot and regrouped with the ambulance staff. We'd tried plans A, B, C and even D. That's when we got lucky. We were racking our brains trying to think of a plan E when a big blue Jag pulled up. A short, greying man in a dark brown corduroy jacket got out and walked up to us. 'I'm a doctor from Copthorne hospital. Can I help?' he asked perkily.

'Can you ever!'

We walked the doctor over to the car to take a look. 'What was she driving, a go-kart?' he asked, deadpan, as we approached.

'It's a Fiesta. Well, it was, until we got our hands on it.'

The doctor introduced himself to the girl and bent down below what was left of the steering column. He reached in and poked the girl's leg a few times. 'Just checking the bones and the lie of the land,' he muttered. Then he gave Barbara a smile and said everything would be all right in a moment. He led us back to his car. He lifted a black Gladstone bag from the boot and took a phial and syringe from it. 'This won't be pretty,' he began, sounding surprisingly cheerful. 'I'll give her a shot of morphine to take the edge off the pain. Then I'll put my fingers alongside the metal bar and inside her leg. When I'm in there, I'll push the bone out of the way so as to free her leg. You'll only have a very short time to get the metal out of there before I have to let go.

The moment I tell you to move, you have to pull the metal, no questions asked. Then I need you to get her off the seat and on to the stretcher fast. There's absolutely no room for error here. Do you understand? Are you all ready?'

Woody and I flashed a quick look at each other. You can't be too squeamish in this job, but putting your fingers inside someone's leg? Without saying a word, we walked back to the middle of the field and prepared for action.

The doctor had a quick chat with Barbara, who gave a series of ear-shattering screams as answers to each of his questions. She screamed when he prepared the syringe. She screamed when he injected it. She screamed even louder when he passed it to the ambulance crew and got ready for the main event. She only stopped screaming when he did an odd stretching exercise with his arms. She stayed silent, probably thinking the man had lost his mind, as he bent his knees as if he was preparing to do the long jump. We all watched, thinking the same as Barbara, as he took a few deep breaths, rolled his shoulders and closed his eyes as though he was going into a trance. Then he stood up tall and gave us the nod. To be honest, I was trying not to snigger. But I soon sobered up when he began his tricks. He put his finger inside the girl's leg, right inside it, right up to the knuckle. That was when she started screaming again. And increased the volume.

'Just moving the bones and making some space so we can get the metal out of there,' the doctor said, jolly as anything, ignoring her cries and acting as if it was the most normal thing in the world. 'Now, gentlemen, it's time to pull!'

We did so. The metal slipped out of Barbara's leg with a gruesome popping sound. In that instant our doctor pulled his finger out of her leg and stood back. The girl was free. The whole thing had taken less than thirty seconds. A few moments later and she was on a stretcher being rushed to the ambulance for a temporary patch-up job.

We got back up to the roadside as the ambulance doors were about to close, ready to take Barbara off to hospital. She didn't seem to be in any hurry to get there. The minute she was free, her personality underwent a complete transformation. No sooner had she stopped screaming than she started flirting.

'I can't wait to tell all my friends that I got rescued by a group of big, burly firemen. They'll die with jealousy over at the solicitors' office where I work. I'm a secretary. I'm really good,' she fluttered. 'Will you come over and say hello so I can prove I wasn't lying? Will you all come and visit me in hospital if they keep me in overnight?'

'We're the men who hacked your dad's car to pieces and left it in the middle of a muddy field,' Dodger told her grimly. 'We're never coming near you again!'

Our next roadside emergency also involved legs – or at least four-legged animals. We'd been called to help out after a minor car crash out on the main road out of Shrewsbury near the quaint little village of West Felton. A long line of stationary vehicles led us up to the crash site. We passed them all, driving on the wrong side of the road and feeling as if we were riding to everyone's rescue like some conquering army. 'There's the ambulance. That must be where we're heading,' John said as we turned a corner and the road opened up straight and wide ahead of us.

'Funny place for a car accident. It's hard to see what might have caused it,' Woody began from the driver's seat as we approached the scene. At that point I knew exactly what everyone was going to say next. It would be a comment I'd made years ago. We'd been called to another car accident, a Jag that time, which had veered off an equally straight, apparently hazard-free country lane. We'd seen the driver off to hospital, secured the car and been talking about possible causes on the journey back to base. 'Maybe some animal ran in front of the car. It could have been a rabbit,' I'd offered as a theory. Or at least, that's what

I'd tried to say. I've always struggled with my 'r's. That day I'd struggled more than normal. So everyone heard: 'It could have been a wabbit.' From that moment on, they all repeated the cry every time we had an unusual case and drew a blank on its possible cause. Today would be no exception.

'It could have been a wabbit!' the four grown men around me yelled, exactly as I expected. I gave them my usual two-word response.

We parked up behind the ambulance. 'Two people in each car. Nothing too serious – a few cuts and bruises, they all got out on their own. We're looking after them now,' one of the ambulance men told us as we walked round the cars.

'Let's just make these vehicles safe,' John said.

We were giving them a quick once-over when a police car drew up.

'Good morning, gentlemen,' said the PC getting out of his panda car. He was one of the local coppers we worked with on a lot of road traffic and other incidents. He was a serious, quite humourless man in his mid-forties. His name was Norman. He liked things to go by the book and he didn't really appreciate horsing around – which unfortunately made us want to take the mickey out of him at every opportunity. 'I'm not having a very good day and I think I'm going to need your help.'

He was sweating buckets and looking unusually harassed as he gave us the details. 'It was a cow that caused all this. Or two cows – a couple of Friesian heifers, to be precise. They broke out of their field and decided to play chicken on the A5. I closed the road in both directions once this first accident happened. I gave chase when I saw them, but I couldn't catch them.'

'No respect for the law, these cows,' said Charlie with a giggle.

'They're as bad as the wabbits,' added Woody.

'What are you talking about?' asked Norman, his face blank.

'They're talking nonsense as usual. So where are the cows now?' interrupted John, trying to stay serious.

'Who knows? They're certainly not in their field. The farmer's nowhere to be seen either. Can I borrow some of your men and try to find them?'

'Be my guest,' John said with a smile. 'If you need me, I intend to be sitting in the engine with the *Daily Mirror* and a nice flask of tea.'

Charlie and Dodger headed up the road while I set off downstream with the policeman. A second police car arrived at that point and those officers began trying to sort out the traffic jam. Norman and I were the first to spot our four-legged suspects. A little further along, where the road dipped slightly into a hollow, they'd taken up residence in the middle of the central reservation, calmly tucking into the tasty – and normally off-limits – grass. The calm didn't last, unfortunately. The minute they saw us they scarpered – out of the dip and back towards Charlie and Dodger and what looked like the broken-down fence they'd climbed through in the first place.

'We need to get them over there – towards that hole in the fence!' Norman yelled as the others joined us.

Dodger ran towards the heifers waving his arms like a mad man. They remained stock-still for a moment before turning tail and heading towards me. It was my turn to wave my arms like a blinkin' idiot. Then the cows decided to give Norman a go, thundering off towards him – and a shiny new Audi that another police officer was trying to walk through the area in an effort to ease the traffic jam.

'Keep those cows away from my motor!' the driver bellowed.

'That's the plan,' Norman yelled, practically doing star jumps to scare the cows. No wonder the poor sod was sweating. 'Back in your field, you bastards!' he yelled as they drew closer.

For one glorious moment it looked as if they might listen to him. The first of them, around four and a half feet tall and probably a few hundredweight of lean, young muscle, was heading towards the grass verge and the broken-down fence. Her pal decided not to follow. She'd spotted a new place to feed over towards Dodger. Soon they were both there, munching away with the cheek of the devil.

'I am not putting up with this for much longer. Let's do this together,' Norman suggested, a note of desperation in his voice.

The four of us put on a united front and ran towards the cows. In a perfect world they'd have turned around and run straight into their field. In the real world they turned around and ran straight for the brand-new Audi. This time the driver let out what sounded like a whimper as, at the very last moment, the cows separated, one brushing past his shiny wing mirror on the left, the other on the right. Ignoring his police escort, the driver put his foot down and shot out of the danger zone at speed.

The four of us spent the best part of an hour haring after the blinkin' things in the heat of that July afternoon. Time and again the cows weaved in and out of the cars being led through what should have been one of the busiest routes in and out of Shrewsbury. We tried scaring them and we tried coaxing them. At one point Charlie suggested shooting them. Nothing worked – and I reckon we'd be there still if the hefty heifers hadn't had their fill of fresh grass and decided to head for home of their own accord.

As they trotted back into their field, leaving the road to the cars, I swear the first of them looked back at us for a moment. 'You daft humans,' she seemed to be saying. It was as if she wondered what all the fuss was about.

Norman picked up a few of the rotten fence posts and we tried to stretch the remaining barbed wire across the gap to stop the cows breaking free again. 'It's not Fort Knox, but it will do,' he said as we headed back to where we'd started from. It was a long walk and he asked us a favour along the way. 'I'm seeing this new girl,' he said haltingly. 'She works in the Baker's Arms.

I'm trying to tell her my job's a bit more exciting than it is. I want her to think I do some really dangerous stuff.'

'More dangerous than chasing a pair of overweight cows into a field on a sunny afternoon?' Dodger asked with a grin.

'Well, that's the point. I don't want her to know about this kind of thing. If you ever come into the Baker's, can you tell her we were chasing a mugger or a crazed gunman or something?'

The three of us looked at each other. 'Of course we can, Norman,' we lied.

4

Driver training took me off the watch for a fortnight in the middle of July. In the first week I'd aim for my HGV licence. In the second I'd do my specialist EFAD training. That was the official test to be an Emergency Fire Appliance Driver or to drive Extremely Fast And Dangerously, depending on your point of view. My trainer, for both weeks, was to be a man called Keith Johnson. I already knew him by sight. He was a short, round bloke of about forty. He had a mop of greying hair that looked as if it had landed on his head from a great height, a pair of big bushy grey sideburns and a near-permanent cheery smile on his face. Keith had been a fireman himself for years, before deciding to become the brigade's full-time driving instructor.

'I'm Malcolm Castle,' I said, extending my hand as he walked across the parade ground towards me on my first morning. My course was due to begin at nine but, not wanting to be late, I'd been hanging around getting excited since eight.

'Good to meet you, Malcolm Castle,' Keith said cheerily. He'd not reminded me of his own name, I noticed. No one ever did back then. 'We'll be driving this little beauty for the next two weeks,' he said. He put his clipboard under his arm and walked us towards the Ford D series vehicle in the front yard of the station. 'Well, it will be two weeks if you're any good. If you're not then it could be just today. We'll see how it goes, shall we?'

'Yes, sir.'

'Driven an engine before?'

'No, sir.'

'But you think you can do it?'

'Yes, sir.'

'And you're all right for toilet?'

I did a bit of a double take. I hadn't been asked that since primary school. 'I'm fine, thank you, sir.'

'Then let's get started, and you can stop it with the sirs, my name's Keith. OK?'

'Yes, sir ... Keith.'

I swung myself up into the cab. I was on the driver's side. It was funny how even that seemed exciting. Just sitting behind the wheel made this a day to remember. Then turning on the ignition? It was the best feeling in the world.

'Let's take it easy for the first half-hour. Get the feel of the beast. Get to know how she likes to be driven. It's got a manual gearbox, as you can see, but if you make it to the end of next week we'll do a conversion course so you can drive the Renaults on a live shout. It's loaded up with a full tank of water and I've had them put some pumps, rolled-up hoses and other equipment on board so you know how the real thing will feel. But remember this was a front-line engine just one year ago. To all intents and purposes it is the real thing. When the public see you drive by they'll see a fire engine. They won't see a training vehicle and they won't see a trainee driver. They'll be expecting the very best from you. So will I.'

I gulped, nodded, checked my rear-view and wing mirrors and prepared for the off. A sideways glance showed me that Keith was still smiling. He looked as jolly and kindly as he had whenever I'd passed him in the station or come across him in town. But as with everyone else in the Fire Brigade it seemed as if there was steel behind the smile. 'One last thing,' he said as I put the engine in gear. 'If you do make it through the week to the first test on Friday you will get a second chance if you fail. But if you fail twice then it's over. Plenty of people do fail. Do not think this is going to be easy. These two weeks are not a holiday. If you want one of those, book yourself into Butlins. Have I made myself clear?'

I squinted into the sunshine out on the road ahead. 'Clear, Keith,' I said.

He nodded. 'Then drive me to Whitchurch.'

A bead of sweat was trickling down the small of my back as I waited for the lights to change just outside of Chester. I'd been driving the engine for over an hour. I'd got us to Whitchurch and back as instructed. I'd headed towards Warrington, and now I was heading back towards Chester again. At my side, my cheery, jolly instructor was still smiling like a very hairy, rapidly greying Cheshire cat. But he was also acting like the sergeant major of some hellish new army.

'No, no, no!' he would yell if I strayed so much as an inch over the centre line of the road or edged what felt like a fraction of an inch too far forward at a junction. 'Change gear, son! Change down now!' he bellowed on the open road as we headed towards traffic. There were no dual controls on the engine but Keith didn't really need them. He slammed his right foot down in the passenger well when he thought I should be braking. He stretched out his right leg when he wanted me to go faster. And he had his mouth in gear the entire time. Instructions, criticisms and comments came thick and fast. Nothing I did was ever quite good enough. At no point did I think I was likely to last the day, let alone the week.

After four hours of sheer, unmitigated tension we stopped for lunch at a café on the outskirts of Shrewsbury. The car park was pretty full, but I gave a sigh of relief when I saw there was one large space right by the entrance. Keith ignored it. 'Park over there, son,' he instructed. I followed his gaze. He was pointing to the far side of the car park, to a space the size of a pocket handkerchief. 'Reverse your way into it. And jump to it. We've not got all day.'

I got the job done and followed Keith into the café. It was packed with shiny white plastic tables laden with sugar pourers and sauce bottles. I ordered myself a cheese-and-tomato toasted sandwich and sat down opposite Keith. He'd been yelling at me and criticising me so much over the past half-hour that I was resigned to having the worst lunch of my life. I felt as if I was facing the firing squad. I tried to control my breathing and keep my face impassive. Any minute now I expected Keith to lay into me anew. But he didn't.

'They do a marvellous soup of the day here,' he began fussily, his Cheshire Cat smile broader than ever. 'The omelettes can be passable good as well if you get the right lady cooking them. The full English is worth having if you're ever here on a weekend. It doesn't matter who cooks that – it's always good. And the lady owner, she's over there, the one with the pen behind her ear, she bakes some fine home-made cakes. We'll be back for one of those most afternoons. Her Battenberg is a particular favourite of mine. You'll find it goes down a treat with a nice pot of tea.'

'So what was it like? How's your instructor? You didn't crash into anything, did you?' Alice was waiting for me at my house at the end of my first day's training. She was wearing denim shorts and a short-sleeved white shirt. Her hair was tied up high on her head and she reckoned she'd spent all day chopping up vegetables to make a super-hot veggie curry. I fell into her arms. I was six foot four and she was only five foot five but I swear she had to hold me up and somehow manoeuvre me towards the sofa.

'It was being beaten up,' was the only way I could think to describe it. 'It was like my first day of fire training over at Chorley four years ago. The instructor started off like the nicest bloke in the world but he turned from Jekyll to Hyde when we got out on the road. He's like two different people. When he's watching me drive he never lets up for a single blinkin' minute.

It's like driving a tank with Sergeant Major in the passenger seat next to you. I've been sitting on my backside all day, but I feel as exhausted as if I've climbed a blinkin' mountain. I can't believe I've volunteered for this. And it's only been one day.'

Alice listened while I relived as much of the day as I could remember. She poured me a glass of home brew but I decided I should probably say no just in case Keith turned up at my front door to criticise the way I was holding the glass and accused me of being a drunk. She laughed when I described how close I reckoned I had come to lopping the wing mirror off an old lady's Austin 1100 when I'd taken the engine out of the Shamrock Café's car park. Best of all, she really did seem to share my enthusiasm for what was due to happen in the remainder of the week. Keith had given me a tatty hand-out detailing the requirements of the official HGV test. They began with the basics like proper gear changing, proper ten-to-two steering-wheel handling and proper indicating. They included observation in front and awareness out behind, safe reversing and all sorts of other manoeuvres. I had a feeling that a lot of it would also involve un-learning the bad habits I'd picked up since passing my ordinary driving test at seventeen. Plus, of course, getting confident handling something ten times as heavy, twice as high and twice as big as most other things on the road.

I slept like a log and dreamed about reversing incredible expanding fire engines into a series of ever-shrinking parking spaces. But it didn't put me off. When my alarm went off at seven o'clock on the Tuesday morning I leapt out of bed, full of enthusiasm and ready for anything. I was at the station by eight thirty – walking up and down, incapable of settling and itching for the minutes to pass so I could get back into the engine at nine.

'Good morning, son. All right for toilet?' Keith asked as he bounded over towards me, big smile on his face as usual.

'I'm all right, Keith, thank you.'

'Then let's see if you've remembered anything from yesterday.'

Mr Hyde took over before we'd even left the station grounds. 'Mirrors, son, mirrors!' he barked, tapping his pen on his clipboard with the ferocity of a ferret in a fox hole. 'And what are you doing this far over on the right? Think you're on the Continent, do you? Going French on us, are you? Get back on your own side before I give up altogether and go back to my desk for the rest of the fortnight.' We headed over to a supermarket car park on the northern edge of town where he had me squeeze the engine into a variety of improbably difficult spaces, much like the dream I'd had the previous night. 'Middling, middling to fair,' he said at one point, which I guessed would be as close as I would ever get to a compliment. 'Now, see the white lines going round that corner towards the exit sign? That's going to be the corner of a factory building. Reverse around it and don't spare the horses.'

After taking a short break for lunch and fitting in more than five hours of complicated manoeuvres we were back in the Shamrock Café. 'A pot of tea and a large slice of that Victoria sponge would be very welcome indeed,' Keith said. He was Dr Jekyll again – and I was so pleased I didn't mind that I was left to pay the bill.

By the third day I reckoned I had Keith's number and could cope with anything he threw at me. But he was one step ahead, the way the old guard always was. I set off at a whip of a pace. I followed all his instructions and got ready for his criticisms and comments. They didn't come. Keith had a new weapon at his disposal. Silence. He didn't say a single word as I drove where I was told. For the next two days I came to dread the silent shake of his head and the long, low sighs of disappointment he made at almost every junction. Worse still was the scratch of his pen against paper. What did I do wrong then? I'd ask myself as he jotted down yet another hasty note. Did more than seven seconds go by without me looking in the mirror?

Did I stop half a foot too soon on that last reverse? What on earth has he spotted and how can I make it better next time?

I'm sure Alice thought I'd done the worst of my moaning that first night. I hadn't. I kept at it every night that week. I berated myself for every real or imagined mistake I'd made. If I thought I'd done a manoeuvre 99 per cent well enough then I laid into myself for missing out on the top score. I loved driving that hefty old Ford D series engine. I felt utterly comfortable in its big, sagging front seat. And I was damned if I was going to pass Friday's HGV test with anything less than flying colours.

'Now, son, this is the full DVLA test. Test conditions shall apply. I take it that you are ready?'

'Yes!'

'Then let's see what you're made of.'

Friday afternoon traffic was building up as I followed Keith's first instructions and took us west along Smithfield Road towards Shelton Hospital. Keith had decided to do the manoeuvres in the large car park at the rear of it, and while it was chocker with cars I managed to avoid hitting a single one. The test took exactly an hour and it ended, just as it had begun, in the car park alongside our main appliance room. 'Turn off the engine, son,' Keith said in a low, solemn voice. I did so. The world seemed beautifully quiet in that moment. Both our windows were down and a glorious summer breeze flooded into the cab. I gulped down some air and tried not to look at the mess-room windows up above. My gang, Red Watch, were on nights so they wouldn't be around for another couple of hours. But I had plenty of friends on Green Watch. I wouldn't want to face them if I'd failed this test. I wouldn't want to face anyone.

Keith let out one of his longest, most disappointed of sighs. He stared at his notepad as if he was trying to rewrite every last word on it. He turned a few of the pages and he sighed again. 'Malcolm …' he said, torturing me with pauses.

'Er … Yes?'

He tapped his pen absent-mindedly on his pad. Then he said it. 'Malcolm, I'll see you on Monday morning at nine o'clock sharp. You'll be sent your HGV licence in the post, but remember it can be taken away at any time. If we don't want you driving our fire engines then it won't matter how many fancy licences you've got in your wallet. Passing this test means very, very little, son. Have a very pleasant weekend.'

I said yes to the home brew that night. Alice had gambled on me getting through the course so she'd invited a big group around to celebrate. Four of us had clubbed together to buy a couple of frame tents and we were planning a camping trip later in the month. We laughed, joked, smoked, drank and sang the night away. At one point, just after eleven at night, I heard sirens, probably on the main road through town a few minutes away from me. It was your bog-standard two-tone nee-naw – so it could have been a police car or an ambulance. It could have been one of the retained crews from Baschurch, Prees, Wem or anywhere else within ten miles or so. But I had a feeling it was Red Watch. Good old Caddie had been on the board as number two on the water tender when I'd poked my head into the appliance room before leaving the station earlier on. So he would be the one in the driving seat trying to get past all the minicabs and drunken revellers in the town centre. I envied him, the way I envied all the drivers. But at least I knew I was one step closer to emulating them. I slept even better for the next three nights. It's funny how quickly you forget the stress and the bad times in any situation. Within a few hours of passing my HGV test the only things I could remember about the training week were the good things. And if the HGV course had been good then I knew EFAD was going to be blinkin' fantastic. Extremely Fast And Dangerous driving, I kept saying to myself. How brilliant was that?

*

I polished my boots, ironed my light blue shirt, attached the epaulettes, fastened my black tie and was at the station by half past eight on Monday morning. I got talking to Trevor off Green Watch and Jamie, one of the retained crew from Baschurch. He had come in to the station to collect a new pair of gloves on his way to his day job at a timber yard on the edge of town.

'You missed a bit of sport on Friday night,' Trevor began. So it may well have been Caddie's siren I'd heard at about eleven o'clock, I thought.

'What happened?'

It seemed someone had set fire to a load of old mattresses piled up outside a shop doorway in the town centre. There was a flat above the shop. It had someone in it.

'Could they get out? Did we have to do a rescue?'

'It was a woman up there – and she got out on her own. It was your bog-standard domestic. She'd dumped him, he didn't like it, so she had to pay the price. The cops were with us and we heard later on that they found the guy holding out at his mum's house over in Telford.'

'What a hero.'

'Always are, aren't they? Anyway, we had even more sport when the family that own the shop turned up – a dad, three brothers and two very angry wives. They were not at all happy about the damage. Had a bit of a scrum with us when we tried to pull some of the ceiling down to make the place safe. Two of them got arrested as well. Biggest night Dale and Norman have had all year.'

We were still talking when Keith bounced up, clipboard in hand and his usual big grin on his face.

I broke away from the others and got ready for the main event. Just as well, as it turned out. For EFAD began with a bang. 'Morning, son. Are you all right for toilet? Good. Then you've got a persons reported in a house fire at Hadnall. Get me there.'

My task was to choose the route and go for it. But Keith had one more trick up his sleeve. 'I think we're going to say that the Heathgates roundabout is completely blocked. I think we'll say that they're repairing the water mains. So you'll have to find us another way to Hadnall and the clock is ticking.' I stole a glance at Keith as I felt the adrenalin and the excitement flow and pulled up some mental maps in my mind. He was holding a stopwatch. So the clock really was ticking. This was going to be fun!

I pulled us out of the station entrance and on to the main road.

'Section 67 applies,' Keith said when I got us on to St Michael's Street. That was a great thing to hear. Over the next five days those became my favourite words. They were my cue to put on the blue lights and the siren and to tear-arse around the countryside in the name of practice. I got us to Hadnall in what I hoped was super-quick time that first morning. Then I got us to Church Stretton, and then right over the Long Mynd and past Oswestry to Wrexham. We ate up the miles that week, covering town, country and everything in between. We went to Stoke-on-Trent, we careered halfway across Wales to the coast at Prestatyn. We sped towards Liverpool, Manchester, Newcastle-under-Lyme. As usual, Keith's particular skill was to pile on the pressure to see how I'd react. He timed everything. He frowned and unfolded OS maps as I drove, convincing me that I must be going the wrong way and forcing me to question every turn that I took. Between the big drives he introduced all manner of other challenges. It was serious stuff. We were doing police-style advanced driving skills, driving at speed in built-up areas, on A-class roads in the countryside and on some of the narrowest dog-leg lanes in the county.

One of Keith's first big lessons was how to read the road ahead, even if I couldn't always see it. 'Anticipation, son, anticipation,' he'd say. 'You'll be going faster than anything else on

the road. You'll do more damage than almost anything else on
the road as well. This is the ultimate responsibility, remember.
If you mess up, if you crash this engine because you don't know
how to drive it, then it's not just you, your colleagues on board
or the poor sods you've hit who are in danger. What about the
people whose house is on fire? They're on the floor, breathing in
smoke and they're dying because you didn't get to them. Babies
in a cot, upstairs in a smoke-filled bedroom. Think of them,
Castle. And what about the people in the car accident you were
sent to attend? They could bleed to death and there's nothing
the ambulance staff can do to help because you crashed the fire
engine and didn't get there in time to cut the victims out of their
car. Your responsibility is to all of these people, son – are you
aware of that? Do you think of it? Do you understand it?'

I wolfed down the cakes at the Shamrock or at any other café
we stopped at each afternoon on EFAD. I stirred extra sugar
into my tea and even ordered a second pot to replace all the
liquid I'd lost sweating out on the road.

'Emergency stops. Ready for one of those? Now – stop!'
Keith roared immediately after tea on our second afternoon.
He slammed his clipboard on the dashboard so hard that
it nearly snapped in two. I hit the brake and felt the adrenalin surge through my body as I lurched towards the steering
wheel and the windshield. 'Think on, son. Think on about
how much momentum this engine has generated. Think about
how much damage it could do if you let it out of your control for
as much as a moment. Now stop!' Keith bellowed once I'd sped
up again and got back into fourth gear.

'I've been waiting for rain but the weather has defeated me,'
Keith pronounced on the third morning after checking I was all
right for toilet. 'But if I can't watch you drive in the wet then we
can do the next best thing. Let's say there's a persons reported
at the quarry over at Haughmond Hill – get me there.' I took a
look at my mental map, plotted out our course and put my foot

down. Keith had a quick word with the gaffer when we arrived and we were waved through the quarry gates. I spent the rest of the day driving – and trying not to skid – on gravel.

For the rest of the day, and the rest of the week, Keith kept the information and the questions coming on the other vital aspects of the fire engine driver's job. I already knew that getting the engine to its destination was only the first part of the picture. On arrival the driver has to operate the water pump and maintain communications with the control room.

Supplying water was clearly a huge responsibility. With a full tank we had 400 gallons on board. That sounds like a lot, but it gets used in double quick time. If you were using a hose-reel at full pressure it could last as long as fifteen minutes. But if you had two of the largest diameter hoses running, the driver had only two and a half minutes to find an alternative supply. It was the ultimate responsibility. The guys who had risked their lives going into a burning property could hardly rely on anyone more. The water might well be keeping them alive. If it stopped, then all bets could be off. Not on my watch, I promised myself under my breath.

'What did you say, son?'

'I said: "Not on my watch."'

Out of the corner of my eye I could sense that Keith had nodded. But he didn't speak for quite a while. When he did, he picked the worst possible time to do so. We had just pulled off the main road to Bishops Castle and were heading up towards the Stiperstones, a vast, stunningly beautiful area of heathland where the hedgerows were high, stretching up and out in all their midsummer glory. The lane ran through a dense copse – the trees hung low over the road, making it feel as if I was driving through a tunnel. Through that shadowy tunnel, from round a blind corner, a flurry of holiday cyclists was suddenly coming full pelt down the hill towards me. 'You get to the address you're aiming for. There's a person reported. What do you do?' Keith

asked as a tractor with a wide-load trailer entered the copse
from a side road fifty yards ahead of us. It swung out to the right
to avoid the last of the cyclists. There was nowhere near enough
room for all of us.

'I drop the tank straight away to get water into the pump.'

'Good. They run off into the property with the hose-reels.
Now what do you do?'

The tractor hadn't slowed down. Another wave of cyclists
had appeared and the high hedge on my left had been replaced by a deep, wide ditch. A glance into the rear-view mirror
showed there was a Land Rover behind me. Up ahead I saw
heavy mud tracks on the road. A concealed entrance? Another
hazard? 'I assess if they'll need supplementary supply. I'll almost
always assume that they will. First up I'll aim to get it from a
hydrant.'

'How will you know where to find one?'

The first of the cyclists flashed past us on the right. 'Local
knowledge. We might have done a check on that street. Or it'll
be obvious. I'll look for the sign. I'll start at the nearest junction,
or outside the nearest house if we're in the middle of nowhere.
Once I've found it I'll run out to it with a hose. I'll connect
the standpipe, connect one end of the hose to it and then join
together however many more lengths of hose I need to get to the
fire engine. Then I'll run back and turn on the hydrant. When I
get water to the pump, I'll close the tank to conserve that supply.'

'What if the hydrant is broken?'

The tractor came within inches of my passenger-side wing
mirror. I tried not to breathe. 'I'll see if I can fix it on the spot.
I'll have a go at cleaning it. If I can't do it straight away, I'll find
an alternative.'

'If there aren't any hydrants? Take a hard left here. Ignore
those cyclists. Head towards Pontesbury. Drive like you mean
it.' We'd come out of the copse and the sunlight was dazzling.

'I'll find a pool, a pond, a stream or any open water supply. I'll use the light-portable pump or major pump. I'll have any spare men help me carry it.'

'What about communications?'

'The officer in charge will use the radio on the journey. When we get where we're going, before jumping off, he'll tell Control that we're in attendance. Then it will be over to me.'

'So what will you do?'

'I'll monitor the radio, of course, so I'll answer any calls we get from Control or anywhere else. If the OIC or anyone else comes out to me with a message or has any update for Control, I'll go on the radio and relay it for him.'

The road ahead was quiet at last. And Keith carried on firing questions at me for the rest of the drive. Sometimes he asked me simple yes or no procedural questions. Sometimes he asked me the best routes from one lonely farm to another. Sometimes he asked about engine maintenance, emergency repairs or almost anything else under the hot Shropshire sun. At first I think I was irritated that he carried on firing questions at me at the worst possible times – as I approached a blind bend, a hump-back bridge or a flurry of oncoming traffic, for example. Then I realised he was testing me. Just like everything else in the Fire Brigade it was all about how you handled pressure. This mild, jolly-looking man could pile it on and turn the screws with the best of them.

'You bring the engine back to the station. What's the first thing you do?' he barked on the penultimate day of EFAD as a flock of sheep blocked the road ahead and I had to try to thread my way past them to reach a fictional persons reported address as fast as possible.

'I plug the engine into the electrics. It's got to be on charge so it's always ready.' The sheep had scattered and I'd found clear road again. Keith sat in silence as I powered along an empty straight road. I took us through Annscroft until I reached Ford, where we were heading straight into the setting sun.

'It's an ordinary day at the station. You're on the board as number two. What do you do at the start of your shift?'

'I do the A routines,' I said, eyes squinting desperately as I tried to confirm to myself that the road ahead was clear. 'I check the lights and the fuel level. I do a visual check of the tyre conditions. I check the fuel levels in the light portable pump and the electrical generator. I look in all the lockers and check there's no missing equipment. Then I sign the logbook.'

Was that another barely perceptible nod of Keith's head as he told me to drive back to the station? Was his smile wider than normal? I wondered if I could allow myself to relax, just a bit, as my final day approached.

The rains that Keith had wanted two days earlier began to fall with a vengeance at around seven o'clock on Friday morning. By the time we got out of the station the roads were swamped. In town I sliced through huge pavement to pavement puddles. In the countryside some of the lanes seemed almost impassable. 'Good practice this,' was Keith's delighted verdict as he reintroduced a few emergency stops.

'It's like driving on gravel,' I told him.

That time I'm sure I got a proper smile.

What helped my mood and banished some of the butterflies from my stomach was the fact that the EFAD test was almost entirely practical. Almost everything was practical, back then. Maybe that's why the job suited me so much. Keith and I talked about the theory, especially as we sat in the Shamrock Café eating our jam doughnuts and drinking tea. But I wasn't tested on it in any great way. There weren't endless written exams to take, nor was there a mass of paperwork to complete. Like everything else in the Fire Brigade back then it was all about the doing. The powers that be didn't need to know that you'd ticked all the right boxes on some super-correct exam paper. All they did was trust Keith to be a proper judge and jury. If he had seen me in action and given me the nod, then that was good enough for them. But would Keith give me the nod?

The test began after lunch. I followed every instruction he gave. I carried out every manoeuvre. At three thirty, bang on schedule, I took a left-hand turn off the main road and brought the engine back to base. I parked it right alongside the appliance room.

'I think we can have the ignition off, son. We'll not be fighting a fire from here,' Keith said.

Silence crashed down on us once the engine was stilled. I could hear my own breathing. I'd had a lunch of beans on toast topped with cheese less than two hours earlier. But I could still hear my stomach rumbling. I could also feel that bead of sweat roll down my back again. The rains had stopped but it was hot and humid. Though my window was open, there wasn't even a hint of a breeze. I watched a couple of bees buzz around the driver's side wing mirror before heading off to a nearby hedgerow. I wished I was like that bee. I wished I was as free. I looked over at Keith. He was gazing into the distance, frowning and looking worried. Time passed as slowly as it had seemed to do at school. There was more of the scratching of pen on paper. Part of me wanted to lean across and try to read what Keith was writing. Part of me didn't want to know. Of all the torments ever devised this endless wait seemed one of the worst. And as if it wasn't bad enough I realised that for the first time in the training course I really did need the toilet.

'Well, Malcolm, I reckon that will do,' was all Keith said when he decided to break the silence. He looked down at his clipboard, snapped it shut and put his pen in his shirt pocket.

I sat motionless. That will do? What did that mean? That will do, as in you're no good, never will be and might as well pack up and go home? Or that will do, as in you're good enough and you've made it?

'Congratulations, son, you've passed. Next time you drive a

fire engine it won't be the training vehicle, it will be the real thing.'

I've no idea what I said in reply. Probably something stupid. I remember shaking Keith's hand, handing him the Ford keys and climbing out of the cab. I began to walk over to my locker to get changed for home. 'Where do you think you're going?'

I stopped dead. 'I'm sorry, I thought I'd been dismissed.'

'You thought wrong, young man. You won't be driving this old bus when you're on a proper shout. It's time to forget the training vehicle. We need to see how you do on the Renault. It's time for you to show the chief what you're made of.'

The station had clearly been quiet that day. The appliance-room doors were closed and all our appliances were inside, freshly washed, ready and waiting for a drive. Keith led me towards the water-tender ladder, the engine I'd travelled on countless times in the back and always dreamed of driving. 'Hop on,' he told me.

The driver's seat felt great. I leaned forward and grabbed the wheel, revelling in the sense of power it gave me. Keith then began a lecture about the Renault, the differences between manual and automatic vehicles and the basic driving techniques of the latter. Everything he said was peppered with questions, the way it always was. But I managed to answer them without hesitation. I loved cars. I loved this engine and I'd watched enough other people drive it over the years to know it inside and out.

Keith no sooner got to the end of his final tutorial and jumped out of the cab than John, George, Ben and Charlie came into the appliance room. John pulled himself up into the passenger seat. The other two got in the back. 'How about you take us over to Leebotwood, jockey?' John said, without even a hint of a smile. 'No pressure. But if you screw up you'll never sit up front again.'

*

Driving an automatic was different. Driving a Renault was different. Driving without jolly old Keith at my side was most different of all. With John in the passenger seat there was no barrage of questions, no endless stream of comment. It was like going from primary to secondary school. I was with the big boys at last. This was grown-up stuff. It was serious. 'Take us back, jockey,' John said when I'd made it to Leebotwood. I thanked my lucky stars that I knew this part of the county like the back of my hand. I swung a turn on to a narrow lane on my right. Three-quarters of a mile later I knew I could join another, slightly wider road. From there I could cross country a bit and climb up into Shrewsbury from the south. As usual, I had to slow down for a fair few tractors and farm vehicles. I splashed through a lot of deep, muddy puddles. But I got us all back to base as fast and as efficiently as I knew how.

'Thank you, jockey,' was all John said when we were back in the appliance room. That and: 'I think this vehicle needs a good cleaning now, don't you?'

I turned off the ignition, climbed out of the cab, plugged the engine into the electrics and got a bucket and a brush. I started to smile the moment I was alone. I'd not expected any of the officers to go overboard congratulating me, saying 'well done' or anything. Nevertheless I felt good. I'd passed the official tests with Keith. I reckoned I'd passed the unofficial one with John, George, Ben and Charlie as well. Other challenges lay ahead. Driving properly with the professional mickey-takers of Red Watch sitting in the back of the engine would be one of them. But I was up for that.

That afternoon I cleaned the engine as if it was made of precious glass. John sent Joe down an hour later to inspect it. He told me I could change into my civvies and head home a full hour before Red Watch's shift was due to end. I left the station in my car as usual. But I was so pumped up with adrenalin and latent energy I reckon I could have run home with the light portable pump on my back. That hot, humid Friday night in July all I wanted to do was celebrate. After two weeks of tea and cakes in the Shamrock Café I was certainly ready for something stronger. Alice and I joined a gang of her mates at a riverside pub right in the middle of town. We got a table on the wooden deck outside. A live band started to play at nine and a group of my old school mates came along and joined us at about ten. I don't know why, but everyone was in as good a mood as me. By chucking out time we were all totally plastered.

5

The two weeks of Monday-to-Friday driver training had pushed me out of sync with the rest of Red Watch so I had a couple of unexpected extra days off to recover from my celebrations. I had plenty of ways to fill my time. Much to Caddie's disgust, I'd long since given up on fishing. 'Maybe I'll do that again when I'm really, really old, like you,' I told him with a smile when I decided to find another hobby. But in all seriousness sitting down beside a pond watching a float bob around all day had never really suited my personality. I needed something that would get the blood and the adrenalin moving. I'd found it. A year ago my mate Steve and I had decided to take up rock climbing. It was one of those crazy decisions you make in the pub one night. We'd been reading a newspaper article about a guy who'd climbed Froggatt Edge in Derbyshire, and we'd said how cool it would be to do something similar. A couple of weeks later we were giving it a try. It went brilliantly. Climbing suited the two of us down to the ground. It was the perfect mix of terror and teamwork. There was a massive sense of satisfaction when you got back to your starting point, looked up and realised where you'd been and what you'd achieved. We'd done lots of local climbs since then in places like Grinshill, Nesscliffe, Forest Glen and Pontesford Hill. The weekend after my driving exams I was heading further afield to Tremadoc just outside Porthmadoc in Wales. The café at the base of the climb was run by Eric Jones, a hero in the climbing world who had climbed the Eiger solo and been a stunt double for Sean Connery. How cool was that? I met some great fellow climbers that trip and when I got to the top of the Tremadoc cliffs I felt like the king of the world.

Back in Shrewsbury I patched up the worst of the cuts and grazes I'd got doing the climbing. Thanking my lucky stars I'd not got any worse injuries – maybe going rock climbing the day before I hoped to drive a fire engine wasn't the best idea I'd ever had – I got ready for work. We were on days again, so I had to be in the muster bay to parade at nine o'clock sharp. I felt as excited and nervous as an eighteen-year-old new recruit – and I just wanted to get on with it.

'Morning, Mike,' I said to one of the Green Watch men as I parked my car at the station.

'You're early,' he said.

'My watch must be fast.'

He was going upstairs for a brew but I didn't follow him straight away. I'd catch up with the rest of Green Watch in a few minutes' time. I could hear their smoky stories of fires fought and crises averted later. In the meantime I wanted to look at the board. It would show me what position I would be working that day and for the rest of our tour. I went into the appliance room, ready to see my name on the board as number two. It wasn't there. John, who had crept into the appliance room behind me, was more than happy to tell me why.

'Driving my fire engine? Will you heck, son. Don't think for one moment you're taking my fire engine out for real. You only passed your EFAD five minutes since. You don't have one half handful of the skills or the experience you need to answer a shout for real. You're a jockey. You're still nothing more than a lad. If you're very lucky I'll think about letting you bring it back from shouts, or later in the month you might be able to drive it over to the school fair over at Bayston Hill. But drive it out to a real shout? You must be joking, jockey. It's worth a good forty grand, that engine. You did all right when you went for your little drive last week, but that was then, jockey, this is now. You think I'm letting you put your sticky mitts on the steering wheel again today? Don't be so soft, lad. You're going to have to wait your turn like everyone else.'

'I just thought—' I began.

'Don't think, jockey, it doesn't suit you. You're number five. Nothing has changed. We don't want you thinking you're anything special because you passed your HGV and EFAD. Now, if you want my advice you'll get upstairs and have a cup of tea before we start work. It's going to be hot as hell today. I want you in here polishing the floor as soon as you've finished your routines. I expect to see it as clean as crystal.'

I headed upstairs with my tail between my legs. Mike and some of the others were in the middle of a noisy argument about politics and I was happy to leave them to it. The minutes ticked away and after my second cup of tea it was time to scoot downstairs and get dressed up for the start of the shift. It was also time to face up to Red Watch. 'Very kind of you to bother turning up,' Woody began when I joined him at the lockers. 'To what do we owe this rare honour? Should we thank you for rejoining the watch after your two-week skive?'

'You should keep out the way or you might get accidentally clobbered on the volleyball court later on.'

Then it was Arfer's turn. 'Well, you've had your nice little holiday swanning around Shropshire in the old Ford. Think you can cope with a bit of real work again, or have you gone completely soft?'

The wind-ups went on for the rest of the day. And I walked right into some of them. 'It's sausage and mash today – who wants three sausages?' Charlie yelled from the hatch at lunchtime.

'Me!' I yelled back, fast as you like.

'Bad luck, jockey. We're one short. Everyone else is getting four!' he crowed as the rest of the watch fell about laughing.

I ate my lunch fast – and I did get plenty of mash, gravy and peas as seconds so I didn't feel too hard done by. No surprise that no one, not even Caddie, said 'well done' or congratulated me on passing the HGV or the EFAD tests. Fortunately they didn't need to. The jokes and the mickey-taking told me that it had been noticed.

A week or so later my disappointment on the driving front would be completely forgotten as I found myself right in the middle of one of the most terrible tragedies I have ever encountered. In the meantime we were kept busy as Red Watch got caught up in one of our busy patches.

'Get your best bib and tucker on, lads. We're off to see the nurses,' John yelled as we hit the pole and slid into the appliance room at the start of our next tour of days. Getting a shout at the Royal Shrewsbury Hospital should have been a more sobering affair. Back then, the Royal was the main hospital covering an area of around 3,000 square miles. Most of the time it was chocker with patients, from Welsh sheep farmers and Black Country hod carriers to local mums-to-be and any number of sick kids. A burning building full of sick, ill and immobile people would be a challenge for anyone. But nine times out of ten the call-out would be nothing more than a FAGI – that's False Alarm Good Intention. If there's even the slightest hint of a fire in any of the hospital buildings the nurses were taught to press the alarm button first and ask questions later. If two seconds after the bells sounded they found out the smoke had been caused by matron having a sneaky ciggie up at the nurses' station, then that was for us to deal with when we arrived. Over a few cups of tea and a lot of good-natured flirting, of course.

That day our investigations took a bit longer, though.

'It's in the storeroom next to the male medical ward. Or it was. I could smell smoke when I went in to get clean towels. Or at least, I think I could. I'm not sure any more. But I got worried. I didn't know what to do. I might have panicked. I'm new. I'm sorry.' A fantastically pretty but clearly scatty young nurse was pushed forward to greet us when we rocked up to our usual spot in the grounds of the sprawling hospital. We, of course, all pushed ourselves forward in a desperate bid to be the one to speak to her. She had wavy blonde hair, full, perfectly shaped lips and her pale blue uniform looked a bit tighter than it needed to be. Which was just about perfect as far as we were all concerned.

'What's your name, love?' John asked, front of the pack as befitted his status as officer in charge.

'It's Katie. Nurse Katie Scoones.'

'Well, Katie, my love. You look like a very professional young woman. If you can smell smoke then I'll bet there's smoke to be found. We'll take over from here. But please don't go any-where as we may need to talk to you again.' He looked at the far less attractive and much older matron-type to confirm that the lovely Katie would still be here when we came out. The older lady pursed her lips and nodded her head. Very little got past her.

The storeroom at the hospital was bigger than any of the stores we had back at the fire station. I reckon you could have played five-a-side football in it. If it had been at the station, I bet we would have done. As well as stacks of towels and sheets it was stuffed full of cardboard boxes, filing cabinets, strange-looking pieces of discarded medical equipment – you name it, we could see it. The only thing we couldn't find in there was any sign of smoke, let alone of fire. And one very obvious problem reared its ugly head as we tried to find the source. Back then we had to rely upon the Fire Brigade's number one, high-tech, smoke-detection tool to get this job done: our noses.

'You smell anything, Windsor?' John asked as we fanned out around the room.

I didn't have time to speak before Charlie interrupted. 'Only Pete's tunic,' he said. 'He went to the kitchen fire over in Harlescott at the weekend. He's had at least six cigs this morning as well.' And that was the big problem. We spent far too much of our time in smoke-filled buildings. Added to which, pretty much all of us smoked. So we reeked of the stuff – and we were virtually immune to smelling it.

'Fresh air, fresh start, lads,' called John. And so the pantomime began. We left the storeroom, headed outside, gave Katie our most heroic grins, filled our lungs with Shropshire's best, then went back in the room to try and smell that darn smoke. Then we repeated the trick, in and out of the hospital like a fiddler's elbow.

'Any of the patients looking at us would think we've got the runs,' Charlie said as we finished the routine a third time, still without success.

'We'll I'm not putting "cause unknown" on the report,' declared John.

We went over everything we'd already done. We re-smelled the light switches, the fluorescent light bulbs, the plug sockets, every piece of electrical equipment we could find.

'I reckon it's this, boss,' Pete said as we got increasingly desperate for an answer. He was kneeling over a five-bar heater that he'd pulled out from behind a load of boxes. 'The back of it is covered in dust. Shall we get the beautiful Katie to tell us whether or not anyone's been using it?' We did. And even though it was the middle of summer the beautiful Katie said she was almost 100 per cent sure that someone had. 'We use it to dry our stockings,' she admitted to much merriment.

'Good enough for me. I think your patients can all sleep well in their beds for the rest of the day,' John declared, signing off our visit with a flourish.

'I'll sleep in Katie's bed any day of the week,' Charlie whispered.

'In that bed I'd be doing something more than sleeping,' Pete added.

Matron, whose hearing was far better than our combined sense of smell, silenced the banter with a look. It was Betty and

Mabel all over again, I thought, as we hung our heads and acted like naughty schoolboys for a while.

'Tea, gentlemen?' she asked, softening a tad.

We were happily drinking it in the warm summer air when it happened. The hospital's fire bell rang out for the second time that day. Five tea mugs were slammed on to the nearest window sill in unison. We edged back towards the fire engine to get any kit we might need. Was this going to be the real thing?

'It's in the operating theatre. It's a big fire. They're in the middle of an operation and they won't be best pleased!' A second matron-type came barrelling out of the nearest doors towards us. Her face was as white as the collars and sleeves on her rich blue uniform. We were already in action. Pete and I were numbers three and four so we had rushed to the appliance to pull on our breathing apparatus. Charlie was grabbing his kit and the others were getting ready to support us. Around us Katie and the other nurses who'd been drinking tea, smoking and chatting with us minutes before were fading away and heading back to their wards and their patients.

The operating theatre was at the far side of the main hospital building. We ran through the shiny, brightly lit hospital corridors, past equally shiny metal trolleys and beds. We slammed through plastic double doors, scattering crowds of staff and visitors who were already looking nervous at the sound of the warning bells going off all around.

'It's on your right. You'll see the sign. But you can't go inside!' shouted our latest guide, a nurse who had better, faster legs than the woman who'd first alerted us to the emergency. We reached the double doors that led into the operating theatre. They formed the sort of air lock or exclusion zone that kept the room sterile. Looking through the glass it was clear that the operation inside was going ahead as if nothing was wrong. What I guessed were two gowned-up surgeons – one turned out to have been

64

an anaesthetist – and two nurses were leaning over their patient and busily going about their business. One of the nurses gave a smile and a nervous thumbs-up when she saw us. Then one of the surgeons tried to dismiss us with a wave of his hand and a shake of his head. I caught John's eye at that point. He didn't like that one bit. I tried not to smile. John was always good value when his temper was roused.

'Does anyone here know what happened?' John barked.

One of the nurses in the corridor did. 'They managed to put the fire out. It was the drapes underneath the patient, and the bed-dress he was wearing. It wasn't alight for long. I don't think it harmed him. They got it on the floor and stamped it all out straight away. That's why they're able to continue with the operation.' She took a step back after giving us the information. John thanked her and we all stood there like lemons for a while. Most of the time firemen can go anywhere they like. We've got all sorts of powers that open doors for us in the name of duty. But there are strict rules about who can and cannot go into an operating theatre during an operation. For once those rules applied to us as much as to everyone else.

'I think everything is all right and you can probably go,' the nurse said nervously after a few tense minutes.

'No, my dear. I think we need to wait here and find out exactly what happened in there and why the fire alarm went off. I'm certainly not having anyone wave me away like I was a damned nuisance,' declared John, still irked by the surgeon's attitude. I felt my grin return. This was going to be fun.

The operation carried on for almost forty-five minutes, during which time no fewer than three nurses offered us cups of tea, all of which John told us to refuse. When the work inside was finally done I braced myself for the start of our own little drama. We stood aside as two orderlies went in to collect the patient and wheel him off to who knows where. The orderlies must have been a bit surprised by the charred material the man was lying on, but they were careful not to show it.

We stood back yet again as the two nurses in scrubs left the room. They kept their heads down and didn't make eye contact as they passed. Interesting.

'I'm the anaesthetist. If you have any questions you'll have to ask the surgeon,' the first of the men said when he left the room. And the second of them, the man who'd tried to dismiss us earlier, clearly didn't want to talk. He slammed his way through the first set of double doors. He didn't acknowledge us and kept his gaze fixed firmly on the stairwell to our right.

I smiled again. There was no way John was going to put up with that.

'I'm John Allen, officer in charge at Shrewsbury fire station. I'll be wanting to talk to you about what happened in there,' John said, blocking the other man's exit.

'You want to talk about a complex operation on a sick man who was having his gall bladder removed? I wasn't aware that members of the Fire Brigade were so medically minded,' the man said patronisingly.

'No, sir. I want to talk about the fire. I want to know what happened and why the fire alarm was pressed.'

The surgeon glared at us as if we were a bunch of insects spoiling an otherwise idyllic summer picnic. 'There was a brief fire. It was extinguished immediately. The operation on the patient's gall bladder was successful. I don't think there is anything else you need to know.'

'I need to know, sir, how the fire began.'

I loved the way John said 'sir'. He couldn't have sounded less respectful if he had tried.

'It's impossible to say how it began. These things can be caused by almost anything,' barked the surgeon.

John, of course, wasn't having that. 'Technically speaking, fires can't be caused by anything. There are three basic requirements: fuel, oxygen and heat, as I'm sure you are aware. That's the triangle of fire. All three will have been needed to start your fire. Shall we look at them in turn?'

The surgeon chose not to. 'I'm sure that's absolutely fascinating, but it is still impossible to say what caused the fire inside my operating theatre,' he said, this time with even more haughty arrogance.

'I think you'll find we have to say. We need to file a report. For everyone's safety, we need to make sure this won't happen again. I will need an answer,' John repeated. He might be on the surgeon's turf, but he'd be up for a fight almost anywhere. The battle of the giant egos was under way. I knew full well that our boss wasn't going to back down.

The surgeon began to pace from one side of the corridor to the other. He walked to the stairwell then stood very still for a moment. He looked to the left and to the right, as if to check there was no one else around. It seemed he had made a decision. 'It is just possible that the fault was mine,' he said in little more than a whisper from the far side of the room.

'I beg your pardon, sir?' asked John.

The surgeon turned to face us. A tortured look flashed on to his face. He walked towards us, still looking from side to side to confirm we were alone. Funnily enough, as he approached he seemed to shrink. Can a man really have his tail between his legs? This man did.

'I was sterilising the patient's skin with alcohol prior to the operation. It is just possible that I didn't wait quite long enough for the alcohol to dry before using the diathermy machine. It is just possible that a spark could have flown. That may have been the cause of the fire.'

The words came quick and quiet. It was as close to an admission of guilt as we were likely to get. John said nothing. He jotted a few lines down in his notebook. He showed what he had written to the surgeon, who read the words and nodded. They had a very brief discussion on the way the fire had been dealt with and the procedures the hospital had in place to prevent it happening again. Then John turned and led us all away. 'We wish you good day, sir,' he told the surgeon over his shoulder. For the first time he sounded genuinely polite and we all knew why. He'd won the war.

6

They were the lazy, hazy days of summer. They were the days I remember from school as being the happiest of the year – mainly because they normally fell in the school holidays. I liked school well enough. I enjoyed woodwork, physics and PE and I got on well with most of my teachers, but I was never one for sitting still for hours at a time. So it was the holidays and the weekends I remembered most from childhood. I remembered the long careless days when my pals and I could wander wherever we wanted across the Shropshire countryside. Our mums and dads never kept tabs on us. If they worried, they never showed it. We were told we had to be home for tea at six, but apart from that we could look after ourselves all afternoon. Sometimes we took sandwiches with us in the mornings and disappeared for eight hours at a time. We had little gangs. We played games. We built dams in streams, we created secret dens in the bracken, we climbed trees and pretended we lived in tree houses. What we didn't know at the time was that we'd been lucky. We had more than our fair share of scrapes, cuts and bruises over the years. We got ourselves lost every now and then. We broke a few bones. But we always got home in the end. Not every kid, and not every parent, was so lucky. For some families, the parched, perfect days of August would always be a time of sadness, a reminder of what might have been.

We were racing out towards Minsterley. The fields on either side of us were a mix of gold and green, a perfect patchwork of colours and a veritable hive of activity. Tractors and trailers were everywhere but we tried not to meet the eyes of anyone we passed. Up above the sky was the richest of royal blues, sliced right down the middle by the sharp white vapour trail of a plane. The passengers up there were so lucky, I thought. They had no idea what was going on down below. None of us were speaking in the fire engine. The mood was as tense as I'd ever known it. As usual we'd only been given the sketchiest bit of information in the original call-out. But earlier in the morning we had heard some of the background from contacts in the local police and ambulance services. It seemed a mum and dad over in a village called White Grit had reported their little boy missing the previous afternoon. Neighbours had helped them set up search parties. The police had taken over as night began to fall. Then, twenty minutes ago, they had finally made a discovery. The boy's water bottle and a plastic sword had been found beside a pile of newly broken timbers high up on the side of the hill above the village. The rolling hills there were a honeycomb of tunnels and underground chambers left from long-forgotten tin mines, lead mines and smelting works. When the miners had departed, many of the shafts had been filled in. Others had merely been sealed with hefty wooden lids. Many of those timbers had now rotted and given way. A couple of years ago we'd been called up on to the hills of nearby Snailbeach to rescue a sheep that had fallen through a pile of timbers and ended up fifty feet underground. It had taken a lot of ingenuity to get the sheep out and I'd been kicked black and blue by the terrified animal after being winched down to get a rope around him. In the end, though, we got the sheep out alive. I don't know why, but somehow I already knew that today would be different.

'There are the cars. Up on the right. That's where it is,' Caddie said as we left the final cluster of houses and turned another corner. A few hundred yards ahead of us there were two police cars, an ambulance, a pair of tractors, a very battered old Land Rover and two other cars. A couple of dozen people were standing around them or clustered in small groups further up the hillside. Whoever the lad's parents were, an awful lot of people wanted to help them find their son.

Caddie parked the engine alongside the ambulance and we climbed down in silence. Two policemen headed over to speak to us. The first of them was Norman, the officer we'd been chasing cows with on a far happier day. His colleague was PC Dale Walsh, another man we knew well from these parts. Dale was plump, for a copper. He was in his late forties and had a completely different personality to Norman. Instead of being serious and humourless he was one of the jolliest of the local constabulary. He liked to stop for a chat, a joke and a cup of tea. He was tough, but he had a gift of diffusing Friday- and Saturday-night fights with a touch of humour. Today his face was tight and he didn't even waste time saying hello.

'The mineshaft is three hundred yards over that ridge. The lad's parents are there, with two of my officers, the family doctor, the ambulance staff and some close relatives. Our torches can just about pick out what looks like a boy's body down the shaft but it's very hard to see. If it's him, then he's only twenty or thirty feet below ground. We haven't been able to get down there unaided and the rocks are too hard to dig into.'

'There's been no sound from the boy?'

'Nothing at all. He could be unconscious.'

'Or he could be dead?'

The policeman flashed a quick glance past us to check no one else was listening. 'In my opinion, he is almost certainly dead.'

Caddie stayed in the engine to monitor the radio. Arfer, Ben, Woody and I collected the kit we were likely to need for a rescue. Then we followed John and strode up the hill with it as fast as we could. I looked away from all the worried, teary eyes we passed as we crossed the dry, unforgiving countryside. Two women, both my mum's age, stood at the crest of the bluff. They bowed their heads as we approached. When we'd passed them we saw the boy's parents for the first time. It was impossible not to know that they were his mum and dad. Although they were surrounded, supported, by several other people, they stood out because they seemed so completely alone.

'Oh God. Oh, please help us. Please help us get him out!'

Everything changed the moment the parents saw us. The mother, a pretty woman not much older than me, launched herself towards us. Her face was streaked with tears. Her eyes were wild with grief and desperation. 'His name is Billy. He's only seven, he'll be so scared. You have to help him,' she said. Then she fell. She fell to her knees, then she fell to the ground. She was crying, a terrible, hopeless cry as the others rushed to her side.

'He's here. He's so close to us. Please. Just get to him.' This time it was a man who spoke. This had to be the boy's dad. He'd moved next to his fallen, broken wife. But he was trying to stand tall. His voice was raw and hard to hear. His face told of his own tragedy. It said he was beaten by his utter powerlessness. His job was to protect and provide for his family. He was the one they should turn to, the one who could make everything all right. Yet all he could do that day was ask us for help. Now it was our turn.

John laid one hand very briefly on the man's shoulder. He said three words. 'We're here, sir.' Then we got to work.

None of us spoke. From then on none of us would speak, until there was something useful or important to say. We set up our 'tool dump', laying a green, reinforced plastic salvage sheet on the ground for all our kit. We had a lowering line, general purpose lines, a first-aid kit, torches and a set of shear legs that were effectively a three-legged tripod with a metal eye at the top, facing down. Meanwhile the two policemen showed us what they had found. Planks of half-rotten timbers had been dragged away from a dark cutting in the stone. The mouth of the shaft was tiny, maybe two and a half feet across at most. There were signs of furious digging across the whole of the top of it.

People had tried desperately to find a way through the rocky earth and to open up the shaft and effect a rescue. The harsh quartzite stones of these Shropshire hills had beaten them back. The mineshaft had been sunk into tough, deep layers of ancient rock. It was impregnable, impenetrable and awful.

Our torches cut through the blackness as we leaned over the top of the narrow shaft. As PC Walsh had said, the body was no more than thirty feet below us. I could make out a pair of dirty white tennis shoes and green football shorts. None of us could see the lad's torso or his head. We clicked off our torches. It didn't look as if he'd moved since he'd first fallen. He must have plunged head first through all the rocks and debris that lined the tunnel. We shouted down to little Billy, the way his parents and all the others must have been doing all along. There was no reply and he didn't move. It was obvious he'd not moved for quite some time.

John looked at the three of us. Our rules in these sorts of situations said we couldn't presume someone was dead unless it was completely obvious. In this case, therefore, we had to perform a rescue as if Billy was alive. Once a doctor could get to the lad, he or she would make the next move. John nodded at Ben, a tough, strong man, but the smallest among us. 'You,' he said. 'We'll lower you down.'

The rest of us set up the shear legs over the top of the shaft. In almost total silence we tied a parachute knot in one of the general purpose lines and fitted it around Ben's body in such a way that he could be lowered in a vertical position. We attached a large pulley to the eye on the shear legs then made sure everything was braced and secure. Ben collected the first-aid kit, a torch, a spare helmet for the lad to wear on the way up and a hand-held radio. He held on to the free end of the lowering line and straddled the mouth of the shaft. Four of us took his weight on the line. On the nod we began to let the line out foot by foot. Ben sank through the rocks and roots and then on down into the darkness. A ripple on the rope and Ben's voice on the radio was the signal to stop. He was there. We stood at the tripod, keeping hold of the line. I focused on the ground in front of my feet as I waited for word from below. Behind and around me I could sense the boy's parents, their relatives and friends and all the others. I could feel the hope, the expectation and the desperation in them all. I couldn't look at them. Not even when I heard the boy's mother start to cry.

Thirty seconds passed. Then John's hand-held radio buzzed back to life. 'He's unresponsive,' Ben said. 'I'll put him in the parachute knot straight away. Haul him up on my signal.'

I flashed a very quick glance towards Billy's parents and their supporters. Had they heard Ben's words? If so, then they'd have been given hope. But I knew it would have been false hope. Something in the flatness of Ben's tone told the real story. He couldn't pronounce the lad dead – and even if he could, he wouldn't have announced it over the radio without knowing who might overhear it. 'Unresponsive' was the only description Ben could have used. We didn't yet know the truth, but the word didn't inspire much hope. In fact it suggested the exact opposite.

'Hold steady,' John said in a low, calm voice as we waited for Ben's next instruction.

The four of us stood motionless as we grasped the line. All of us fixed our eyes firmly on the ground beneath our feet. Time seemed to pass more slowly than ever. At one point a dozen or so lapwings flew by, oblivious to the horror beneath them. The sudden burst of birdsong cut through me. It was too normal, too ordinary for a day like today. It seemed wrong to hear it. Wrong to think how beautiful it was.

The boy's mum had stopped crying and I blinked hard and kept my eyes on the ground. Every second passed so slowly. But we got Ben's signal in the end. We began to pull, slow and smooth. This was the turning point. In a few moments' time everyone would know the worst.

'Hold my hand, Julia. Hold it as tight as you like. Hold on. It's OK.'

In the background I could hear different voices trying to calm the lad's parents.

'The firemen are in charge now. This is what they do. Give them space. They just need a few more minutes.'

But we didn't even need that. We were only a few seconds away from pulling a small, broken body out of the mineshaft. I held the rope firm as Arfer and Woody moved in to release the lad and hand him over to the awaiting ambulance crew. He was laid on the ground right by my feet. I didn't want to look, but I couldn't look away. The doctor and the ambulance staff knelt beside him. As they leaned over him they blocked my view and I could no longer see Billy's face. I said a prayer of thanks for that. I said a bigger one for Billy himself. Surely this wasn't too late? As the sun shone on that glorious August morning I wanted to know that there was still hope.

There wasn't. If we hadn't had a doctor on the scene the ambulance crew would have had to rush Billy to hospital for the official confirmation of death. As the family doctor had joined the rescue operation this confirmation could come straight away. There was no way of knowing which scenario was for the best. I joined the others in fitting Ben's line back to the pulley and hauling him out of the shaft. Just like the boy, his hair, his face and his clothes were covered in dirt, dust and mud. But at least his eyes were open as he broke through into the fresh air and the sunshine. We pulled him clear, still without saying a word.

Our part in this tragedy was almost over. All we had left to do was to clear up our equipment and walk it back to the engines. Some workers from the council were on their way to put a fence around the hole to prevent further tragedies till a more permanent solution could be found. But before then a new wave of horror was about to break. The doctor, a tall, angular man in his fifties who had a slow, sad manner that perfectly suited the situation, began to speak.

'Mr and Mrs Atkinson, I'm so very sorry but Billy is dead. We'll take him to the hospital and we'll find out more. But I think he was killed instantly in the fall. He wouldn't have felt anything. He wouldn't have been in pain. He wouldn't have been scared. Mr and Mrs Atkinson, your son wouldn't have suffered.'

The doctor's voice was clipped but kind. Billy's mother didn't hear him. She broke away from the arms of those around her. She was on the ground by her son's body. She lost control and began to scream, a savage, brutal cry that echoed over the hillside. Her grief, her anger and her despair was like nothing I had seen or heard before.

'Mrs Atkinson, Julia—'

Nothing anyone could say could turn the tide. The young mother was lost on the ground, gulping in air, looking for someone to blame. She watched as her son's body was lifted on to a stretcher – an adult stretcher, horribly, grotesquely large for this damaged little body. Then she found the target for all her anger: herself.

'I told him, "Go outside. Don't play in the house. You can't spend the day inside. Play in the garden. Go for a walk on the hill." I told him. I made him. It was me that made him go.' As her son's stretcher was carried away from her, she was on her knees, rocking back and forth. Every inch of her body was racked with sobs as she forced the words out like bullets. 'I'm going to kill someone for this. I'm going to kill someone.'

The woman's husband was at her side. His face was as pale as chalk. His mouth was narrow, his jaw fixed. He too was struggling to breathe and he looked as if the shock and the anger might never leave him. He was gazing out into nowhere. Focusing on someone or something he could hurt.

'Mr and Mrs Atkinson, if you want to come with us to the ambulance ...?' the doctor said quietly.

Neither of them gave any sign that they'd heard him. It seemed that nothing could penetrate their terrible grief. But in the end the man snapped into action. He stood up straight. He nodded at the doctor and turned towards his wife. He reached out his hand. And she didn't take it.

I learned something as we all tried to give the couple some privacy in those awful, endless moments on the hillsides of Shropshire. I learned that husbands can't always comfort their wives. Wives can't always comfort husbands. When you have lost a child you are entirely alone. Mrs Atkinson broke away from everyone around her. She stood on her own and wrapped her arms around herself. It was as if she wanted to pull herself so small and so close that she could disappear into the very hill-side that had claimed her son. She took a few paces forward, then stepped a few paces back. She was going nowhere. She was directionless, lost. Yet she couldn't stay still. I stole a glance at her husband. He, too, was lost on his own island of grief. He seemed to sway without her support. Would he fall? Should we go to him?

In the end the parents' families, neighbours and friends took control and led the pair back across the hillside. No more than a couple of minutes had passed since Billy's body had been brought to the surface. It had felt like several hours.

None of us spoke on the journey back into Shrewsbury. Nothing could have been said. Most of the older men on the watch were fathers or even grandfathers themselves. I was only twenty-two but I already knew I wanted kids of my own one day. I wanted the kind of family that the Atkinsons had built. Now I knew that if I were ever to achieve it I shouldn't take one single day of it for granted.

Bad news travels as fast as good in the Fire Brigade. By the time we got to the station the rest of the watch had clearly been told what had happened. So no one really spoke there either.

There was no gallows humour, none of the usual jokes or banter that help us cope with the occasional horrors of the job. Today had taken us well past that point. Everyone knew it. Everyone respected it. We climbed off the engines and checked that the contents were clean and properly stowed. We made sure that everything was in place and ready in case we got another shout. Then we left the appliance room. We never had official debriefs back then. At most we might talk things over while we had a cup of tea. But we didn't do it that day. That was the day no one wanted to speak at all.

Up in the mess room Betty and Mabel served a lunch of roast pork, boiled potatoes and veg without comment. I swear I caught sight of a tear in Mabel's eye at one point as she looked out on her unnaturally silent dining room. A moment later I saw Betty reach over and give her older colleague's hand a brief squeeze. The pair of them turned to the stove and began to get our pudding ready. For the first time it hit me just how intricately involved those two wonderful ladies were in our work. They too sensed its peaks and troughs. I hoped that they too had a way of dealing with those times when it threatened to overwhelm us.

Seconds were served and over at the far end of the table Pete was trying to restore a sense of normality to the occasion. Bless him, he began talking about the weather. He thought that the rains might return tomorrow. The summer had been too hot for too long. It wasn't normal. He thought temperatures might drop by the weekend. Possibly there might be fog... Grateful for these first steps away from the tragedy of little Billy, we began to pitch in a few comments of our own. Softly spoken conversations sprang up further down the table. Betty and Mabel had made a second pan of custard for our blackberry pies and they came out to serve it to us rather than asking us to line up for it at the hatch. Martin, one of the least effusive men you could ever meet, told them it was the smoothest he had ever tasted. Joe told the ladies that the pies themselves had been just as good. We talked about food for a while and we got through it. Those were the moments that helped me see these people were more than colleagues, they were family. That bond would see us through until we were able to laugh at things again.

7

'A cat up a tree?' bellowed John. 'A cat up a bloomin' tree? Is this a late April Fool's Day joke, or what? This cat had better belong to the Queen. Is someone trying to put us on or something?'

It was two shifts after the little Billy Atkinson call-out and I was relieved when the team started to respond to John's outrage with some of the old banter.

'The Queen has corgis, not cats,' Charlie told him helpfully, when he could get a word in edgeways.

'Well, at least a corgi up a tree would be worth looking at. Cats are supposed to be in trees. That's where they go. Why the bloomin' heck have we got the call?'

'It's someone from one of the pet charities that's called us,' Pete shouted from the watch room.

We had regular calls from all sorts of animal charities. Sometimes it was one of the big national organisations that called us, sometimes it was a small, local outfit. Many of the same volunteers helped out at all of them. And one volunteer in particular always stood out from the crowd.

'Oh God, not Mad Pam?' John asked. Mad Pam was one of our favourites. She was obsessed with animals. She probably preferred them to every human being she had ever met. As far as she was concerned, every last mole, sparrow and goat had its own distinct personality. Every one of them was a tortured soul that she alone could fully understand. She was in her fifties with masses of flame-red hair, worse masses of make-up and, if she thought it would help her beloved animals, she would be

wildly flirtatious with anyone in authority. Which in these cir-
cumstances almost always meant us.

Once a call has come in we have to answer it, however ridiculous it sounds. So as soon as we'd been given our instructions we
headed off, taking bets along the way on which one of us Pam
would cuddle up to if she didn't get her way. At Uffington the
first person to speak to us was your standard-issue, mortified-
looking elderly lady. She was wearing a beige patterned dress
that resembled a very old sofa. 'It's my cat, Sinbad. I can't quite
believe the fuss, but you have to help get him down,' the old lady
said when we approached.

That was when Mad Pam intervened. She was resplendent in
a tie-dyed blouse that was a riot of reds, oranges and greens. She
was wearing green wellington boots and was holding a large tin
of cat food. 'I'm terribly worried that poor Sinbad might starve,'
she said, breathlessly. 'Mrs Spicer says he's not eaten since yesterday. He didn't touch the meal she put out for him this morning. And he's got nothing to eat up there.'

'He didn't pack sandwiches?' Charlie asked with a sly grin. 'A
packet of crisps? Maybe a flask of soup?'

We tried not to snigger as we looked up. And up, and up.
For of all the trees in all of Shropshire Sinbad had managed to
choose one of the tallest. It was a knobbly old beech tree stretching a hundred feet or more into the sky. Sinbad had made it well
over halfway up. He was balanced, somewhat precariously, on a
lone branch that spread out almost directly overhead.

'Does he often climb this tree? Won't he come down on his
own?' John asked the old lady hopefully.

'No, he hardly ever comes out to this side of the house. It must
have been a dog that scared him. I heard barking, I swear I did.
They must have chased him. Sinbad would only have climbed so
high if he was scared and he wanted to get away from it. There's
horrible, nasty dogs around here. Something should be done,'
she said, aiming an accusatory look at some of her neighbours.

'We tried to coax him down, of course,' said Mad Pam, putting her hand on John's arm and gazing directly into his eyes. She had picked up a toy mouse that looked as if it had been made out of an old football sock and she pointed to an array of cat dishes and other treats laid out in Sinbad's sightline on the ground.

'No dice?' asked John.

'No dice, officer. He won't move at all. The ladder I've got in my car is far too short, I'm sorry to say, so I couldn't do anything myself. I was entirely powerless. You gentlemen were my only hope. I hate to disturb you. I know how busy and important you all are. But I had no other choice. I do hope you understand, officer. I do hope you don't mind?'

'Well, our ladders might just about reach him,' John admitted grudgingly. 'It'll be a challenge though.'

'You will rise to it. I know that you alone will rise to it,' Pam said even more breathlessly. She was looking up at the boss through thick, batted eyelashes now she was close to getting the result she had hoped for. The rest of us, already grinning like idiots over the 'cat up a tree' scenario, began to snigger like a group of schoolboys on the back seat of the bus.

'The 13.5 metre ladder, if you please,' John barked, slightly more brusquely than normal. Had our redoubtable lady from the animal charity made the Station Officer blush? The ripple of schoolboy laughter became something of a wave. We lifted our longest ladder off the appliance and began to position it at the base of the tree. This big ladder is the one we train on constantly during drills back at the station. It's the heaviest and the hardest to manoeuvre so it's the one we're lumbered with whenever the boss wants us to sweat a little. Funnily enough it's very rarely used on a real-life shout. There aren't that many situations where we need to get that high, that fast. Since signing up nearly four years ago I'd only used it once before in anger. All the other times had been back at the station, where it was always stood on solid, flat tarmac and leaned against the full-square walls of our training tower. Setting it up on a far from level front garden and balancing it on the bouncy branches of an old beech tree was another matter altogether. Especially as the moggie's owner had started to cry and the usual rent-a-crowd had turned up to watch our every move. The schools hadn't gone back yet so there were dozens of kids gawping. One of them had even nipped home to get her camera. Which was particularly bad, bearing in mind what happened next.

'Extend the ladder!' instructed John in businesslike fashion. The ladder consisted of three key sections. When it is positioned vertically one of us 'foots the heel', standing at the base with their foot on the round beam below the bottom rung to keep it still. A second keeps the handling poles steady, two more pull like billy-o on the extending line that links all of the extensions via a series of pulleys. This sends the next two sections skywards. On the parade ground it all happens very smoothly. Up against that tree was a different matter. The extra extensions had to push through a mass of branches, snapping some off and being temporarily held back by others before they sprang out of its way and let our ladder get as close as necessary to poor old Sinbad. The plan, at that point, was to send one of us up the ladder to grab the grateful cat and bring him down to his even more grateful owner.

'One more pull, lads!' John yelled as the final extension stretched out. 'Keep pulling!' We'd hit a particularly tough obstruction. It was a very springy branch that refused to bend out of our way. Pete and I used our full bodyweight to pull on the extending line, and at the very last moment, just as the branch pinged back like a catapult, something very bad happened. Sinbad chose that exact moment to hop on to it. Of all the branches. Of all the moments.

'No!' I heard John shout from behind me.

'No!' Sinbad's owner wailed.

'No!' wailed Mad Pam even louder.

'Yes! Oh yes! Look, Mum – it's flying!' yelled the girl with the camera from rent-a-crowd.

To the sound of a massive twang from the branch the cat was propelled through the air at what looked like subsonic speed. But while he was moving fast, everything else seemed to go very slow. I swear I could sense Sinbad's moggie brain whirring into action in those first desperate moments. He seemed to stretch out all four limbs horizontally in a desperate bid to increase his surface area and slow his descent. It was almost as if I could see Sinbad's little white teeth grit themselves as he realised it was all to no avail – and that he was going to hit the deck with an almighty thump!

'Thump!' There it was. Sinbad landed on the other side of the garden hedge, just ahead of the fire engine. The crowd of onlookers drew in a collective gasp as everyone waited to see if he got up again. His owner let out yet another horrified wail. Mad Pam clutched her throat and gasped in dramatic, theatrical fashion. But Sinbad did us all proud. Not only did he get up, he got up fast. He sprang to his four feet. He gave all of us what looked to be a very harsh, very affronted stare. Then he scarpered, shooting off like a whippet with wind. He aimed for the nearby woods and had soon disappeared amidst the bushes and trees.

'Sinbad – darling! Come back! Come back to me!' his owner cried, setting off after him at a fraction of his pace. Poor old John, trying desperately not to laugh, had to follow her. We couldn't really let an elderly member of the public disappear into a wood on her own. And he probably needed additional information for the incident form as well. With so many neighbours and onlookers around, the rest of us should have remained model professionals in his wake. Like heck. As usual Charlie was the first to crack. I was next. Then everyone was doubled up, making jokes about how many of his nine lives Sinbad might have used up today and how cats really can fly.

'You remember the woman with the cat up the chimney over at Whitchurch?' I yelled out on the journey back to the station. It was one of the favourite incidents from my first full year in the brigade. John, Charlie and Pete all let out massive groans of agreement.

Dodger, though, hadn't joined us at that point. 'What cat, what chimney?' he asked. The rest of us were more than happy to fill him in. Charlie began the tale, constantly interrupted by Pete.

'It was a little old woman. Probably seventy. Lovely old dear. She'd never called the Fire Brigade before in her life and she was dead upset about troubling us then.'

'Every second thing she said was an apology, bless her cotton socks.'

'So was her cat up a tree or what?' Dodger asked.

'The cat was trapped up the chimney. And like this lady today she'd tried to tempt the thing back with its favourite food, saucers of milk and squeaky toys and the like, but she'd not got anywhere. Its name was Newsy or Newby, if memory serves.'

'Newby,' said Charlie. 'And the old lady was called Flora.'

'You remember every shout we've ever done, but you forget your mess money almost every week and you go months without settling up at the bar. That's quite incredible,' said Pete. 'Anyway, dear old Flora reckoned Newby had been scared by a car backfiring. So he'd shot up the chimney and stayed put. She could hear him mewing away and she reckoned he was trapped or in trouble somehow.'

'Wasn't the living room full of junk? Loads of porcelain trinkets and horse brasses and ornaments on the shelves all around the fireplace? We had to do quite a clear-out job before we could get close enough to the fireplace to hear what was going on,' said Charlie. 'Pale cream carpets as well, if I remember right. Fireman's nightmare.'

'Plus, we thought the cat was dead. We couldn't hear a darn thing. If it was still up there, it was keeping its mouth shut. My money had been on him coming out of there in a cardboard box.'

'We were all set to break the news when George reckoned he'd heard something.'

'None of us heard it. None of us heard a thing,' said Pete firmly.

'Well, George swore blind the cat was there. He reckoned it was alive and well but trapped inside the chimney.'

I decided it was my turn to take up the story. 'We shone the torches up the chimney from the bottom to try and see the cat or show her the way out. Nothing at all. So we got the ladders out and climbed up on the roof. I went up there with Charlie. We shone the torches down from the top to see if that would do the trick. Then we started with the water. We dragged a hose-reel up on to the roof then we dribbled a bit of water down to tell Newby it was time to move.'

'Hadn't we just got new radios back then?' asked Pete. 'When nothing happened down below, we radioed up and got you to send a bigger burst down. No cat. So we got a second bigger burst. We'd had to put sheeting down on the old lady's hearth and everything. We could all hear the cat by then so we knew it was alive. Thing was, it only mewed every now and then. But the damn thing wasn't coming out of the chimney. So we had a third burst and one last gush. We had black water streaming down into our buckets by then. But no sign of Newby.'

Charlie pulled the fire engine wheel around and set us straight on the main road back towards Prees and on to Shrewsbury. 'That was when Brian Reeves showed up,' John shouted from the front seat next to him.

The rest of us all groaned. Brian was one of the officers from Headquarters. He was tall, arrogant and not much liked. He was on duty that day and he'd been listening in on the radio and heard our messages about the job. He'd only gone and turned up.

'What's up, gents? Not got it down yet?' mimicked Charlie in Brian's distinctive upper-class twit accent. We all groaned yet again at the memory.

'He got all officious and made out he was in charge. We wanted to deck him,' said Pete. 'Reeves reckoned he could hear the cat's meows himself. I remember he stood up all tall and thrust out his chest and said he knew exactly where the cat was and what we had to do.'

Charlie did another impersonation. 'Surely it's obvious! There is a shelf in the chimney about four feet up. Cut a hole in the chimney breast and fetch the cat out that way.'

I laughed as I recalled what happened next: 'We asked the old lady if we could do it and she said yes straight away. She'd have let us knock the whole house down if it had saved Newby. So we started knocking out the bricks. Dust bombs went off with every whack of the chisels. All Flora's framed photographs on the dresser, all the fancy lace cushions, all her china knick-knacks and odds-and-sods were covered in it. Our clean-up job was going to take as long as the rescue. But Reeves was convinced he was going to be a hero by solving the problem – and for a while I did believe him.'

'It was you that put your arm into the hole, wasn't it, Windsor?' Pete asked.

'It was indeed. Reeves was desperate to do it himself, but I reckon he thought Newby might bite his fingers so he made me do it. And there was no cat there. I felt right round. Nothing doing. Reeves didn't believe it, of course. He said I was a fool or something. So he pushed me aside and reached in the hole himself.'

'And did the cat bite his fingers? Did it draw blood?' asked Dodger hopefully.

'No such luck. No, there was no cat. Or at least, not at that exact moment. Reeves was reaching into the chimney, giving it one more go. The kettle had boiled in the kitchen so Flora had left the room to make us all a brew. That's when Newby let out his loudest meow yet. The only problem was it didn't come from the chimney breast. It came from the log box on the side of the grate. I opened it up, just as we heard the kitchen door open and Flora approach. Newby was right there, half asleep, a bit fussed about being woken up and as clean and happy as the day he was born. He'd been in there the whole time.'

'Quick, give me that damn cat!' said Charlie in Reeves' voice as he finished the story. 'He grabbed it off you, didn't he, jockey? He stuffed the poor blighter inside that hole in the fireplace. He jiggled it around inside the soaking wet, dirty chimney for a few seconds while it probably got the fright of its life. Then he pulled it out the very moment Flora walked back into the room. It had turned into the dirtiest, soggiest moggie you'd ever seen. "Flora, I've rescued your cat from the chimney breast. She's safe and sound now. All is well," he said. Cheeky blighter!'

We carried on laughing for the rest of the journey back to base. And I carried on smiling for the rest of our shift. Because John had given me some good news on our return. If we didn't get a shout tomorrow, he wanted Caddie, Dodger, Des and me to head out on hydrant duty for two hours in the morning. And he wanted me to drive the fire engine.

8

'Right, Windsor, just remember that if there's a smudge, let alone a scratch on that paintwork when you come back then there'll be trouble. For starters, I'll be after your blood, then I'll bring in Betty and Mabel. I'll tell them you criticised their steak-and-ale pie. You won't stand a chance. They won't show you an ounce of mercy. So you look after my fire engine like your life depends on it.'

I waved John away without a second thought. No one's jokes could burst my bubble that day. Nothing could take away the excitement I'd felt all morning as we'd done our station checks and our routines. We'd done our drills, drunk a pint of hot, sugary tea and half-killed each other on the volleyball court. I was wide awake, even though I'd barely slept the night before, to be honest. I'd been out to the local pub with Alice and I'd hardly sat still.

'You're like a little boy on Christmas Eve. A six foot four little boy of twenty-two who really should know better,' she'd joked with me.

Back at my house I'd ironed and re-ironed my shirt for the next day. I'd polished my boots and even my buttons. I'd set two alarm clocks and rung up the phone company for an official alarm call, just in case. Nothing, I swore, absolutely nothing, would get between me and the driver's seat of the fire engine the next day. And shortly after eleven fifteen the following morning there I was, ready for anything, ready to go.

I reached up to the driver's door and pulled the handle. I swung myself up into the cab – good news that I'm so tall because it was quite a height. Then I settled myself down on the shiny black seat. Over to my left Joe was climbing on to his seat as number one, our officer in charge. We were a five-man crew that day, so behind us we had Caddie and the new guys, Dodger and Des. It's funny, but I could sense that they were looking forward to a morning of hydrant duty the same way I was looking forward to driving. I'd been excited about hydrant days when I first joined the watch. Now I'd passed that enthusiasm on to them and I was moving on to the next big adventure. This really was the best job in the world.

Hydrant duty never really changed back then. We were given a patch to cover – that day it was one of the modern residential estates off Sutton Road. We had to take the engine out there. I would park up alongside each hydrant on our list. Dodger and Des would jump down, unload the standpipe, key and bar then carry them to the hydrant. They'd screw the standpipe on to the water outlet and turn it on to check the flow. If all was well they'd disconnect it, reload the equipment on to the engine and give the hydrant post and lid a fresh coat of yellow paint to ensure it was easy to spot in an emergency. If there was a problem with the water flow or if the hydrant was blocked or broken in some way they'd do whatever it took to solve it. As we left and headed to the next hydrant the trick was to remember exactly where the previous ones had been. That way at least someone would be able to find one in a fire. Today's fire crews have electronic devices that tell them exactly where to find water. Back then we did have paper maps, but the main thing was to rely on local knowledge.

Down in the appliance room Woody was pulling the rope and opening the doors for us. 'Are you all right for toilet?' I asked myself as a joke, thinking back to Keith and my training drives.

'Don't forget about the camber on the main road. They're all going to be watching you from the mess room,' Caddie muttered as I turned the ignition, took a deep breath and released the handbrake. I turned the wheel to the left as the engine came out into a patch of weak summer sunshine. It was typically kind of Caddie to give me that last reminder. But I'd not forgotten the way the road curved just ahead of me. I'd certainly not forgotten that I'd have an audience.

The road was annoyingly busy that morning. I let a couple of cars go by from the right as I idled on the edge of the main road. Then half a dozen more cars came from the left. I looked to the right as the last of them passed. Two more cars were coming. It wasn't this tense in training, I thought to myself. It hadn't felt anything like this bad. But at last we had a quiet patch. The road was clear. I took a gulp of air and sent us forward. There was no stall, no kangaroo start, just a textbook smooth drive. I said a little thank you in my head and picked up the pace. We were out on the open road for real. This was it.

'Right, lads, you know what you're doing?' Joe was leaning around and talking to Dodger and Des in the back. It took the focus away from me for a moment. Deliberate or not, I'll always thank him for that. Though, to be honest, I wasn't having any problems. In fact it was the exact opposite. I was trying not to relax too much. I didn't want to tempt fate or get my come-uppance too soon. But oh boy I was loving it! I felt totally, utterly, completely at home behind the wheel of the fire engine. We were so high up there. We were the true kings of the road. I could feel the power that was harnessed within this incredible, seemingly indestructible truck. I could sense what it could do. Sure, it was heavy and sluggish at first, but I could give it momentum. I could give it power. We owned the roads we drove along. It was only five miles to our first set of hydrants. I would happily have driven fifty.

The hydrants are pretty close together on new housing estates so the lads got through around twenty inspections in two hours that first morning. Every time I moved the engine on and parked it the lads jumped out and did their stuff, flirting with the passing housewives in the residential streets, same as I used to do when I'd been in their place a couple of years earlier. The final two inspection points were down a couple of country lanes. My breathing picked up at one point when I saw an overhanging branch ahead of us. For all his jokes, I knew John really would go over the engine on our return with a fine-tooth comb looking for smudges and scratches. I was determined not to provide any. So I exhaled sharply when we passed the hazard without taking a hit from anything much more than the lowest hanging leaves. 'That's job done. If we head off now we'll still be back in time for lunch,' said Caddie when Dodger and Des came back on board after spending a good quarter of an hour digging silt out of one of the last hydrants on their list.

I drove the same crew out on hydrant duty the next day as well. This time we headed towards Bomere Heath where the hydrants were few and far between. We probably only got around five done that morning. Most of the ones the lads found were in a bad state. Out in the sticks we often found that hydrants would be filled with mud and need digging out. Others might have their lids stuck down fast and need a bit of brawn to release them. Still more could be lost in the undergrowth and the lads would have to hack away at the bushes before the inspection could begin. Throughout all of that day's inspections I stayed put in the driver's seat. I was acting like the boss – and I felt like I was the bee's knees.

John made a few jokey jibes about the number of flies on the windscreen when we got back to base, but that only made me smile all the more.

'You look like someone who's lost sixpence and found 'alf a crown,' Mabel said as she topped up my lunch plate with thick onion gravy.

'I've been out driving the fire engine. It was good.'

'It's good to see someone so happy in their work,' she said. 'Let's hope it lasts.'

It didn't, unfortunately. I'd sort of got it into my head that while I wasn't going to be doing an emergency drive any time soon I would get to drive on all of our non-urgent jobs. The following day, a Saturday, we turned up to be told that the retained crew from Baschurch were up on a watching brief at a field fire in the hills way out west of town.

'The lads were called out before dawn. They've done five hours without a break. They need feeding,' John declared in the middle of the morning. 'Woody, take the engine into town and get them some grub.'

I was on Woody's appliance that day, as number four to his number two. John didn't ask us to swap places. So I sat in the back sulking as Woody drove us into town and we waited for the Golden Fry chip shop to open. I was still feeling sorry for myself when the owner pulled up the shutters and we collected eight large cod, ten portions of chips, a bottle of ketchup and eight cans of drink. We put the fish and chips in the hot box and headed up to the hills. I only really cheered up when we got right out into the countryside. It's hard to be unhappy when you're in such a beautiful place. The fields were rough, ragged but nonetheless enchanting. For hundreds of years they'd survived every extreme of weather. Those fields would never change. I looked at the richness of the greens in the grass and the hedges, the deep greys of the stones, the occasional dark browns of bare earth. The land rolled down from the heights and stretched out towards Little Stretton. Occasional trees stood proud and important like soldiers. The air was dry and full of pollen. I took a lungful of it and realised, to my surprise, that I'd not felt travel sick once on the journey. Maybe I should get angry more often, I thought. Maybe that took my mind off things.

We leapt down when we got to the retained crew's fire engine. I was looking forward to spending more time with those guys. Big, wide-open counties like Shropshire relied hugely on retained crews. They all had full-time jobs else-where but signed up to help us out by being on call for twenty-four hours a day – sometimes seven days a week. They had to carry an alerter on their belts. If it went off, they had to get to their local station like a greyhound out of a trap. As soon as the minimum complement had turned up they'd be sent out on the call. Sometimes they were called into our station, to stand in for us when we were all out on shouts. Other times they got shouts themselves. Without the retained crews we couldn't cover the whole of the county. They gave us manpower all across the region without the expense of having full-time crews in each and every hamlet. They got a bit of cash for simply making themselves available, which was fair enough as their lives weren't their own when they were on call. They also had to do loads of training so they could pull their weight in an emer-gency. What made me laugh was the way they had to click into fireman mode at a moment's notice. Mostly this meant running to their local station and pulling their fire kit on top of what-ever they happened to be wearing at the time. Last summer I'd done a heath fire with the retained guys from the Prees station. We'd all been sweating like pigs. When the fire was under con-trol we took our tunics off. It was as if we were at a fancy-dress party. One of the retained guys was wearing pyjamas under his kit, one of them was in bloodied butcher's overalls, another had a T-shirt with a slogan on the front you wouldn't want your grandma to read.

'How's tricks?' we asked the Baschurch guys when we dragged the hot boxes over towards them.

'Can't complain,' said their OIC, before settling down to do just that. 'It's tough, trying to make a living out there. Don't you watch the news? The country's going to hell in a handcart. You lot with your big fireman's wage and your cushy second jobs on the side – you don't know you're born.'

'We brought you chips, what more do you want?'

'A couple of pickled eggs would have been nice.'

'Well, we'll try to remember that for next time, you ungrateful sod.'

We stole some of the lads' chips and loafed around chatting for a while. Then, when we decided we couldn't postpone it any longer, we got ready to head back to base. The retained crew threw their used chip wrappers on to the embers of the fire they'd just put out, assured us that everything was under control and waved us off.

'Lucky so-and-sos. Earning a nice bit of extra dough for sitting around at a glorified barbecue. You can't beat a good watching brief on a summer's day,' Woody said as we drove away.

'At least you're not in charge of them. Remember the watching brief we did one night last year? You still owe us for that one, old man. We could have lost our backin' jobs,' Arfer said.

I laughed along with the others at the memory of it. We'd been sent to a barn fire high up on Clee Hill. We'd tackled it by midnight, but as the winds were predicted to rise we'd been told to stay watching over it for a few more hours. Our OIC decreed that as long as one person was awake at all times the rest of us could take two-hour catnaps. Woody had offered to take the first slot on the watch. 'I'm off for a fag, so I'll stay awake. I'll give you a shake at three o'clock and we can swap round,' he'd told us. But Woody had fallen asleep as well. Three o'clock had come and gone. So had five o'clock. And six o'clock. We only woke up when the local retained crew arrived to relieve us at seven.

'Every single one of you was snoring your heads off,' we were told. 'But you' – he pointed at Woody – 'you were snoring louder than anyone. We could hear you before we'd even left the station.'

'At least we got woken up by other firemen,' Woody countered defensively. 'Remember that time we did the night-time salvage over at Stoney Stretton?' He turned round to me, the one person in the cab who hadn't been there. 'We'd been working like pigs all night. We had the salvage sheet laid out on the grass, we'd been lifting and carrying for hours. It was hot and sweaty and we took a break, leaning on our helmets and closing our eyes for a few moments. Next thing we knew we were all fast asleep.'

'So who woke you? The chief?'

'Worse than that.'

'Betty?'

'Steady on. No, it was a golden blinkin' retriever. He was out on an early morning walk with his owner. Slobbering over us with a tongue as rough as a scrubbing brush. I've never been woken up by having my face licked before.'

'You haven't lived, mate,' Ben called out as the conversation began to degenerate the way it so often did.

We plumbed new depths as we passed the Lion Hotel in the heart of Shrewsbury, a jewel-box of a place that had been considered ancient and interesting when Charles Dickens had stayed there a hundred or so years ago. A little further up High Street we were silenced by the radio coming to life. There's always an extra jolt of excitement when a call comes through while you're already out on one of the appliances. At times like these the job was at its most intense. 'House fire on Belvidere Road, persons reported,' came the call. I could sense Woody doing a mental calculation to work out the best route. He put his foot down and sped us up through the town's one-way system and headed back the way we'd come. The siren and the blue lights clicked on as we reached our first junction. We were on our way.

'Persons reported' – those two key words ensured this shout would have our full and undivided attention. They meant exactly what they said. Someone was reported to be in the building that was on fire. The police and an ambulance were automatically mobilised for persons reported calls. When we got them, the pressure on everyone was intense. But it was toughest on the driver. Every second he delayed was an extra second someone was potentially breathing in smoke. It was an extra second that a fire could spread or some other hazard could prove fatal.

I looked at my watch as we thundered through the late-morning traffic. Half past eleven in the morning was getting on for prime time for a kitchen fire, though there was no way of knowing what we might be facing. Woody picked up speed as I got kitted out in my breathing apparatus in the back. I fastened the shoulder and waist straps, checked my torch was on the shoulder strap and the fireman's axe was on my waist. At my side Charlie was getting kitted out in the same way. In the second fire engine that we knew would have been mobilised from the station the others would be preparing too. We must have all thought that we were ready for anything, the way we always were. What we didn't know was that today was different. There was a shock ahead that no amount of training or experience could prepare us for.

'Oh dear God, I don't believe it. It's Mabel,' Joe said as the engine slowed to a halt. Ben, Charlie and I, all facing rearwards, tried to twist around and see what he was talking about.

'What do you mean?'

'It's Mabel. It must be her house that's on fire. She's standing in the street. She looks in a bad way.'

Things were a bit of a blur after that. There's no one we won't help as the Fire Brigade. We offer the same professional service to everyone. But it feels different when it's one of your own. It means more somehow.

Joe was off the engine before it had stopped. So were we. He strode up to our lovely, proud, mouthy chief cook and reached out his hand. She all but fell into his arms. It was the most extraordinary, unlikely scene from two people who had rarely if ever shown any vulnerability before. 'You OK?' was all Joe said at first.

'I'm fine. I'm just so stupid, so silly, so embarrassed.'

'What happened?'

'I was making chips when I answered the front door. I was the stupid, silly, dippy housewife who went to the front door when she had a chip pan on the hob.'

'Is there anyone else in the house?'

I was almost certain that Mabel's husband had died years ago, but I had no idea if she lived with any other relatives. 'It's just me. I was cooking for my lunch. What a stupid old woman I am. I can't believe I've been such a prize fool.'

Joe told her to stop worrying and as the second appliance arrived we started to act. Mabel's house was a well-kept semi-detached, the kind we knew well and visited all the time. The kitchen was at the back and had a door leading out into the garden. 'I did shut the kitchen door behind me. That was the only clever thing I've done all day,' Mabel called out.

That was good news. As well as holding back the flames it should have stopped the smoke from spreading and doing too much damage to the rest of her home. That was particularly important in chip-pan fires. Not only do they leave smoke marks on every surface, they leave grease. Cleaning up afterwards is absolute hell.

By this time Charlie and I had stormed in through the back door with a fire blanket for the burning pan. We had to fight our way through thick acrid smoke. The fire blanket did its job straight away – every kitchen would have one, if I had my way – and when those flames had died Charlie carried the pan and all its boiling oil right out to the safety of the back garden. That's when the next job had to be done. Unfortunately for poor Mabel, the fire had spread to her kitchen curtains and begun to burn several of her wooden cabinets. With the boiling oil out of the equation we could bring in the cavalry: the water. We hosed the inside of her kitchen and quickly put out the flames, but the fire had already done a heck of a lot of damage.

'Mabel is not going to like the look of this,' Charlie whistled as we shut off the hose and surveyed the scene. There was water and burnt stuff everywhere. China dishes and anything else that wasn't nailed down and had been involved in the fire, had been blasted on to the floor and smashed. 'She doesn't like it when you put a fork in the knife drawer back at the station. I reckon you should be the one to tell her about this, Windsor. You're her favourite. Go on, you go and get her.'

We both went. But in the end it took quite a while before we could attract Mabel's attention. Out in the street she and her neighbour were having a bit of a barney about who was to blame for the fire – with both of them wanting to take the rap.

'I should never have come around at lunchtime. I should have known you would be cooking,' said the neighbour, a round, kindly-looking lady around Mabel's age who had a stricken look on her face and seemed to be on the point of tears.

'You weren't to know I had a pan of chips on.'

'I should never have kept you talking for so long.'

'I should have known better than to answer the door at all – me, who's worked at the fire station for so many years. And I don't have a single penny of insurance for this either. I never thought I'd need it. I never thought I'd be such a silly, stupid, foolish old woman.'

I stepped forward to try and comfort her. 'It's not so bad. You did the right thing to shut the kitchen door, Mabel,' I began. 'That kept the worst of the smoke in there. You'll need to have a bit of work done to get your kitchen back the way it was, and the water hasn't helped. It's done a lot of damage, to be honest. But there's next to no damage in the hall. Even in the kitchen the flames didn't get through the ceiling, so you were lucky there as well.'

'And we'll fix it all up for you,' added Martin, who'd been on the second appliance. 'We'll get you some brand spanking new units in there, we'll get a lick of fresh paint on the walls and it will be good as new in no time. We'll start on Tuesday and we'll finish when we go on nights again at the weekend. Won't we, lads?' Everyone roared their agreement and I stole a quick glance at Martin as Mabel began to cry for real. Who would ever have thought that of all of us it would be the gruffest, most taciturn man on the watch who managed to say the exact right thing at the exact right time?

'Lynda, can we go to your house and make my boys some tea?' Mabel asked her neighbour when she was finally able to speak. By the time they had come back with the mugs Mabel had dried her eyes, brushed her white hair and painted fresh red lipstick on her face. Some of her old spirit had returned too. A lady from one of the houses opposite brought out a packet of custard creams from Spar. Mabel gave them a witheringly dismissive glance. Her friend Lynda did exactly the same. So another lady darted back into her own kitchen to fetch a tin of very posh Scottish shortbread. The usual one-upmanship was alive and well in Shropshire that afternoon. We were more than happy to take full advantage of it.

All told, around half a dozen elderly ladies had joined the rest of the rent-a-crowd by the time we were gearing up to leave. It was extraordinary, watching them rally around their friend, listening to her explanations of the fire, discussing what they planned to do to save the food in her pantry and explaining how they would help her cook her meals until the repair was done.

'There's no stopping women like that when they get the bit

between their teeth. No wonder we won the bloody war,' Arfer muttered as one of the ladies brought Mabel a deckchair, an umbrella to use as a parasol and a blanket for the shock.

We didn't see Mabel back at the station for another six days. We were on nights until the following Thursday, then we had our usual four days off. When we were due to see her again, at the start of our next tour of days, we were more than ready for her.

'There's an old lady at the front door wants to speak to you, Mabel!' Woody yelled when she was in the kitchen, getting ready to cook our lunches as normal.

'Come back, Mabel, the kitchen's on fire!' we all added as one. Mabel might be pushing seventy and one of the nicest women in the world but we weren't going to let a mickey-take opportunity like this pass us by.

'None of you are too old to go over my knee for a sound smacking!' she retorted, brandishing a wooden spoon with intent.

'Promises, promises!' was just one of our very predictable responses.

We kept the jokes coming for quite a while, but if Mabel had any doubts about what we really thought of her she only need look at her new kitchen. We'd raised a bit of money among the various watches and everyone had pitched in to sort out her sodden electrics, put new doors on her cupboards and cabinets, hang some brightly coloured new curtains and give the whole place a complete facelift. We even bought a flower in a pot for her window sill.

'I'm cross with all of you and I want you to know it,' she declared after we had taken the mickey out of her one more time. 'But if you tell me what you want for lunch I'll see if I can find my way to making it.'

'Pete, you're mess manager so it's over to you to sort all that out,' said John. 'But remember I like a good beef-and-ale pie. We haven't had a decent toad-in-the-hole for some time either. And a chicken curry never goes amiss.'

As John headed down to the station office, Pete took a seat at the end of the mess-room table with Mabel. He'd just collected our usual £3 a week mess money so his next job was to work out what we would eat for the next four-shift tour of duty and what we needed to buy. As mess manager Pete got paid over-time to buy the food in his own time. In my four years at the station I don't think that had ever happened once. No surprise that as soon as we had done our drills Pete called four of us to the engine.

'Jockey, the boss says you can drive,' he told me.

'Brilliant.'

'Everyone rigged and ready in case we get a call on the way?'

'Ready.'

'Then let's go shopping.'

I drove us into town and out towards the Co-op shop we always used. I parked us up at the far end of the car park and sat back as Pete and Dodger marched off towards the store trying to impress as many housewives and small children as possible along the way. When they were back with enough food to feed our little army we stowed it in the lockers so it would be out of the way if an emergency call came through. Then I manoeuvred around an obstacle course of badly parked cars and took us back to base.

'That's six times I've driven the engine now,' I said to myself as I plugged the engine into the electrics back in the appliance room. Six times spread out over nearly three weeks. Did the thrill of driving fade the more often I did it? Did it heck! I had been as excited driving back from the supermarket as I'd been that first day on hydrant duty. More importantly, my ulti-mate goal, driving out to a real shout, was surely getting ever closer.

That afternoon we headed over to what we thought was an office fire in town. It turned out to have been a false alarm – some dirt or dust had got into the fire alarm, so all we had to do was clean it out and head back to the station. Just before we departed, John turfed Ben out of the driver's seat and said I should drive us home. Looking back, that was no big deal. But it felt like one at the time. Yes, it had been a false alarm, but it was a proper job all the same. We'd all been pumped up and ready for action on the way out. We were still pretty fired up on the way back. Plus, of course, there was the thought in the back of my mind that if the radio came alive and we got an emergency call there'd be no time to switch to one of the more experienced drivers. That day it would be my engine, my responsibility. I gripped the steering wheel tighter. This was every bit as exciting as I'd expected it to be. It was brilliant.

'Shame we didn't get another shout, boss. I was ready for it,' I told John cheekily when we were back at base.

'Yes, but was Shropshire ready?' he asked.

At least he was smiling. For all the jokes, I knew I was slowly being accepted by the watch as a pretty decent rookie driver. Day by day and shift by shift there were fewer faces at the mess-room window watching me pull out on to the main road at the start of each drive. There was never any malice in it, but I was pretty certain the jokes had already been written: if I were to hit a kerb while driving I'd be Kerbie Castle or Windsor Kerbie for the rest of the drive. So thank God I never hit one. Thank God I never stalled the engine either. With no smudges or scratches to be examined when I brought the engine back I didn't provide any ammunition for dinner-time mickey takes either. No one con-gratulated me on any of this, of course – I'd probably have fallen over in shock if they had. But bit by bit I felt I was making it. As the summer stretched on towards autumn I knew I was being treated as a fully-fledged member of the driving team – the one thing I'd fought for since joining the watch four years ago as a green-as-grass eighteen-year-old. I remember how pleased I was at being accepted. So I decided to take advantage. For pretty much the first time on the watch I needed to ask someone a favour. Forget the sixteen-ton fire engine. What I really wanted to do was borrow Caddie's car.

9

The money I was making from my building jobs let me upgrade my faithful but ageing Ford Cortina. When it had been parked up outside my house or in the station it had certainly looked as if it could do something. In truth, it was getting a bit tired. I called it my sheep in wolf's clothing. I searched in the *Autotrader* until I found just the right replacement. A 3 series BMW. White with the full Alpina body kit and stripes. It was quite a step up from what it replaced, and I was now convinced that I had the best-looking car on the watch. Or I was, till Caddie changed his and went from a Morris Oxford to a 4.2-litre Jag. It was his new pride and joy. And it was mine too. I loved that car from afar, well, from across the car park, at least. It was mustard colour and it had a white leather interior. Alice had gone over to Nottingham for a couple of days to find somewhere to live the following term. I was going to drive over and bring her back in time for a party I'd organised for her twenty-first birthday. That Jag, as a birthday surprise, would be the perfect car to do it in.

'So let's get this clear. You want to use my new car, to show off to your new girlfriend?' Caddie said when I finally made my request.

'That's pretty much it, yes,' I said, honesty being my only available policy.

'Why the heck would I agree to that?'

'Because Alice would be really pleased. I know she would.' That was the first card I had decided to play. Everyone on the watch fancied Alice, but Caddie, old enough to be her dad, had the softest spot of all.

'She likes cars, does she?' he asked, faltering.

'She loves them,' I lied. 'And she thinks you've done an amazing job restoring that Morris Oxford you had. She's always talking about it. I know she'd be really grateful if you said yes.' Caddie's mind whirred away, but I knew I was winning him over.

'I suppose there's no harm in a wee trip over to Nottingham. Just this once, mind.'

'I'm sure Alice will come over and buy you a drink to say thanks,' I said. That was my ace. Caddie folded and the game was over.

'It's worth ten of you,' he said, handing me the keys on the day of my trip. 'One scratch, jockey, one scratch and I'll have your house.' I gave him a salute and got behind the wheel. It was a great car. I fired it up, got into gear and roared off down the street. The last thing I saw in the rear-view mirror as I turned off towards town was a very worried-looking Caddie.

Whoa! When I overtook my first car I over-steered massively. The motor was so much more powerful than anything I'd driven before. I stormed past the car and weaved back on to my side of the road. A little later I hit an even higher speed as I dipped down towards Cannock. As I cruised along the A38 I felt as though the road was mine. Forget being a fireman. I was a racing driver. The trip to Nottingham would normally have taken an hour and a half; I got there in less than an hour.

I'd arranged to meet Alice outside the university, so I rocked up, parked the Jag and stood alongside it, leaning on the bonnet trying to look like an English Danny Zucker. I reckon I could pretty much pull it off. I was Alice's boyfriend. I had a proper job, I was a fireman. To those student types, I reckoned I was the business. Who knows what they really thought. But I was feeling best in class as she rushed towards me with a couple of her pals. The surprise worked. She was in awe of the car, but more importantly, with me, that I'd gone to so much trouble for her birthday. We went for something to eat, had a wander round the city, then headed off home. One of her friends was as keen on fast cars as me. 'Give it a go, let's see if this thing can fly!' he yelled from the back as we joined the dual carriageway. I went for it. We hit sixty then seventy – and then it all went wrong. There was an almighty bang. Then there was a horrible, metal-wrenching crash. Then things got even worse.

I'd hit the brakes at the first bang. I swept us off the road and we all got out to survey the damage. The back silencer box had only gone and fallen off. So when we got under way again we went from cruising along in a smooth purring cat to thundering along in something that sounded like a Tiger Moth on a dodgy landing strip. And the faster I tried to go the worse the noise became.

'Malcolm, it sounds like it's going to blow up!' Alice's other friend screamed at one point.

'What do you think Caddie is going to say?' Alice yelled above the din as we finally made it back to Shrewsbury.

'Nothing. Because he's never going to find out,' I shouted back, crossing my fingers in hope. I kept the speed down, desperately hoping that Caddie wouldn't be out walking – or even within earshot – as we got into town. Fortunately there were plenty of people who could help me out. Archie, who ran the workshop in the fire station yard, already had a great reputation patching up dents or scratches on the appliances before the chief got to see them. He was a tall, gangly man who had a cigar permanently welded to his bottom lip. I headed straight for him after dropping Alice and her friends off at her parents' home.

'Caddie will not be best pleased to see this. Not best pleased. Not best pleased at all,' Archie said in his typically fast, machine-gun-style voice.

'I know. That's why I was hoping he wouldn't have to see it. Have you got the parts? Can you get them?'

'Aye, I can get them. It won't be cheap, mind. Won't be cheap. You know that, dontcha?' I knew it. The price we paid for illicit work like this depended largely on the degree of secrecy required – and on the amount of stick we'd get if we were found out. No surprise that my bill for keeping Caddie in the dark was high. I had to shell out a shocking £28. I was gutted. That was more than the entire exhaust system on my old Cortina. Still, I paid up and thanked my lucky stars that the job had been done so fast. I cleaned the car, top to bottom, back to front, inside and out. I filled it up with a full tank of petrol and Alice and I bought Caddie a big bottle of whisky. He wasn't fooled for a moment. But as she came over to the station to thank him in person I just about got away with it.

Getting through the weeks took a bit of juggling now July had turned into August. I was finding plenty of work for my building business. One of the first people I'd done the pointing for at the start of the year had got in touch and asked me to lay a patio outside his kitchen. His next-door neighbours had asked me to put up a new garden fence for them. I'd done some basic plumbing work for a friend of my mum's. Even John had put work my way when he'd been overloaded earlier in the summer. The end result was that the cash was building up. The country and the economy were all over the place in the early 1980s, yet somehow I managed to do OK. I'd been paying 15 per cent interest on my mortgage when I'd bought my house. Interest rates had fallen massively since then so I had more money left at the end of the month. Our wages were doing OK too, so I ignored all the negative headlines and booked my first ever skiing holiday for the following spring with a group of my old school friends who worked the production lines at Rolls-Royce. I tried to see as much of Alice as possible before she headed off for the new term in Nottingham. Oh, and I had a new hobby for the days when I thought rock climbing was too tame. I'd taken up hang-gliding.

I had contacted an instructor called Mick Skinner and booked a course over at Long Marston Airfield just outside of Stratford. The whole thing was initially challenging but a lot of fun. Mick had mounted a winch on to the back of a home-modified Hillman Hunter estate. After a few low-level tows to get used to controlling the hang-glider, it was time to go higher. I clung to the A-frame of the training glider that he connected to the car via a bridle. Mick then sped off in the car, paying out a set amount of cable as he went. In the process the glider and I began to soar up into the air. It was the most exciting thing ever – apart from driving a fire engine, of course. And it got better. When you reached what you reckoned was the pre-agreed height you flicked the release cord with your right hand and you were free. From then on you had up to five minutes to glide back down to land. Once you had, you put the A-frame control bar on to the specially made bracket on the back of the car, jumped aboard holding the nose of the hang-glider close to the car's roof then you got driven back to the start.

'You'll either love it or you'll be so terrified you'll hate it,' Mick had said on the first day. I loved it. I did a few more glides over at Long Marston. I even blagged a few flights in one of the microlights that were kept at the airfield. Then I joined the Long Mynd Hang-Gliding Club so I could fly off the top of hills for real. The Long Mynd is one of the best places in England for hang-gliding. It's all to do with the direction the ridge faces and how long it is. If all goes well you can glide for seven miles up and down the ridge. On a good day you can fly as far as the east coast of England!

I was thinking about hang-gliding as we headed past the Long Mynd to Carding Mill Valley the following week. I wished I was up there, because that way I'd be in another world. All of beautiful Shropshire would be laid out beneath me, everything looking orderly and calm. You always have a fair few butterflies in your stomach when you glide. You don't go thousands of feet up in the air with only an aluminium frame with a scrap of material stretched over it and not get nervous. But at the same time you feel calm. You can't be that cut off and that far away from your hectic life and not be calm. That's why I wanted to be up there. Because it was anything but calm in our fire engines on this particular day.

On our last tour of duty, out of nowhere, Ben and Simon had come to blows. As far as we could tell it was triggered by the kind of horseplay that went on all the time at the station. Most of us had been asleep on the last night shift of our tour when Ben had pulled Simon's quilt off his bed and threatened to throw it out of the window. It was a silly prank, but Simon went ballistic. The lights in the dorm went on as the shouting began. The pair of them fronted up and then started to go at it, hammer and tongs. It was a fierce, full-on fight. They lunged for each other and managed to land a fair few heavy punches before the rest of us could dive in and pull them apart. Ben was taken downstairs to the control room while Simon was dragged off to the muster bay, and they both received a serious talking to from the boss. The rest of us remained upstairs, pretty much in shock. It wasn't so much that flare-ups like this didn't happen, it was more that they *couldn't* happen. Yes, there were some on the watch who were liable to get into a fight on a Friday night. Ben was one of the worst offenders and he was forever telling tall tales of the action seen by the metal comb he carried in his back pocket. But Friday-night barneys on our own turf were another matter. The one simple, unwritten rule of the Fire Brigade was that we didn't fight each other. Bringing that into the station was totally out of line. You can't lay into someone today when you could be on a job with your life depending on them tomorrow. You couldn't bear a grudge against someone you needed to rely on as your wingman. So no surprise that John ordered the pair to sort it out – and fast. They had duly apologised to one another and the tour of duty had ended without further incident, but on an uneasy note.

Today, as luck would have it, Ben and Simon were number three and number four respectively on the water-tender ladder. I had a feeling that everyone was being tested as we raced out across the countryside. The atmosphere was unusually tense. And we weren't even sure what we were facing. A hiker had reported seeing smoke billowing out of a lonely house way above him in the hills. He'd made the call from a local farm. The farmer thought the house was unoccupied, that no one had lived there for years. All the same, we were heading into the unknown and we had to be ready for the worst.

In the back of both appliances numbers three and four were in full BA sets by the time we got to Church Stretton, Shropshire's own Little Switzerland. We gained more altitude as we turned into Carding Mill Valley. The fire was in a long, narrow stone cottage. It looked as if two homes had been knocked into one. Two windows upstairs were partially open and smoke was pouring out of them. It was leaking out of cracks in the windows and window frames around the rest of the house as well. Ben and Simon were sent in through the front door, yelling out to see if there were any occupants as they went. At the same time Woody and I were sent in through the back. We dragged the hose-reel round the side of the house and sprayed down the back door before trying the handle. It wasn't locked so I pushed it open. Smoke billowed out but the door got stuck almost straight away. I put my shoulder against it and the extra inches I got gave us enough room to squeeze in.

We were in a room full of smoke, but no flames. Were we alone though? Standard procedure when you're searching a room is to start off by heading to the left, so that's what we did. Like most house fires, the smoke was incredibly dense. The old comment about not being able to see the hand in front of your face must have originated in a house fire, not a fog. That day, in the back of that house, there wasn't any point in using torches. Even with the strongest beams available we couldn't see as much as a foot beyond our noses. Still, the room had to be searched and searched fast. I took up position alongside the wall. Woody was at my side, reaching out and stretching into the middle of the room. We searched using our hands and feet, keeping our weight on our back foot, leaving the front foot to search at ground level and check the integrity of the floor ahead.

'You got anything yet?' I called out at the first corner of the room.

'All clear,' Woody yelled back. Communication in thick, acrid smoke was incredibly tough. Reliable, working radios you could use in a fire were still just a glint in the Fire Brigade's eye back then. If you could see at all then you had to rely on our own brand of sign language and a dose of common sense. If not, then it was a case of shouting your head off. When two firemen were going round a room like this we were supposed to stay in physical contact. But back then, it was looked on as a sign of weakness if you held on to your partner, so we tended not to – ridiculous, looking back. We took the mickey out of each other about enough things already without holding hands all the time. So contact tended to be verbal, which was why Woody just swore very loudly when he stumbled on a nest of tables that could have doubled as a bear trap. I stepped around a sofa I had come upon against the wall of the room then passed a glass-fronted cabinet. Woody swore again as another coffee-table contraption got in his way and I nearly fell when I reached out to feel and put my weight on what turned out to be a rocking chair. In the shortest possible time, though, we were on to the last of the four walls and looked set to call the room clear and continue the search through the rest of the house. But before we could do so we had one more obstacle to negotiate.

*

We were almost back at the door we'd come in through. Our plan was to open it to help with the ventilation then head on into the hall and the rest of the cottage. Suddenly my left foot came into contact with an object on the ground. Wondering what the hell I'd kicked into, I leant down. The lower you go the thinner smoke will be. That's why it pays to keep down if you're trapped in fire. That's why it's only in Hollywood films that hunky firemen sling beautiful women over their shoulders and carry them out to an adoring, cheering crowd. In reality, being put on someone's shoulder lifts you up into the danger zone. Here in the real world we're far more likely to drag you out along the ground. It's not very glamorous and you might pick up a few bruises that way. But your lungs will be a whole lot better for it. Anyway, back in our burning cottage, the air was a lot clearer lower down so I could identify the final obstacle to step over. Of all things it was a mannequin dressed in an odd-looking suit and tie, with the smooth waxy face and wildly unfashionable hair that dummies always had. It was in one of those ridiculous theatrical poses you see in shop windows as well: one arm sticking out, the other slightly to the rear, the head looking straight ahead like a World War Two hero on a battleship.

Woody stepped over the dummy and pulled the back door wide open behind him. 'Room clear!' he shouted.

With some much needed extra visibility we were able to carry on with our job. The smoke was still thick out in the hall and we did a bit of a dance with a coat stand as we approached the front of the property. All the doors in the hall were closed; after checking for hazards we managed to search them fast. There were only two small bedrooms upstairs and they were both clear. The one bathroom was downstairs and it was empty too. With a final 'Room clear!' we headed into a cramped junk or boot room to the side and met up with Ben and Simon, who had finished tackling the fire and were now carrying out their search from the front. The fire had been small, fierce and the kind of thing we saw all the time. It appeared to have begun on the cooker. 'A pan of spuds,' Ben reckoned. When those get forgotten about, they burn dry then when they catch light they generate a lot of heat and masses of very nasty smoke. In this case one of those old-fashioned clothes racks that hang from the ceiling had caught alight and added to the drama. No one would be cooking or washing in that kitchen any time soon. But at least no one had died.

We all headed out through the front door to report to John. Five minutes later, when the last remnants of smoke had cleared, Woody and I went back inside to help make the property safe. The others had already turned off the electrics. We now pulled a section of the kitchen apart to check for hidden embers. We dragged the wooden clothes rack off its hinges and checked nothing was smouldering in the ceiling. Then we went outside for the final time.

'God knows where the owner's run off to,' mused John as we re-stowed our equipment on the engine. 'Could have been tramps or youths who broke in and did a runner, I suppose. The place doesn't look like anyone's lived here properly in years. Go in and lock the back door, Windsor, then we can think about going on our way.'

I headed through the house to lock the door from the inside. It was then that I took my first proper look around the room – and I got a massive, horrible shock. Looking back, it was obvious. At the time it was just terrible. For it wasn't a tailor's dummy we'd stepped over. It was the poor, lonely old man who had lived in the house. I knelt at his side. Even now, even without all the smoke, he didn't look real. The heat had seared out all the lines and wrinkles in his skin. His body fat, bubbling through the skin, had given him the false, waxy appearance. He looked absolutely the same as the things you see in shop windows. And even the theatrical pose began to make sense. I felt a catch in my throat as I worked it out. The poor old man had been trying to escape from the fire. He'd made it as far as his back door. He'd been reaching out towards it. He'd been so very close to safety. But his heart, his lungs, or his luck had given up on him and he had collapsed to the ground right there, in that contorted position, on the wrong side of his own back door.

'Boss, you need to come and look at something,' I bellowed. The others filed in and we stood looking at the homeowner in silence.

'Dead as a door nail, poor old codger. But we'll be needing a doctor all the same,' John said quietly.

Caddie radioed to check up on the whereabouts of the ambulance. When it arrived the crew put the old guy on a stretcher and drove him off to hospital where a doctor could follow procedure and pronounce him officially dead. I remember that his right slipper fell off as the crew moved him out of the room. His bare foot lay before me, and it was quite different from his face and hands. His foot had been protected from the worst of the heat by the shoe. It hadn't changed its form quite as much. It was what it should have been: an old man's foot, with yellowing toenails and patches of rough, hard skin. A complete contrast to how young his face looked after the heat of the fire. I don't know why that struck me as so odd and so sad as I looked down on it. But everything about that day, and that fire seemed strangely sad.

The feeling didn't leave me as I joined the others and stood outside the cottage on a perfect late summer's evening. It was getting dark and thick horizontal lines of dark blue and richest purple looked to have been painted across the horizon. The country lane was coming alive with insects and the faintest breeze was blowing clouds of petals and pollen across from the nearby fields. We were on our own outside the cottage, which despite its lonely location was still far from usual. No cars had come by, no neighbours or nearby farmers had headed over and no family members had been alerted to the tragedy. This poor old guy had lived and died alone. Would he be buried alone? I'd recently been out with some of Alice's old school friends who worked for the council. One of them organised funerals for people who died with no family to look after them. She put notices giving the funeral's date in the local papers in Shrewsbury or anywhere else they thought would help. Often not a single person showed up on the day. I hoped this old man didn't suffer that fate. He'd been so close to escaping with his life. How sad that he should be so alone in death. Were any of the others thinking the same thing? It certainly wasn't anything we were likely to discuss. But maybe this experience did remind us of the value of friendship. There were no handshakes and no profound speeches, but by the time we got back into the engine Ben and Simon had started to talk about a decorating job Ben was in the middle of. By the time we got to Shrewsbury we were all discussing tactics for our next volleyball match. It was peace in our time. Life could go back to normal.

10

I used to joke that I'd joined the Fire Brigade at eighteen because I wanted to be a hero and rescue lots of pretty damsels in distress. Over the years, far too many of the damsels concerned turned out to be of the four-legged variety. But now I was finally going to encounter the genuine article.

After a couple of dull, rainy weeks, the good weather was back with a vengeance. 'An Indian Summer, my favourite time of year. The days are long and the skirts are short,' Charlie declared to universal agreement. At which point we got the dream call-out. A sunbather needed our help. A female sunbather. And we were being paid for this! Just how good could life get?

The number of men and the number and type of appliances that get sent out to a shout depends on the nature of the emergency, as well as on the availability of suitable manpower. For a typical house fire we would normally have five on the water-tender ladder, four on the water tender. For a simple domestic emergency with no lives in the balance it could just be the water-tender ladder, and we could sometimes send that out with only four of us on board. Regardless of the number of men needed for a shout, the entire gang would jump down the pole or run into the appliance room. The extras would come along in case someone stumbled, twisted their ankle or needed to be replaced at the last minute.

When we got the call about our lady sunbather the extras were keener than usual to jostle for position and climb on board. But in the end it was Caddie driving the main appliance with John at his side and me, Charlie and Pete in the back. We were all smiles as we waved the others a cheeky goodbye and hit the road.

'What exactly does "trapped in a fence" mean?' Charlie asked as we digested the nugget of information we'd been given on the situation facing us. 'We had that dog trapped in a fence a few years back. Its head got stuck. Why would a woman put her head in a hole in a fence? Could this be a wind-up? Are we on our way to meet Jeremy blinkin' Beadle?'

John kept things serious and brought us back in line from his seat up front. 'This lady could be trapped in barbed wire. She could be impaled on metal railings. This could mean any number of things. I don't want anyone horsing around. This is a serious job. It is most certainly not a joke.'

We shut up, kept our heads down in the back and sweated. Even with all the windows wide open it was boiling hot on the fire engine. Everyone we passed on the streets was in shorts and light-coloured T-shirts. We were in our full kit: thick blue leggings, black leather boots and our thermal fire tunics.

I started to get travel sick again as we drove towards Harlescott Grange. I'd not had an attack of it for a while, so this was probably due to the heat as much as anything else. The engine had been relatively cool in the shade of the appliance room. Now we were out in the early afternoon sun it was baking hot. I tried to look out to the distance to calm my stomach. The countryside looked beautiful. The fields were full of ripening corn and the trees were in full leaf. The sun was glinting on a stretch of water far out to the east. It looked like a sparkling strip of silver. Everything seemed heavy and bloated and relaxed. I took a big gulp of air as we swung into a housing estate. I didn't time it very well. The smell of melting bitumen in the tarmac was intense. We headed round a couple more tight turns before coming to a halt. I closed my eyes for a fraction of a second. My motion sickness started to pass, the way it always did. I was ready to get on with the work in hand. I had a gorgeous sun-bather to rescue!

Down on the ground we walked past an ambulance outside the house in question then headed towards the side gate. The back garden was jam-packed. All the poor girl's neighbours had trooped through the gate and were clustered around her in the back garden. They stepped aside as we approached, leaving us to walk towards a lone lady in denim shorts and a bright red bikini top standing right against the fence.

'Bingo!' I heard Charlie mutter as we approached. Bingo indeed. No barbed wire, no one impaled on metal railings. Just a very beautiful, half-naked woman who needed our help. This was why we'd all joined the Fire Brigade!

'What's your name, love? What's happened?' John asked, clearly trying not to laugh.

'It's Jennifer. Jennifer Jacobson. I live here. It's my finger. It's trapped.' She moved her body away from the fence and we took a look. She had the index finger of her right hand wedged into a knot hole in the fence. 'I don't know why I did it,' she continued. 'I'd been sunbathing. I'd just stood up to have a drink and I saw the hole. There was a knot in it and I pushed it through to the other side. Then I realised I couldn't get my finger back out. It's bleeding and it hurts. It's the most stupid thing I've ever done.'

A quick examination showed why. Her finger had hit a nail on the other side of the fence. It had dug into her finger when she'd tried to pull it free and now she was caught like a fish on a barbed hook. 'I tried everything to get myself free on my own, but in the end I had to call for help.'

'I heard her. I live two doors down and I was the one that dialled 999. I'm Mrs Lloyd,' said a fierce, competent-looking older lady with short greying hair and a faded, floral dress.

'I'm from number 46. I brought some butter,' interrupted another, far friendlier lady. That explained the slightly rancid smell, I thought. 'We tried to ease her finger out, but the nail was in the way.'

'I brought my dad's hacksaw,' said a young lad proudly. 'I live next door to Mrs Lloyd at number 43. I heard all the noise. I wanted to cut the lady's finger out. I can do it now, if you let me.' He bent down and brandished the saw with intent.

Jennifer gave a shriek. 'Derek, I told you to put that away!' She looked over at John. 'I told him no. I thought he'd have my arm off. He's only eleven. He's shorter than I am. Even the saw is taller than he is.'

'I can stand on a stool,' the lad said defiantly.

John took the hacksaw out of the lad's hands without a word and passed it to me for safekeeping. Then he took control. He led us all next door so we could look at the nail from that angle. It was short, rusty and was there to stay. In its own way, this job was gearing up to be quite a challenge. We headed back round to Jennifer's garden. John explained our plan to her while the rest of us prepared. The idea was to cut a panel a foot square around Jennifer's finger. Once she was free of the fence she could go to hospital where they'd have more delicate tools to finish off the job.

We got ready. Charlie and I grabbed our short ladder and some other kit to brace the fence and keep it still. Then Pete came forward with our air-operated Cengar saw and began fitting a new blade to it. The contraption dwarfed the hacksaw the lad had brought over from his dad's toolkit. It looked a pretty serious tool, especially to Jennifer.

'Oh God. Is that what you're going to use to cut me out?' she asked.

I spotted a twinkle in Pete's eye as he moved alongside our sunbather. 'It is, my dear, but don't worry about a thing. I'm getting much better using it now I've cut back on the drinking. Seven out of ten times I reckon I get the aim just right,' he joked.

Poor old Jennifer let out an even louder wail and the rest of us tried to keep a straight face. 'Jennifer, please, I've not had an accident in weeks now. Not a really serious one, anyway,' he said, before John shut him up with a look.

'My friend is joking, of course,' John said firmly. 'As I said before, he's not going to cut your finger out of the fence altogether. He won't even come close to your hand. All we're doing is getting you ready for the ambulance. They'll do the rest in hospital. They'll probably advise a tetanus injection, but I'm sure they'll explain all that to you in their own time. Now, if you're ready, let's begin.'

Charlie and I held the fence still while Pete fired up the saw. It made a real racket. All the neighbours jumped back in shock. The little lad's eyes widened, partly in horror, but mainly out of the sheer thrill of it. This was probably the most exciting thing that had happened to him all holidays. I know I'd have been the same at his age.

'Don't let it slip!' Jennifer begged Pete. She was nice as well as stunning to look at. And her eyes were genuinely scared all of a sudden. Maybe the jokes had gone too far. Pete gave her his kindliest smile.

'Don't you worry, miss. Jokes apart, I'm very good with this equipment. You might want to close your eyes, in case there are splinters. But it will all be over in a jiffy,' he said.

He was right. The saw made a heck of a noise but it sliced through the fence fast. Soon Jennifer, with a big square of fence round her finger, was free again. Mrs Lloyd ran inside the house to get her some extra clothes, much to our disappointment. Then Jennifer walked out of the garden and towards the ambulance out front. She said 'thank you' around a dozen times in a couple of minutes. For all his dodgy humour earlier on, I reckon she'd have thrown her arms around Pete and kissed him if she'd not got that fence panel attached to her hand. We yelled out good wishes as she disappeared round the side of her house. The ambulance man wanted her to hold her right hand up to help stem any bleeding. She looked as if she was balancing a square wooden plate on her finger like clowns do in the circus.

After we'd made sure the fence was secure and collected all our equipment, the last word went to Derek, the four-foot-three lad from number 43. He looked longingly at the timber-cutting blade on our saw. He looked at the hole it had cut in the fence. Then he looked at me. 'I could have done that,' he said despondently as I walked him home and put his dad's saw back in his garden shed.

We spotted the next damsel in distress on a country lane well out towards Llynclys where the road signs began to be written in Welsh as well as English. She wasn't the tall blonde beauty I was always hoping to rescue (well, she might have been blonde, but when we first saw her she was wearing a motorbike helmet so it was hard to tell). Nor, to be honest, was she particularly keen on being rescued. 'It's new. It's broken down,' was all she said, sulkily pointing towards her gleaming black moped. She took off her helmet – she was blonde, funnily enough – and pursed her lips.

'Patricia, it's George. How are you?' George called out from the back seat next to me.

If Patricia had been annoyed at needing our help before she was even crosser to have been recognised.

'Oh God, it's you. The whole world will know about this now. This is the last thing I need,' she pouted.

'Well, let's get you on your way as soon as we can,' George offered, sounding a lot kinder and more conciliatory than he ever did at the station. 'What happened? Have you got enough petrol?'

'Of course I've got enough petrol!' she snapped. 'I can't believe you asked that. Would you ask a man that question? You wouldn't, would you? Have I got enough petrol indeed!' She stood up tall. 'It just seized up. It was going fine. Then all of a sudden there was a terrible noise and the whole thing just seized up. It's the first time I've been out on it. I got it from the bike shop in Oswestry. It was delivered new, in its box, first thing this morning. I did everything the manual told me to do. I read every page. That's something a man wouldn't do. But it's still seized up on me and I don't know why.'

We pussyfooted around her for a while, asking a few questions and trying not to offend her. We're not the AA and strictly speaking roadside rescue wasn't our job. But having stopped we were committed. And there was no way our male pride would see us beaten. We tinkered with the ignition, took a look at the spark plug and after ten minutes or so we drew a blank.

'Lads, I reckon we can get the bike in the back of the engine,' Joe, our OIC of the day, said after a while. 'Patricia, if you don't mind sitting up front with me, we can take you to the bike shop and get them to take a proper look at it.' We did so and it's fair to say Patricia's mood didn't improve much on the journey. She was planning to use the moped to get to work every day. Now she thought she'd been ripped off. 'They sold me a lemon,' she kept muttering. 'It's because I'm a woman and they thought I wouldn't complain. They sold me the Friday bike. They knew it hadn't been made properly.'

'Good luck, love,' George yelled out once we'd dropped her off at the bike shop and were heading on our way.

'Don't call me love,' were the last words we heard from her.

A week or so later we heard what had happened. Unable to resist, George had popped into the bike shop for an update. He had the biggest grin imaginable on his face when he arrived at the station the next morning.

'You'll all want to hear this,' he began. 'That girl on the broken-down moped? Turns out she didn't have any oil in the engine.'

'That's what I said,' Joe protested.

'You want to know why? Remember she said she read every page of the manual and did everything that it told her?'

'Which no man would do. Yes, we remember that.'

'Well, the page about the oil said to remove the dipstick and check there was oil on it up to the line. She'd removed it and as there was no oil in the tank the dipstick was clean as a whistle. So she got a can of oil and put a bit of it on a cloth. Then she dabbed it on to the dipstick, right up to the line as instructed, put it back in and headed off on her first big ride.'

'Bloody hell, did the mechanics dare to tell her?'

'Would you?'

Fifteen months ago we'd been an official part of the entertainment over at the big West Midland Show down by the River Severn on the outskirts of Shrewsbury. We'd had a high old time trying to impress the ladies with our training routines – dragging ladders around and climbing up and down them like heroes. Then we'd taken the turntable ladder right into the middle of the main arena and sprayed jets of water over the crowds from 100 feet up. It had been a real hoot, even though the weather had been lousy and most of the audience were already sheltering under umbrellas. Now it was time for the annual Shrewsbury Flower Show and the weather was dry as a bone and boiling hot – and unfortunately we weren't planning on taking an active part in the proceedings. A whole host of other acts were there to entertain the crowds. So why were we there? As far as Arfer was concerned, it was to offer an extra climbing frame for snotty-nosed, sticky-fingered kids who'd spend all day begging to be allowed to climb into our cab and turn on the siren. 'Can we agree on this before we get there?' he'd said at the station. 'The little blighters can do a bit of climbing if their mums are decent lookers. But if they scratch or break anything we're allowed to run them down. And none of them touches the siren or the lights. Agreed?'

He was right about the children: they swarmed all over us like a cloud of gnats from the moment we arrived. But the real reason we were at the show was to keep everyone safe. There are always dangers in big crowded events like these. Smokers drop cigarettes in litter bins, children get too close to the water's edge, and almost anyone can have a few drinks too many and end up in all sorts of trouble. There was a country show once where we had to cut the wedding ring off a farmer's hand after it got trodden on by one of his prize cows while he was trying to clean its hooves. More often than not our biggest challenge is to sort it all out with a straight face. It isn't always easy.

'Remember the time that posh woman fell through the bottom of a picnic chair at the West Mid Show?' Woody said as we headed off on a patrol round the showground.

'The one who didn't want her friend to know it had happened? So we had to get the Cengar saw into the tea tent and cut her out while her friend was in the queue for the loo?'

'How about that school fair where the prefect helped us do a safety demonstration and ended up getting a fire bucket stuck on his head?'

We were laughing as we ambled through the crowds. The show was laid out all over Shrewsbury Quarry, the beautifully wide, undulating park carved out of the curve of the River Severn in the middle of town. It was the middle of a gloriously warm afternoon and the park was packed to bursting. Woody's family were helping out on a bric-a-brac stall somewhere in the very middle, so we headed that way next. Along the way we saw several familiar faces: Mr and Mrs Thom stopped us for a chat, the nut-brown farmer from the telegraph-pole fire outside of Stapleton shook our hands, and the lady from the Gold Fry chip shop blew us a kiss.

The bric-a-brac stall was surprisingly busy, so once Woody had said a quick hello to his wife and kids we headed back to the fire engine to see how Arfer was getting on. He was looking distinctly unimpressed as we approached, swatting away the latest wave of excited-looking kids.

'What time do you call this? Leaving me with these monsters for the whole backin' afternoon.'

'We've been gone less than half an hour,' Woody said, looking at his watch.

'That's half an hour I could have been in the beer tent. They've got local home-made cider on a stall over by the showground. I notice you didn't think to bring me a glass. Or to get me a beef burger. Or anything at all.'

'Well that little boy is about to put his toffee apple down on the passenger seat. Ask him if he'll sell it to you,' Woody said with a malicious glint in his eye. Arfer let out a terrifying roar and leapt forward to protect his fire engine from this latest threat.

We tried not to laugh as Arfer scooped up the squealing kid and deposited him a safe distance from the vehicle. As he did so, John came back from his own patrol of the grounds and Arfer headed off to get us all a cup of tea. No surprise that he got cider instead, saying the line on that stall was shorter. The four of us then settled down to while away the afternoon in the camping chairs we'd brought along specially. I sat back, stretched and soaked in the sunshine. A lot of firemen hated these public events, preferring to be in the station or out on a 'real' shout instead of mingling with the local population. Basking in the sun, sipping cider, I reckoned they were out of their minds.

'I think it's my turn to do a patrol of the ground,' Arfer announced an hour or so later when the shadows had begun to creep over our patch of grass.

'Paying particular attention to the beer tent and the hot-dog stall, no doubt,' said John. 'Tell you what: I'll go with you.'

Woody and I packed up the chairs and climbed up into the cab. The sun was going down fast, dropping out of the sky like a big, golden coin. The air was still warm and rich and there wasn't even a whisper of a breeze. If anything it felt as if it was getting hotter as the festival went on. There was a live band playing in the bandstand and they were attracting quite a crowd. After a lull around teatime the spectators' area had begun to fill up again. Everyone wanted to be in a prime position for the evening's big finale – the gala firework display.

I'd just finished my second cheeseburger and was draining a plastic cup of Heinz tomato soup when the festival organiser came on the tannoy. The newly crowned Miss Shrewsbury would kick it all off by doing the countdown, he said. Then she'd hit the big red button to start the display.

'Well, lads, nine times out of ten this will all go as smooth as clockwork, but we'd better be ready just in case it doesn't,' said John.

We couldn't see Miss Shrewsbury, more's the pity. But she did her job well. The crowd counted down, she hit the button and the first rockets shot up into the clear evening sky. Thousands of people went 'Ahh!' on cue as the fireworks exploded into a mass of reds, blues and greens. Another set of rockets went up. This time the sky was alight with a wave of huge, ever-expanding circles of coloured light. Next we had some amazingly loud bangers. Then the reds, blues and greens were back. There was a brief hiatus while what was supposed to be a massive white Catherine wheel spluttered and took an awfully long time to start to turn. But the pace picked up again as music blared out over the tannoy and the biggest wave of rockets yet blasted up to the sky. They burst into a series of blindingly white stars that trickled down from the heights, gradually fading and dying as they fell back down to earth. Or at least, that was the plan. Halfway through this final part of the display something went wrong with one of the rockets. It should have powered its cargo hundreds of feet into the sky. It didn't. It pootled its way a hundred feet or so above the showground then seemed to hang there in suspended animation.

'Uh-oh,' Caddie said quietly.

Uh-oh indeed. The rocket might not have got very high, but it was determined to put on a show all the same. After the pregnant pause it blew itself apart the way all its fellow fireworks were doing, releasing a vast circle of bright white stars to twinkle and trickle slowly down to earth. Except, of course, that this particular rocket had not got far enough away from the earth. The embers were still very much alight when they reached the ground. The heads of fireworks are specifically designed to burn hot, hard and violently. That's what makes them beautiful. That's why they're so dangerous if they touch something they shouldn't.

'The marquee's on fire! Windsor, Woody, get over there with extinguishers and a beater!' John yelled out the command. We'd already started to move. And John and Caddie had begun grabbing kit of their own. For it wasn't just a case of one ember starting one fire. The marquee looked to be alight in three different places. A clothing stall had also taken a direct hit and started to burn far over to our right. And a pile of hay and straw was burning at the edge of the showground where a troupe of Shetland ponies had been strutting their stuff only a few hours earlier. Five separate fires were blazing simultaneously. And there were only four of us on duty to try and sort it all out.

Fireworks were still going off overhead, the music was still blaring out and the crowds were screaming and screeching in a mix of worry and excitement as Woody and I thundered up the hillside with our equipment. The marquee was not looking good by the time we arrived. It was made of some sort of shiny, plastic-based material that was clearly nowhere near as fire-proof as it should have been. The embers from the fireworks had shot right through the roof in three different places. The tent was full of wooden chairs and tables and the bar was made of bales of straw, several chunks of which were already on fire.

'I'll take that side, you go for the corner. We'll tackle the back of it last,' I yelled at Woody as we arrived. 'Get out of the tent!' I yelled at the people milling around. 'Everybody out! Move right away now!'

I pulled the pin on the first fire extinguisher and blasted the worst of the blazes. That done, we hit the remaining fires with the beaters. As they've got such short handles you have to keep low and lean in very close to the fire when you use them. It means you get hot as anything and can get singed eyebrows as well as a bad back. But if there's a big grass fire on a farm or out on the heath, or in a public place like this, then they're hard to beat, if you'll excuse the pun. That night we got the marquee under control in double-quick time; you work fast when the adrenalin and the training kick in. We did have help from the police, though. PC Dale Walsh and another officer I didn't know had stormed in and were handling crowd control while stamping out as many rogue embers as they could find.

'Keep an eye on it all! We've got to go,' I yelled after scanning the scene one last time and judging it to be safe. The fireworks had stopped and the evening's soundtrack had been turned off, so we weren't doing all this to music any more. Without the flashing lights and explosions it felt less like a war zone. I scarpered across the fairground towards the clothing stall while Woody headed off in the direction of the showground.

'There's an extinguisher here,' someone shouted at me as I passed. I skidded to a stop and turned around to pick it up. It was heavy as heck, but I had a feeling we might need it. This particular stall was one of the worst possible things to have taken a hit from the firework. It was laden with woolly sweaters and piles of paper and plastic bags. John and Arfer had been forced to pull the whole thing down in an effort to contain the flames. By the time I got there they'd beaten most of them out. The extinguisher helped kill the remainder. Our problems weren't over yet though; there were two fire engines on their way to join us, but they'd not arrived so we were well overstretched.

'Your man over there by the parade ground, he needs some help,' a teenager shouted out to us. He'd come running up from the far side of the field and raced back down to take us to our next big challenge. Fortunately, Woody wasn't tackling the fire on his own by the time we arrived. A whole group of people, men and women, young and old, were giving it their all as well.

'Watch yourselves! Get back!' John bellowed as some of them began stamping on a pile of embers on the edge of the fire. Most of the men were in shorts and a few of the women were in long, floaty cotton skirts that could easily have been touched by the flames. Most surprising of all were the people trying to kick the life out of the fire in plastic flip-flops.

'I'll take the fire beater and help Woody,' I shouted at John as he tried to protect the most vulnerable of the volunteers. On the other side of the track that the ponies had been trotting round Woody was fighting what could easily have become a losing battle with the fire. The straw was tinder-dry. In the last few minutes, at the worst possible time, the wind seemed to have picked up again. Now it was whipping up the flames and blowing sparks towards an even larger pile of hay behind us.

'I'll take this side,' I told Woody. He moved to his left and we began to make a pincer movement on the fire. Arfer joined us and when John sent volunteers to fetch us more fire extinguishers we finally got it under control.

'Five fires, four men, and all of it tackled in less than ten very busy minutes,' John said, wiping sweat off his face and looking at his watch with satisfaction as we leant on the beaters and took a breather. 'And now the cavalry arrives.'

We looked out across the showground to the main road. The other fire engines from Shrewsbury (one with the full-time crew on it and one with the retained firemen), had finally turned up. We watched them as they got parked up and the two officers in charge headed in our direction. John briefed them on events then walked back to their appliances with them so he could see the flower-show organiser along the way.

'Well, I don't know about you lot, but I'm sweating cobs. Anyone fancy doing a detour around the beer tent on the way back to the engine?' Arfer asked when the rest of us were on our own. We all fancied it, funnily enough. Fortunately, it was still open. The crowds that had taken flight at the start of the fires were already beginning to filter back. John joined us shortly afterwards. He was with Dale Walsh, the policeman in charge for the evening. They had both spoken to the organisers and, while there was some concern about the fireworks planned for the following evening, they'd decided that the show would go on as planned. By the time we'd sunk our first free pint, Queen was blaring from the PA system as if nothing had happened.

'Help! We need help over here! Someone's drowning. Help!'

Four heads jerked forward on the fire engine. We'd long since re-stowed all the equipment we'd used fighting the fires and we were having a bit of a rest before the show's official finish time of ten thirty. Surely nothing else could have gone wrong?

All four of us opened our doors and jumped to the ground. I turned out to be the closest to a scared-looking girl of about eighteen. She grabbed my arm. She was breathing fast and she reeked of cigarettes and booze. Her eyes were wide open and afraid.

'Who's drowning? What's going on?'

'My friend. My boyfriend. He said he could swim to the other side of the Severn. I told him not to try it, but he did and he's gone under. I can't see him. You have to help him.'

I was a lot taller, faster and steadier on my feet than she was so I left her in my wake and ran off in the direction she was indicating. Three other teenagers were swaying around on the water's edge. They all seemed to be laughing.

'Is someone in the water? What's going on?' It was impossible to sense which of them was the least inebriated so I barked the question at the group in general.

'It's Shortie,' one of the two men said through his giggles. 'Can't you see him? He's hanging on to that branch over there. He can't swim.'

I looked out across the water. The lights from the show had mostly been turned off, but it was still quite easy to see who they were talking about.

'What's his real name?'

'It's Shortie.'

I cursed under my breath. I'd been a bit wild as a teenager myself, but I swear I'd never been as stupid or unhelpful as this. 'Shortie, can you hear me? Can you swim?' He too seemed to be laughing. 'Whoever you are, are you able to swim? Can you get out of there on your own?'

I'd actually answered my own question before I'd finished asking it. If he was as drunk as his mates he couldn't do much on his own. He could be Mark Spitz and he'd still need a rescue. I turned round. John and Woody were at my side. Arfer was in the cab ready to radio for help if required. 'I suppose this is one for me?' I asked John. I knew the answer before I'd finished speaking. This was years before the age of risk assessments and health and safety. A man was in the water and someone had to fish him out. This, along with so much else, was the Fire Brigade's job. I pulled off my tunic, emptied my pockets of anything valuable and handed it over to John. I kept my shoes on – swimming in them would be hard as hell, but if I had to wade around I didn't want to stand on any rusty bike frames or supermarket trolleys. I took a breath and went for it. I'd certainly needed the breath. It might have been a warm July night but the water felt as cold as the grave. It winded me, took the air right out of my lungs as I plunged in. The kid I was heading across to rescue must have been incredibly drunk. I reckon the water was cold enough to sober up anybody.

'Stay holding on to that branch. I'm going to grab you in a minute, then I want you to let go and I'll pull you back to the edge. Do you understand me?'

Shortie didn't give much indication either way. He did, though, continue to think it was all a huge joke. His teeth were chattering and he thought that was as funny as everything else. He was laughing like an idiot when I grabbed him, more forcefully than was strictly necessary, if I'm honest. 'Right, we're getting back to the shore.' I was on my back, kicking like crazy and holding him under his neck in proper lifesaving style. The current was stronger than you'd think in that stretch of the River Severn. There was no way I could get us straight across to the point I'd jumped in. Instead I relied on the fact that the river curved pretty sharply and as long as I kept us moving we'd soon end up on the bank a hundred yards or so downstream. We did, I'm pleased to say. I wrenched Shortie around so he could kneel on the riverbank and then pushed him out while John, glaring at the lad as if he was a particularly unattractive insect, pulled at him from above.

'What were you thinking? Going in the water in your condition?' I asked the boy.

'I thought I was superman. But you're my hero,' he smirked. He stood up, then he almost fell over in a fit of coughing and laughing. 'I'm effing freezing. Let me go get my coat from my friend,' he said. 'I'll bring you a can as well. It's the least I can do.' He stumbled over towards the foursome he'd been drinking with, reached down and picked up a six-pack of beers. He peeled one can off the end of it. Then he put it on the ground, put the others under his arm and he and his mates all turned tail and ran off through the last of the crowds leaving the show. We never saw them again. Though to this day I swear I'm still looking.

11

Forty-eight hours later another big night went spectacularly wrong for a different set of partygoers, this time the residents and guests of a huge country house out by Wroxeter. Their main event was also being held in a marquee, though fortunately for them this one didn't actually catch fire. The message we got on the call-out was typically vague. 'Person trapped under large straw bales.' Six very intriguing words. And mysterious ones as well. If it had been a farming accident it would normally have happened in daylight while the farmhands were at work. We'd got the call-out around nine at night. It was the wrong time of day, the wrong time of year and the wrong type of people for that kind of 'person trapped' call. So I for one was looking forward to answering it, and finding out more.

'They can easily weigh a ton, those straw bales. If we have to move them, then can I get a note from my mum saying I'm excused?' Charlie joked as we turned right out of the station and headed towards town. Wroxeter was six miles away on the other side of Shrewsbury. We'd have to go through the town centre, out over the English Bridge and then on the A5 towards Wellington. With a fair wind we'd be at the address in less than ten minutes. Or we would have been, until we hit the town centre.

'What the hell are you doing? Get out of the effing way!' Ben yelled from the driver's seat as he slammed on the brakes and did a nifty swerve. I could guess what was happening but I twisted around to check all the same. I was right. We were passing a couple of the town's dodgiest pubs. The first wave of Saturday-night revellers were already taking over the streets, drunkenly yelling at us or staggering across the road and getting in Ben's path. 'Move it! Now!' he yelled, winding down his window and giving some very clear, not exactly Fire Brigade-approved gestures to the people in front of him. John then took the nuclear option. He turned on the siren. I couldn't see the drunks' reactions but that sudden noise from that close can wake the dead. I bet they all jumped out of their skins – and jumped back on to the pavement. 'A bunch of drunken, slobbering idiots the lot of them. But, Arfer, it was nice to see your missus out there with her new fancy man,' Ben said as we finally picked up speed and headed out of town.

The rest of the journey was incident free and we carried on joking and taking the mickey out of each other until just before we reached Wroxeter. At that point an ambulance and police car picked up on our tail. Maybe this incident was more serious than we'd expected. The big house we were looking for was on the right, at the end of a long drive, a few hundred yards away. But at the last moment it seemed we were going elsewhere.

A man in a dinner jacket and dickey bow flagged us down in the lane, yelling up at Ben: 'He's not in the house. He's in the farmyard opposite. I'll show you.'

He climbed on to the running board and we headed into the farmyard. Once there, we were surrounded by a flock of men in penguin suits and women in fancy long dresses. Everyone had clearly tried to sober up fast, but not all of them had quite managed it.

'Can you tell me what happened?' John asked the first man as the police and ambulance staff rushed up to join us.

'It's one of my friends. He was on top of the bales. He fell down somehow. He can't get out and we can't get to him.' Up ahead of us was a stack of huge bales. Each one was about five foot in diameter by five foot high. Charlie was very probably right. They'd be as heavy as anything. Plus they were stacked four high. The whole structure looked a bit like Shrewsbury Castle. It looked impregnable.

'What's your friend's name?'

'Stuart. Stuart Treneman.'

'Can you hear me, Mr Treneman? It's the Fire Service. Are you OK in there?'

'No. Not OK,' came a slurred voice.

'He doesn't know what he's saying. He's perfectly OK. We've been talking to him since he fell. He's fine. He just can't get out and we can't move the bales,' we were told.

'And is this your farm?' John asked.

The man in front of him didn't get the chance to reply.

'No, it damn well is not his farm! It's my farm. What the hell is going on?' This, clearly, was the farmer. He was a surprisingly plump, unhappy-looking man wearing a checked open-necked shirt and a dark brown donkey jacket. He was none too pleased to see his farmyard invaded by a fire engine, a police car, an ambulance and a swarm of well-dressed, half-cut partygoers.

'We tried to rescue him ourselves. We threw him a rope,' the first man said, ignoring the farmer completely. Then he stole a glance at the people around him. No one met his eye. He looked down at the ground and shuffled from one foot to the other. I wondered what it was he didn't want to tell us. Had they broken into this farmyard before? Had they done real damage in the past? There had to be something.

'So why couldn't he climb the rope?' barked John.

'He couldn't reach it,' the man said unconvincingly after a very long pause.

A woman in a rich, claret-red dress pushed past him. 'Please,' she said. 'You're wasting time talking. The poor man is injured. We think he nearly died. Please, just get him out.'

I think we all did a double take at that point. It was hard to work out how the man could be badly injured. The gap between the bales was minimal. To be honest, it was amazing he'd fallen all the way to the bottom at all. He'd certainly not have fallen very fast. He'd barely have broken more than a fingernail in the process. So why did this woman say he'd nearly died? John stepped right up to the edge of the bales. 'Mr Treneman, we've been told that you might be injured. Can you confirm or deny that for me?'

'Confirm! They tried to kill me!' That got us interested. The police officer stepped up as well. He took a firm stance between the partygoers and the bales of straw.

'Mr Treneman, can you repeat that last statement?' he asked.

'Tired. Too tired. Don't feel well,' was all we could hear.

As the policeman moved the crowd back, John spoke to the farmer and told him we'd have to pull his giant haystack apart. After a few angry moments he gave a shrug and stepped aside. When John gave the nod, Arfer and I took the short extension ladder off the engine and raised it up to the top of the bales. I monkeyed up first with Arfer right at my toes. Caddie moved the ladder away as we took a closer look at the top of the straw mountain. The gap between the bales was as narrow as I'd expected, though there was just enough room at the corners to see where the unfortunate Mr Treneman had slipped through. Arfer looked over at me with his tired, heavily lidded eyes. 'Ready?' he asked.

'Ready.' I looked down at all the others. 'Everyone clear?' I yelled.

'Clear!'

So we began to push the top layer of bales out and off the edge. It took quite an effort. It was dusty and uncomfortable and precarious. Plus, of course, as each bale probably weighed more than my car the actual manoeuvre was taking all our strength. Still, after a good few minutes we'd got things moving. A few minutes more and we'd dislodged the first couple of bales on the top layer. With a bit more effort we got them rocking on the edge. Then with a roar we gave a mighty shove and watched them thump down on to the farmyard floor. When the dust had settled, we scrambled down a level, slid our legs into the gap between the next set and tried to kick them in the same direction. I could feel the sweat drip down my back as I worked. At one point I almost felt myself fall into the gap but grabbed a handful of straw and held on for dear life while I caught my breath. Landing on top of the man I was supposed to rescue was hardly part of the plan. I weighted fifteen stone in my socks – a lot more in my boots and all my fireman's kit. If this man was as badly injured as he claimed, my unexpected arrival could finish him off.

'It's going! It's close! Clear!' I yelled as my second bale hit the deck. Down below, Woody and Pete from the other appliance moved forward to roll it out of the way and make room for the next one. 'Mr Treneman, we're close now. Are you still OK? Can you hear me?' I shouted down through the straw at my feet.

'Don't feel well. Going to be sick again,' he replied.

Arfer had moved alongside me and the pair of us started to lever out the final bale we planned to move. Once we'd got this level clear we reckoned one of us could slide down to push Mr Treneman up from below while the other dragged him up from above. Woody and Pete were already lining up a ladder with the top of the lowest layer so they could help bring him down to the ambulance.

I unhooked my torch from my shoulder and shone it through the bales. Kicking away the loose straw, I could make out Mr Treneman. He was crouching a foot or so over to my right, so I eased myself down to reach him. That's when I got a real shock.

'Blimey, you've been in the wars. You really are injured,' I heard myself say – probably not the most diplomatic statement I'd ever made. But the man's head was almost completely covered in blood. So was his white shirt. He'd clearly been sick several times. Clumps of hair looked to have been pulled out of his head. Most worrying of all was the wide open wound above his right eye. He looked as if he'd been in a car crash, not fallen down a few bales of straw. 'We need to move him fast!' I shouted to the lads standing in the yard. I checked his vitals as fast as I could. 'Can you move your hands? And your feet?' I asked. He could. So thankfully he didn't appear to have any spinal injuries that would force us into a Plan B. I took a deep breath. It was absolutely boiling down there in the bowels of the haystack. I checked the area for hazards then I grabbed the man round the waist and manhandled him up towards Arfer's waiting arms. Less than a minute later he was safely down in the farmyard. I sat back and tried to catch my breath as I heard the ambulance crew take over the operation.

'You all right, Jockey? You don't need a rescue of your own, do you? Better move fast as the ladder's going back on the engine in sixty seconds,' Pete yelled.

I stirred myself into action and climbed out of the dusty, scratchy prison, shinned down the ladder then threw myself on the ground outside the barn to fill my lungs with clean, fresh air. A few minutes later, desperate for water, I headed to rejoin the rest of the team. The ambulance guys reckoned the man had concussion as well as severe lacerations to his face and head. They shut their doors and scooted him off towards the lovely nurses of Copthorne Hospital. We hung around to hear the police officer get the story for his official report.

'Lionel didn't mean to do it,' said the lady in the claret dress.

Lionel, the man who'd been doing all the talking earlier on, was pushed forward again to take up the tale. 'We could hear him, he was in absolutely fine fettle. He wasn't injured at all. He thought the whole thing was hilarious, to be honest. He made a couple of jokes about being eaten by cows at feeding time. He thought the farmer might have him arrested for trespassing.'

'I still might,' came the fierce interruption.

'Well, we decided to rescue him, of course,' Lionel continued. 'We climbed up to the top. We worked out exactly where he was down below and we tried to get him to pull himself out of there. But he couldn't. He said we had to throw him a rope. So someone ran off to the house to get one.'

'It took a bit of finding,' one of the others said. 'But in the end we found a few lengths of some sort of plastic rope. We tied a couple of strands together till it was long enough.'

'That's my bailer twine! You stole that from me! That's my bailer twine!'

Lionel ignored him again. 'Trouble was, once we'd got the rope ready, we couldn't get it down to him. It kept on getting blocked and jammed in all the straw.' There was a pause. 'It was obvious that we needed a weight.' Another, longer silence. 'A weight would get the rope down to Stu. Then he could climb up.'

'Did you find a weight?' the policeman asked, as no one seemed willing to break the latest silence.

'We found a brick,' Lionel said, very quietly. 'We tied it to the rope. But we didn't tie it very well.'

It was the angry, red-faced farmer who stepped forward to sum things up. Hands on hips, his chest puffed out, he said, 'So what you're telling us is this: your friend trespassed on to my farm, climbed up on to my straw bales and then you stole a bunch of my bailer twine and dropped a brick on his head. You were trying to rescue him and instead you hit him on the head with a bloomin' brick!' For the first time all evening his face broke out in a huge smile.

The seasons were changing fast. I'd been spending my four days off between shifts, and the days when we were on nights, working on an old wreck of a house in Dorrington. I was sharing the job with Charlie, Woody and one of the guys from Blue Watch.

The old lady who'd owned the property had recently died and her kids wanted to do it up so they could sell it as soon as possible. We had our work cut out. Nothing had been done to the place for years. None of the doors shut properly, it had rotten window frames, a dodgy roof, creaky floors and every type of damp you could name. The others were working inside, ripping out the old kitchen units, sorting out the plumbing and trying not to get killed as they fixed the DIY electrics. I was outside, replacing the worst of the cracked tiles and securing a chimney stack that was doing a decent impression of the Leaning Tower of Pisa. There were precious few clouds up above that morning, but the sky was still more white than blue as I rubbed my hands together and began hammering at the slates. By the middle of the afternoon I could see my breath out in front of me as I looked at my watch. Two and a half hours till I was due at the station. I finished off, headed home for a shower and was in the muster bay bang on time.

It was a Saturday, so we didn't do as many drills or routines as on weekdays. Joe simply got us to check all the appliances before the fun part of the night could begin. We had a fast and furious game of volleyball, then headed upstairs to relax. It was Arfer and George's turn on kitchen duty and they were making a vast fish pie with a thick potato crust. Alice and some of the other men's wives and girlfriends were due to come by later on for a few drinks in front of the mess-room telly. As it was a Saturday there was a chance guys from the other watches, plus a few of the retained firemen from the local stations, might drop by. I was looking forward to a relaxed, social night when Arfer gave the call that dinner was on the hatch. We raced up to grab our plates. I piled my fork up high and took my first few mouthfuls. It was terrific. 'Great grub,' I told George, who was in his usual seat on the other end of the long table, trying to look modest.

'There's plenty more where that came from,' he said. 'And a blackberry-and-apple pie for afters.'

That was one of my favourites. But it would be a while till we got to taste it. Everyone on the watch always ate as if a famine was on its way. We shovelled food down our mouths at a ridiculous speed. But we'd still not cleared our plates when a call-out message blasted over the tannoy.

'Blinkin' typical,' Caddie sighed, cramming one more forkful into his mouth. Then he wrote his name on his plate like the rest of us, and thrust it aside.

'And it's going to hit my profits behind the bar if we don't get back soon,' Pete moaned as we all headed towards the pole. 'I was hoping to take a hundred pounds in bar takings tonight. We'll have to make up for it later, OK? I'll be wanting some professional drinking done when we get back.'

'You can rely on us, boss,' Charlie told him as he disappeared down the hole in the floor.

The pole is one of those old inventions that will always stand the test of time. There's no quicker way to get a group of men down from one floor to another. The first person to reach it simply jumps on and disappears. If you're next, you jump on, and in a split second you can tell if the man below is moving out of your way; then you relax your grip and shoot down. Everyone above you repeats the trick till you're all done. We didn't get trained on it or advised on it back then. We just did it. It made sense. And it worked. Half a dozen or more men can get from one floor to another in little more than ten seconds. In three-storey stations with two poles you go down the first, step a couple of paces across the floor and leap on to the second. We can get down both poles in around four seconds. Getting down two flights of stairs would take at least twice or three times as long – and you get a lot more injuries running down stairs than you do hitting the poles.

That early autumn night we got to the ground floor like a well-oiled machine. Then we raced across the appliance-room floor to take our positions on the engines. During waking hours like this we were given a mere thirty-three seconds from the call-out time to get on the engines and be ready to roll. Despite our full stomachs we beat the target with a good five seconds to spare that night and headed out on to the main road. That's when things calmed down a bit. This drive wasn't a race against time. The shout was to a 'fire in the open' over at a school in Springfield. No one's life was in danger. So none of us were particularly surprised when the eagle-eyed Woody yelled that we should slow down as we headed through Shrewsbury town centre. 'That looks like a hen party going into the Yorkshire House pub,' he said. 'No need to race past them like Niki bloomin' Lauda, it's not a persons reported. Let's slow down and enjoy the view.'

We were still in a good mood when we got to our destination. A man who could have been the headmaster but who turned out to be a real sergeant major of a caretaker guided us past the first few buildings and towards what looked like the sports grounds.

'A bunch of local toe-rags have set fire to a trailer tent,' he told us in clipped, military tones when we'd parked up and jumped down. 'I can't say exactly when they did it, but I run a tight ship and keep my eyes and ears open here. I believe I spotted it very early on. I'd say it's been burning for fifteen minutes. Twenty at the most. The little thugs pushed the trailer out on to the pond at the edge of our land. That area is normally used for biology and general science studies, so it's mightily overgrown. There are plenty of tall trees overhanging the pond and there's a wooden fence that's covered in ivy running past them. We've got outbuildings and the changing rooms downwind of it all. When I investigated the scene, the flames were licking the branches of the trees and getting darn close to the fencing. It could just burn itself out, but we all know how dry it's been this year. I called for help because I thought things could still get out of hand. There's a lot of plastics in the tent so the fire could turn out to be more volatile than it looks. I certainly hope I did the right thing.'

'I can assure you that you did,' said John, impressed, as we all were, at the detailed description we had been given. 'We'll take a closer look and see what we can do.'

'And if you find any of those low-lifes smirking in the bushes, tip me the wink. I'll soon give them something to smirk about.'

We told the man we couldn't promise anything, unfortunately, and headed off towards the fire. Leaving the sports pitches behind us, we wound our way through a maze of paths towards the pond. The remains of the trailer tent had beached and were now floating like a funeral pyre on the far side of the water. As the caretaker had reported, the flames were licking the branches of the trees that overhung the pond. On a windy night like this it would be easy for them to jump on to more dangerous ground and do real damage elsewhere.

'Right, lads, let's do this as quickly as we can. Get the 45 mm hose out there,' John commanded.

We headed back to the engine where Caddie had opened the onboard water tank in anticipation. Woody and I got the hose off and rolled it out towards the fire. The 45 mm gave us a lot more firepower than the ordinary hose-reel – and as the fire was still packing quite a punch it was clear we'd need it. It took us three or four minutes to get in position at the edge of the pond. 'Water on!' I bellowed back to Caddie on the engine. When the hose came alive we aimed the water at the base of the flames and gave the tent a good covering. Nothing happened for the first few seconds. Nothing ever does on fires as big as this. Flames seem to cut through and shrug off everything we're throwing at them. But a couple of seconds later we start to see progress – and it's the most satisfying feeling in the world. You slowly but surely control the fire when you extinguish it like this. You direct the water. You see the flames in the areas you hit start to keel over and die. You move the stream from one area to the other. Wherever you take it, you see results. You're in charge.

For a very brief period, in these perfect conditions, you can control nature.

My job was done in about four intense but satisfying minutes. 'Thank God for that,' Woody said as we looked out at the pile of soaking, smoking embers. I knew what he meant. We only have a fixed amount of water in the engine. If we'd needed more, there was an obvious, easy source of it: the pond right in front of us. We'd have to get the Light Portable Pump working. But to use it we'd have to carry our not-so-light, not-so-portable pump through the bramble bushes and over to the water's edge. We'd lugged that monster around a few times too many in training drills lately. The last thing any of us wanted was to have to lug it on a shout.

Woody headed back to speak to the boss and the caretaker as I kept an easy watching brief from the side of the pond. After three days climbing over the rooftop of the house in Dorrington, my body had plenty of aches and pains. So it felt good to sit back on the grass and relax on this dry, peaceful night. In a funny sort of way it also felt nice to have brought a bit of normality back to this quiet corner of Shropshire. Fires can be as beautiful as they are deadly. This one had been particularly memorable. The fingers of rich oranges, reds and whites as well as all the less expected blues, purples and violets had stretched into the sky – and been reflected on all sides on the thick black surface of the pond. Handfuls of sparks had been thrown into the sky with every crack and bang of the fire. They too had cast sudden, sharp shadows on the surface of the water. Everything about that fire had been alive, from the constantly shifting kaleidoscope of colours at its edges to the pulsing, hypnotic richness at its heart.

Now that the fire was out, night had returned. The contrast between the old brightness of the fire and the new blackness of the night was acute. Every few moments bats darted across the sky between the overhanging trees. In the quiet that had replaced the crackling of the fire, I could hear even more of the night: the insects, the bugs, the rustling of the leaves. I stretched my sore muscles. It was getting cold but I would have happily stayed out there for hours, enjoying the peace as midnight approached.

'Windsor! Get your blinkin' skates on and make up the hose!' John yelled from the engine, breaking my spell in spectacular fashion. I sighed. I still didn't want to move, to be honest. I was totally relaxed, drinking in the peace and quiet. But I reached down for the hose and began to roll it. That was when I realised there was a slight problem. Finding my way through the bramble bushes towards the fire had been easy. There had been two of us, we'd had an obvious target to aim for and a huge bright fire had cast light on the scene. Now I was on my own and I couldn't tell where the hazards were. All I could see ahead of me were rich dark shadows. The clouds were low. There was no moon and no stars. The only help I had, from far ahead, was a faint orange glow from distant street lights on the far side of the school grounds. I crouched down and began rolling up the hose. Straight away I walked head-first into my first set of blackberry bushes. 'Blinkin' heck!' I swore at nothing and no one. I stood up and tried to see where the next set of vicious, low-hanging branches might be. They turned out to be just ahead of me as I followed the path of the hose round the next corner. 'Ouch! Blinkin' blinkin' heck!' I cursed again. Then again. A few minutes later I was right in the thick of the maze. The hose had got itself dragged right into the middle of some of the bushes and as I fought to rescue it my face must have been cut so many times I could have gone to Casualty at the Royal Shrewsbury and said I'd been in a car crash. Each time I got the hose free and stood up, pushing the branches away from me, the blasted things would fly back and hit me. Then I'd duck, swearing, and stand up again to get my bearings. Fortunately the orange street lights seemed to be getting closer. I appeared to be on the edge of a nice straight, easy section of the path. So off I went.

That was when Simon jumped out at me from behind the next set of bushes. He let out an almighty roar and leapt up high, raising both his arms. All I could see, silhouetted in the lights from those street lamps, was something out of a horror movie. So what did I do?

I'm embarrassed to say that I screamed like a girl.

12

'So, have you forgiven me yet, Windsor? Did you know it was me jumping up at you – or did you think it could have been a wabbit?' Two nights later and the jokes kept on coming. Simon and the others must have relived the incident a dozen times already. Mabel and Betty and Babs and Maggie had been treated to detailed re-enactments. The lads had even invented a reason to visit Mr and Mrs Thom in the frozen-food store outside the station so they could pass the story on to them as well.

Fortunately I was more than happy to play along with it all. Don't they say that the only thing worse than being talked about is not being talked about? A big part of fire station life was survival of the fittest. If you couldn't take a joke, you wouldn't survive.

'Simon, you'd better change the record. Keep this up much longer and you'll be the loser. When we come back for nights I'm in charge of the bar, remember. Tell that story one more time and you won't want to look too closely at what goes into your pint glass,' I told him with a grin. He smiled as well, did one last rabbit impression then he came over to help me get ready for my new job. Pete had been feeling like a break, so for the next few months at least I was taking over as the official Red Watch barman. Pete talked me through the basic stock control he did for the booze, crisps and nuts, and the even more basic accounting he did for the money. He showed me how to do the weekly clean of the pipes. Then he handed over the Cash & Carry card and the door key to his empire.

'Congratulations, jockey. You now run your own little pub,' he said.

'That's as good as winning the football pools.'

Two days later when we were back on nights I made it even better. I brought in a top stereo from home. We had some proper music blaring out for a change that night – and from then on. I played a bit of The Police, The Jam, Blondie and The Pretenders rather than the 'old man's music' like Tom Jones and Manfred Mann that the others had always chosen. Alice came in to watch me pull pints one weekend when she was back from university. She was looking even more beautiful than normal, tossing her hair back, laughing at Caddie's ancient jokes and making me feel like the luckiest man in Shropshire.

My luck seemed to hold on the kind of shouts we got that autumn as well. Of all the places, one of the first fires we had to tackle that month was in a pub. It meant that when the call came in I pulled the shutters down on one bar and headed off to another. How lucky is that?

The call-out came from the Windmill, a pub most of us knew quite well about eight miles west of Shrewsbury on the Welshpool Road. The car park was busy when we rolled up – and so was the public bar when we got inside. 'It's the chimney,' the publican told us as he led us through some of his most dedicated drinkers. So it was. Even above the noise of the pub we could hear the sound of flames in the chimney. It had been dark outside, but we'd seen smoke billowing from the chimney pots – far more than you'd expect from a nice warming fire in the grate.

'First time you've lit it since last winter?' John asked.

'First time.'

'You put the fire out straight away?'

He indicated the ashes in the grate.

'We used a bucket full of water, just the way we're supposed to.'

'I was right here, ready to dampen it down with a bit of this if required,' chipped in one of the drinkers, indicating his pint of bitter.

'Well, I'm glad it didn't come to that. Criminal waste of beer, that would have been.' John turned to me and Dodger. 'Looks like a textbook chimney fire. I'll go out to the engine and get the spotlight aimed at the top of the chimney to check the smoke. You lads go and fetch the chimney gear.'

We followed him out to the engine to get the kit we needed – a 360-degree nozzle, a set of chimney rods, a stirrup pump, a tarpaulin and a couple of empty buckets.

'Is it OK if we hang around and watch? Conversation's dull as ditchwater in the lounge bar,' one of the regulars asked as we came back with the equipment.

'It's fine with me. Make sure you stay by the bar, don't get too close – and get someone to fill this up with water for me,' I said, handing over the biggest bucket. Dodger and I then made sure that the fire in the grate was fully out and turned our attention to the chimney. Fires like these are normally caused when a dried-out piece of soot or clinker from the last time the fire had been lit catches light halfway up the flue. It then sends fingers of fire up towards the roof, sucking in oxygen, triggering fresh fires and generating ever more heat along the way. Our task was to send the 360-degree nozzle up the chimney on the end of an ever-increasing length of chimney rods. As the nozzle made its way up towards the sky we'd be pounding the stirrup pump over the bucket of water down at the grate. The water would spray out in all directions and put out the fire. By the time it got to the top it would be job done. Well, that was the plan.

'Blimey, thirsty work, this,' Dodger said hopefully when we'd got the nozzle halfway up the chimney. No one at the bar responded. 'A man could die of thirst in here,' he followed up a little later while we were waiting for the bucket to be refilled. Still none of the drinkers took the hint.

I'd put the last of the chimney rods on and got Dodger to keep working the pump as I brought the nozzle back down to earth. I had a frown on my face. By now we'd normally expect to see water dripping down the chimney into the grate. The first of the sprays from the nozzle would extinguish the fire and disappear up and out of the chimney in steam, but once the fire went out it would start to flood down. That was why we'd put a couple of tarpaulins on the pub carpet and positioned an empty bucket in the grate. Out in the engine Caddie was checking to see if it was smoke or steam coming out of the chimney. As it was clearly smoke he knew things weren't going to plan. 'Get a move on in there. Have you lazy buggers done a single stitch of work yet? Smoke's still billowing out the chimney like a game of Cowboys and blinkin' Indians,' his voice boomed over the radio to much hilarity from the pub regulars. I pulled the final chimney rod away and rested the nozzle on the ground.

'I'll go out and have a word,' I told Dodger.

'That's a lot of smoke. And it's thick and not disappearing, so it is smoke and not steam,' said Caddie, standing next to Charlie on the running board of the fire engine in the pub car park. 'Whatever's been burning hasn't begun to go out yet. You're sure the nozzle's been all the way up and back?'

'Twice. We've done it twice.'

'Yet still she burns. It's time for a real expert to take a look.' He turned to John in the cab. 'If you're OK to man the radio, boss, I'll go back in with Windsor and show the youngsters how it's really done.'

John sent us both off with a smile – and I did learn a decent lesson when we were back in the pub. Caddie examined the chimney breast from all angles then stood back and gave his verdict. 'You've had the cowboys in here,' he told the publican. 'My guess is that some dodgy so-called builder must have replaced the old chimney flue with a new one. When did you take over here?'

'In seventy-eight.'

'And you've not had any work done here yourself?'

'We've not had the money. Chance would have been a fine thing.'

'Well, this problem's been building up for quite some time. A fire like this was bound to happen. Your cowboy builder didn't see fit to meet and seal the new flue to the original. Soot and clinker and debris has been falling down between the two of them ever since. The fire is in the old chimney. We're going to have to do a fair bit of knocking around to get to it. We'll have to bash the heck out of your brickwork and see what's on the other side. It'll open up quite a hole, make a heck of a mess. You're all right with that?'

It wasn't really a question as one way or another we had to put the fire out. But when you're planning a demolition job like this then it's good to get your property owner on side.

The publican nodded his approval so we got going. We got our tools from the engine and had a high old time knocking merry hell out of the fireplace. Some of the bricks were loose and were easy to lift out of place. Others took a bit more of an effort. 'Now this is thirsty work,' Dodger repeated, this time with desperation in his voice, as a huge cloud of soot and ash landed on his head. At long last, and stifling a lot of laughs, we were finally asked what we'd like to drink.

Half an hour later we'd removed what felt like a ton of bricks, a load of rubble, masses of soot and clinkers, and even a couple of old crows' nests. We'd replaced the chimney nozzle with an ordinary alternative and forced it through the gaps. After a fair few squirts of water we looked to have extinguished the fire. Caddie radioed in from outside to say that the chimney was finally clear of smoke. Then he wandered in to check up on progress from inside. When he got into the bar he gave a long, low whistle. I took a few paces back to see what he was looking at.

'Blimey O'Riley,' was all I could think of to say. It seemed that

Dodger and I were well on the way to changing the entire look and shape of the bar. We'd taken down most of what were clearly two false walls on either side of the new chimney. We'd opened up what looked to be a huge Inglenook fireplace instead.

'I reckon that's big enough for me to get inside,' said Dodger. He climbed in, and reached up to pull the last few chunks of flammable rubbish from above.

'I reckon that's worth a few more drinks,' said the pub owner. He was looking at our discovery in utter amazement. 'That's incredible. You've found me a proper fireplace. That could be hundreds of years old, couldn't it? It's a feature. I can't believe it was there all along.'

His regulars, most of whom had got bored earlier on and drifted over into the lounge bar, came back to gawp. Everyone was impressed.

'Must be your dream job, this – a fire in a pub,' one of the regulars pitched in as the owner lined up a series of pints on the bar for us.

'It's not so bad,' Charlie admitted. 'But it's not our favourite.'

'Why? What could be better than this?'

'You'd have found out if you'd seen us on the night shift back in May, wasn't it, Windsor?'

'Certainly was. Hard to forget that one.'

'Just before six in the morning, if memory serves. It was an AFA – an automatic fire alarm,' Charlie told the regulars.

'So how did that beat a fire in a pub?'

'Because it was an automatic fire alarm in the Radbrook Nurses' Home. Dozens and dozens of pretty women. All woken out of their beds before dawn by the alarms. All rushing out of the building in their nightdresses and various other states of undress. And it wasn't even a fire. It had gone off by mistake. We didn't have to do a stitch of work. We just had to stand outside the building enjoying the view. Happy days, lads.'

'Happy days, indeed. My name's Alf. You've not got a vacancy for a sixty-two-year-old with a dodgy ticker, a bit of arthritis and chronic gout, have you?' echoed the man at the bar wistfully as he got a tired-looking fiver out of his pocket and stood us another round.

When we'd sunk them, and confirmed once again that there were no smouldering embers left in the newly extended fireplace and that it was safe to go, we headed back to the engines in the car park. Two women were getting out of a car and they couldn't take their eyes off Dodger as he walked past them. He swaggered a bit and flashed a proud glance at the rest of us as we got to the engine. He was still preening as we pulled out of the car park. At which point Caddie decided to put him straight: 'It's not your youthful good looks they're admiring, laddo. You should have taken a glance in the mirror before you left the pub. You're head to toe covered in soot. You look like something off of Mary blinkin' Poppins.'

It rained almost every day in November. Guy Fawkes' night came and went with hardly any call-outs. Most people in Shropshire struggled to light their soggy, water-logged bonfires. No one needed much help putting them out. Most Novembers we get a lot of false alarms as well. People see distant bonfires reflected in the windows of empty houses and call them in thinking the houses are on fire. That November we didn't get a single one.

I did get to drive the fire engine to a couple of volleyball games, though. We were doing pretty well in our local league. We rolled up in the fire engines, a couple of the old-hand drivers stayed in the cabs to monitor the radios and the rest of us legged it into the sports centre to play our games. If we'd got a call-out halfway through the game we'd have stormed back to the engines in our shorts and T-shirts and got changed in the back while the drivers went hell for leather towards our destination. In most cases we'd have got on the road just as fast as we would have done from the station.

One quiet Saturday afternoon I was on the point of driving out on a supermarket run to restock the bar when we got a proper call-out.

'I can't drive us there?' I asked John hopefully as I got ready to switch seats and hand over the ignition key to Simon.

'You know the answer to that as well as I do, jockey. Simon is number two today. Get in the back.'

I probably sulked a bit as we headed off through the countryside. It wasn't as if we were heading out to a fire or to protect people or property. It was one of the stupid call-outs we got every so often. The calls we got because we were the Fire Brigade and people came to us when no one else could help. We were racing across Shropshire to save some sheep. To be fair, even John was annoyed about it.

'Stranded sheep? I can't believe we're giving up an afternoon in front of the telly to rescue stranded sheep,' he said, looking at his watch. 'Does nothing catch fire in Shropshire any more? Has the whole world gone mad or is it just me?'

'It's just you, boss,' Charlie told him helpfully.

The others all laughed but for once I couldn't bring myself to join in.

We were heading upstream of Shrewsbury to an area called Melverley. The River Severn meanders through a wide floodplain there. It normally flooded a few times each year, but that year, that particular flood, was one of the worst anyone could remember. Even the smaller rivers we passed along the way had been transformed. Pretty little babbling brooks were now swollen and dark. Thick, dirty water swirled up round tree trunks and bushes that normally stayed dry. From the safety of our cab you could sense the remorseless power of nature that day. Even the smallest of streams were flexing their muscles. The countryside was alive. It wanted us to be on our toes. It was showing us what it could do.

The world was calmer but no less unusual when we got to

Melverley. Joe parked the engine on the edge of a ghost land-scape, a still, weird-looking water-world. It was getting late on a cold, overcast and suddenly windless afternoon. Out there the river wasn't crashing over rocks and squeezing between tall, tight banks. It had spread out in all directions. It appeared to be at rest. It had produced a flat reflective pool that covered a huge swathe of the countryside. Every here and there the water was pierced by telegraph poles, trees and the occasional tall hedge. They looked incongruous, unlikely and strangely sinister. Or maybe that was just because I was in such a bad mood.

The farmer who had called us out met us underneath a sign-post to Shrewsbury where he was sitting on the steps of a Land Rover having a cigarette. He was very young, very shiny and very posh. 'The damn sheep are over there. They're rare breeds so they're worth a pretty penny. You think you can get them back for me?' He didn't wait for John or Joe to reply. 'Good men. Well, I don't expect you'll thank me for nagging and looking over your shoulders every ten minutes. So I'll be orf and leave you gentlemen to it,' he said before getting into his shiny new four-by-four and disappearing round the next bend.

'Backin' cheek, backin' lazy bugger,' was Arfer's reaction from the back of the cab.

We looked across the field. The sheep in question were hud-dled together on a patch of raised ground 200 yards away. Their island had long since been cut off by the swirling waters that had crept across the fields in all directions. 'It's getting dark and the water level's still rising,' Joe pointed out. 'Their patch of land will be gone sooner than the light.'

We all instinctively turned to John for his view on the situ-ation. 'Well, we don't know how deep it gets between here and there,' he said slowly. 'There could be any number of dips or trenches underneath all that water. There could be any amount of barbed wire. We've no boat and no help from our friendly farmer. It's freezing cold as well. Windsor, I don't suppose you fancy swimming over there and bringing the sheep back one at a time?'

I tried to get my usual sense of humour back. 'I'd swim there to rescue Daisy Duke or Heather Locklear one at a time. But not to rescue a few scrawny old sheep.'

'Not even if they're worth "a pretty penny"?' said Joe, mimicking the posh farmer.

'Not even then.'

John took charge again. 'Let's just consider the kit we've got to play with and come up with a plan.'

The five of us retreated to the warmth of the fire engine. To be honest, it was quite fun trying to think of something. As our flood victims were sheep rather than people there wasn't the usual sense of urgency, and after a while my bad mood passed. Everyone pitched in with ideas, and as usual they went from the inventive to the downright ridiculous. We discussed making DIY boats, building rescue rafts, creating floating bridges, using winches and a variety of ropes and all sorts of other crazy structures and systems. I reckon we could have made a lot of them work if we'd put our minds to it. But all that for a posh farmer we didn't much like and a handful of his fancy sheep? It was never going to happen. 'OK, back to the water's edge. I want an idea of the depth. And we can give the problem a couple more coats of looking at from there,' John said, jumping back down from the warmth of the cab.

Arfer was the first to speak when we got to the water's edge. 'Where's the bleedin' sheep gorn?' We all looked across the water. The island was deserted. Somehow, while we'd been talking in the fire engine, the sheep had taken their future into their own hands – or their own feet. 'They're over there!' Arfer shouted. So they were, shaking themselves dry and having a graze a few hundred yards downstream from us, on a continuation of the same ground we were standing on. 'Come on, lads. Let's round them up. I reckon we can take the credit for this,' Arfer declared.

He was right. We formed a pincer movement, shooed the sheep back into the field they were supposed to be in and pulled the gate shut behind them. Then we drove the fire engine up to the farmhouse to bask in glory and report a job well done.

'I must say I'm mightily impressed. So tell me, how exactly did you get to them?' the posh farmer asked, his suspicions perhaps aroused by how dry we all appeared to be.

'Well, sir, we simply take advantage of the skills we learn in our training,' said John vaguely.

'And those skills are what, precisely?'

'They're complicated. And confidential,' said John, nodding like a wise old man. 'And that would go down a treat. Thank you so much, my dear,' he said, taking advantage of the distraction when the farmer's wife joined us in the yard with a tea tray. It was more than we were used to. Forget cracked, dirty mugs and a single sugar spoon that gets passed round the crowd. She brought a big china pot, a set of proper cups and saucers with a matching jug for milk and a little silver dish for the sugar. 'Best behaviour, lads, and I don't want anyone nicking the spoons,' Joe whispered when she headed back inside to refill the pot.

Our posh young farmer turned out to be a relatively decent bloke after a few cups of tea and a fair few slices of his wife's home-made coffee cake. He also turned out to be a close friend of Shropshire's Chief Fire Officer, so overall it was quite a result to have saved his sheep and left his yard having only broken the one china plate between us.

'Hey, Windsor,' John called out as we walked back to the engine. 'You've had a face worse than a slapped fish all afternoon. Take the keys off Joe and drive us back to the station so I can see how you manage in the dark. And cheer the heck up, will you?'

Joe threw me the keys and I pulled myself up into the driving seat. It hadn't occurred to me before that I'd done my training in the summer and done all my non-emergency drives when the days were long. It probably would be a useful challenge to be on the roads at night for a change. Our headlights cut a huge gash through the darkness from our vantage point high above the road. They stretched out, carving silver lines across the flood waters. I swept us down through Melverley towards Montford Bridge and on to the A5. Traffic was building up and I enjoyed threading our way through it. I still got a thrill on every job I did on Red Watch, but everything felt so much more exciting when I was behind the wheel.

It was almost knocking-off time when I turned us into the station yard. John grabbed the radio and gave the call: 'Closing home station' to Control. It was the message we had to send to Control whenever the engine got back from a shout so they'd know to turn us out over the tannoy not the radio from then on. For months now someone had relayed that message when I'd brought the engine safely back to the station. But it had only ever been on these dummy runs. John had cheered me up a bit by getting me the keys earlier on, but I'd started to sulk again by the time I changed into my civvies at the end of our shift. How long could this trial period possibly last? When would I get to drive the engine for real?

13

The winds hit in early December. They whipped across the hills from Wales. They gained pace on the undulations of the Berwyns, and they did damage almost everywhere, with fallen trees blocking roads, hitting cars and pulling down power lines all over the county. Before we'd even had dinner it was clear it was going to be one of the busiest nights of the year. As the shouts added up, the retained firemen were called in to work all over Shropshire. At first they just slotted into the stations the full-timers had left behind as we headed out on calls. Then, when the first of the retained crews got used, the next set were drafted in behind them. When the last of them was in place, decisions had to be made about getting extra cover from neighbouring counties.

We'd been out making safe a mass of scaffolding that had come down outside a village shop and were heading back to base when we got our second, biggest call of the night. It was almost midnight. After some of the strongest winds yet, a tree had fallen on a bungalow over in Belle Vue. The damage was said to be extensive. And there were persons reported – four of them.

'Shit. We need to turn this thing around,' Martin swore from the driver's seat. Turning a fire engine around on narrow country lanes is harder than turning an oil tanker around in the middle of the sea. Harder still when the clock is ticking and you know every minute's delay could cost someone their life.

'Take it up another half a mile towards Lyth Hill. There's an old manor house up there on the left that's got a big, wide drive outside it. You'll be able to turn there,' advised Caddie, proving yet again that there was nothing as useful as strong local knowledge. John fired up the siren as we came upon a couple of cars around the next bend. There wasn't a lot of space but the drivers did the right thing. They pulled over, carved up the grass verge and narrowly avoided toppling into the ditch. We powered past them.

'Where's this effing driveway then?' Martin barked as the half-mile point came and went.

'It's right there.'

Martin slammed on the brakes. 'I can't get round in one go. I'll have to turn it,' he said. The three of us in the back jumped out and took up positions around the engine. Martin flicked on the hazard warning lights to warn any approaching cars to slow down. He pulled into the driveway, probably giving the people in the house a hell of a shock if they'd looked out of the windows. He thrust the engine into reverse and moved till Caddie banged on the side and yelled enough. I was up front as the engine went forward. I made sure he didn't hit the row of ridiculous cement toadstools that lined the drive. Caddie guided the next short reverse. Then we all leapt back on board. The lights stayed on as we thundered back the way we had come. The radio crackled to life as we swung past another flurry of cars. John clicked the siren off. It was impossible to hear the radio, let alone send messages on it, when the siren was on. 'Seven Zero to fallen chimney' was the first message we listened to, telling us that the crew from Telford were needed at a domestic house. Then there was another. This time one of the retained crews was being sent out to Cardington where a shop sign had landed on a parked car and sent debris all over the road. I exchanged a look with Caddie and Des in the back. This was shaping up to be quite a night.

The main road to Shrewsbury opened up before us. Overhead the night skies were alive with colour and drama. Thick streaks of purple appeared one moment, only to be wiped away by waves of heavy black clouds the next. Rain was thrown against our engine windows as we thundered down one road, only to be blown away on the next. The tall, proud trees of Shropshire were being forced to dance. They were moved this way and that. The whole countryside was alive.

We thundered into Belle Vue and headed towards the street address we'd been given at the start of the shout. It was a long, twisting road and the houses were large and quite spaced apart. Up front, Martin and John were looking out for the bungalow.

'Bloody hell, that's going to be it,' John said as Martin pulled us across to park on the right-hand side of the road.

We twisted around to look. Even in the darkness it was obvious what had happened. A huge tree – an ancient and, as it turned out, largely rotten horse chestnut – had crashed on to the bungalow alongside it. The main trunk lay across almost the entire house. From this central point thick branches had stabbed through the bungalow's roof in half a dozen or more places. The tree was temporarily at rest that way, hovering over the house like a giant spider. But as the wind howled there was no way of knowing when the tree might move again, or how much more damage it might do.

John was first off the engine. Four figures rushed towards him from the shelter of a garage in front of the house. Wrapped in long coats and blankets they looked like druids. 'This is your house?' John asked the largest figure.

'Yes. This is my wife and our two kids. We're all OK.'

'You're the only people in the house?'

'Yes.'

'We were asleep. We were all in bed. It was like the world had ended. It made the loudest crash I have ever heard. It was terrifying – like a bomb going off.' His wife stepped forward, her arms wound tightly round the two smaller figures.

'You're going to freeze,' John said. The kids' teeth were certainly chattering – half because of the cold, half, probably, from the shock. 'How long have you been out here?'

'I'm not wearing a watch. Ten minutes? Fifteen at the most. Only since we dialled 999.'

'The phones were still working. I don't know how, because the lights had all gone out. I got the kids while Terry made the call.'

'Do you have gas?' John asked.

They did and without being asked the dad explained where all the mains connections for gas, electricity and water could be found. John turned to Des and me. 'Get inside. Check the electrics and the gas.' Then he turned to Caddie. 'Get them in the engine. Turn the heating on full blast.'

Des and I headed towards the front of the bungalow. The first extraordinary thing we discovered was that we could walk straight through the front door. The entrance porch was entirely unscathed. A hat stand, laden with coats and hats, stood in the corner as normal. Shoes and wellington boots were lined up neatly on the ground. We saw our reflection in a mirror on the wall. It hadn't even been cracked, let alone broken. We clicked on our torches and stepped through the inner door into the hall. It too was open and undamaged. But from then on the picture changed. The light of our torches showed that a hefty branch of the tree had pierced through the ceiling in the far corner. The leaves blew in the wind and cast a net of noisy, ever-changing shadows. We forced our way past it and got into the utility room beyond the kitchen. Everything turned on its head again because that room, like the porch, was unscathed. Des clicked the gas and water and we pulled the fuses. From now on things should be that much safer.

'Let's search the place,' I said. We went back into the hall and through the first door to our right. It was one of the kids' bed-rooms. What we saw was breath-taking. An even larger branch, probably at least two feet thick, had slammed into the ground right next to a child's bed. The sheets were crumpled. This must have been where one of the kids had been sleeping. 'That has to be the luckiest child in the world,' I said. In the light of our torches we could see the ceiling had been almost completely brought down by the tree. Yet next to no debris had landed on the child's bed. We went next door. Another child's bedroom, another lucky escape for the child. It was almost exactly the same in the mum and dad's room across the hallway. It too had taken a direct hit from the tree, but once again the branches had missed the bed by a matter of feet. The family had lost their house. For all that, they were still the luckiest people in Shropshire.

The wind was whipping around the bungalow when we headed back outside and reported to John. He had been stand-ing on the step of the fire engine talking to the family inside through the tiny open crack at the top of the window. Caddie and Charlie, who had been sent to examine the house from the outside, joined us. We were explaining how close some of the branches had come to the family's beds when John hushed us up. 'I think we've got company,' he said. 'The cavalry have arrived.'

An elderly couple had appeared from round the corner. They were pounding down the country lane towards us at a cracking pace. A stout, determined lady who looked to be in her mid-sixties was in the lead. She was wearing a long, dark sou'wester, a big waterproof hat and in her hand was a hefty torch.

'We only just saw your lights. What's happened? Is it the Walports?' She looked past the fire engine at the house. Her hand flew to her face. 'Are the children all right? The poor little imps – they're only seven and nine. The Walports are our neighbours. Oh, please. Please don't say they're trapped in there?'

The parents and kids started to bang against the fire engine windows. They obviously couldn't find the door or window handles, so Martin reached over and helped them open the doors. The family tumbled out, no mean feat from the height of the engine, and ended up in their elderly neighbours' arms.

'We're all absolutely fine. It was the horse chestnut tree. You can see what happened. It was the most frightening thing in the world.'

'We heard a crash.' The elderly lady turned to look at us, her face stricken with guilt. 'We're a long way round the corner and down in a dip. We didn't know what the noise was. We had no idea.' She looked back at her neighbours. 'We're so sorry. We had no idea. It was only when Kenneth went to look out the window on the landing that he saw the lights from the fire engine. That's when we got dressed and came out here.'

'You'll freeze. You shouldn't have come out.'

The old lady hugged the two young children. As she did so her husband spoke for the first time. 'Of course we came out,' he told his neighbours. 'You must have been terrified. We only wish we had been here sooner.' Then he turned to John, instinctively picking him out as the officer in charge. 'I flew Spitfires in the war. I'm a retired caretaker at the railway station. How can I help? What can I do?' The man was standing tall, almost to attention. He must have been seventy if he was a day.

Des and I took floodlights and chainsaws into the bungalow. The wood chips flew as we lopped off some of the most dangerous branches to protect what was left of the home's structure. We went from room to room doing what we could. By the time we headed back out into the stormy night the elderly neighbours, who'd introduced themselves as Mr and Mrs

Robson, had taken the children down the lane to warm up in their house. Mr Robson had come back bringing towels, hats and gloves for the Walports before taking Mrs Walport to her kids. They'd been gone about five minutes when Mrs Robson came into view. On this stormiest of dark nights she was walking down the lane carrying a tray laden with eight mugs of tea. In the pocket of her sou'wester was a packet of digestive biscuits.

'Mrs Robson, you really should be inside,' John began. She dismissed him with a look.

'I've put sugar in all of them. On a night like this everyone has sugar in their tea. I'm sorry the mugs don't all match. It's many years since my husband and I had this many visitors.'

We drank the tea then headed back towards the house. The police had arrived and we joined them making the property secure. I'd have bet a pound to a penny that local kids would try to get inside to take a look once morning came. I'd probably have had a bit of an explore myself if all this had happened near my house at ten years old. The bungalow would be boarded up and covered in warning signs. But we had to do a bit more safety work in case anyone did manage to get inside.

Most of the clouds had been blown away by the time we got out. The moon was three-quarters full and it shone a decent light upon the scene for the first time. The bungalow looked as ghostly as a haunted house on a seaside pier. In the silver half-light the branches stretched out like witch's hands. It was as if a giant from a horror film had tried to grab the bungalow, pick it up and shake it to hell and back.

'It's been quite a night,' I said as we collected up our stuff, stowed our torches and prepared to leave the scene. But it wasn't quite over.

As usual, our number two, Martin, had been sitting tight in the engine and monitoring the radio while the rest of us worked.

He called us over as we said goodbye to dear old Mr Robson and tried to persuade him that his work was finally done. It seemed we'd had another call. 'It's an RTC over on Pim Hill, no persons reported. The police and ambulance teams have done their stuff, but they're a bit stretched what with the bad weather. They want us to go over and make it safe.'

We were there in less than ten minutes, arriving as a weak, watery sun began rising up in the east. The cars themselves were safe and out of the way of any traffic, but a heck of a lot of oil and petrol had leaked out over the crash zone. 'You know what to do, lads,' John said. We did. Caddie headed to the car to make sure the leaks were fixed while Des and I got spades out of the lockers, began digging heavy, rain-sodden soil out of the grass verges and spreading it over the mini oil slick. We pushed the earth around so the clods soaked up as much of the liquid as possible. Once we'd flattened it out, the police deemed the road safe to use and what little traffic was on the road was free to move.

'No calls?' asked John as we re-stowed the shovels in the lockers on the side of the appliance.

'No calls,' Martin confirmed. 'The radio's been quiet for over an hour now. Red Watch Telford, and the retained crews from Prees and Baschurch are all back at base. The wind's dropped and the light has come up. I reckon the worst is over.'

'Well, I think a round of bacon sandwiches wouldn't go amiss on the way back to the station, so I suggest we stop off at the Stagecoach Café and join the rest of the early morning crowd,' John said as we pulled down the lockers and checked we were ready to move. 'Windsor, you fancy taking over from Martin and driving us there?'

'I'd love to, boss, if it's all right with Martin.'

'Fine with me.'

'Then yes please.'

'And, Windsor, drive carefully. If you get the engine back safe and sound then I reckon it's time you did it for real. I'm thinking of putting you on the board as number two when the next tour begins. Think of it as an early Christmas present. You ready for that?'

I'd never been as excited in my life. 'I'm ready.'

14

It was the second week of December and the second day of our latest tour of duty. More importantly it was the second day when I'd walked in to the appliance room to see my name right there in the number two position on the board. Yesterday had been unusually, irritatingly quiet. I'd done my drills, slammed the volleyball around the court like a demon, wolfed down my lunch and felt as ready to go as a bullet in the barrel of a gun. I'd looked at my watch every ten seconds, I'd barely focused on anything the others were talking about and I don't think I relaxed for a single moment. But there was nothing doing. I couldn't believe it. It was a long, boring nine-hour shift without even a hint of a call. Fortunately I knew that couldn't last. Shropshire was never quiet for long. So the second day I had my moment. The tannoy burst into life when I was in the mess room drinking tea around nine thirty in the morning. I was down the pole faster than ever – and I'd never exactly been a slouch.

No surprise that John was my officer in charge that day, so he sat in the cab to my left. Behind us we had Caddie, Pete and Charlie. I discovered something new in that moment before we left the station. As an ordinary member of the squad I'd only ever been aware of my own actions at this part of a shout. Was I moving fast enough, did I have everything I needed, was I in place on time? Today, for the first time, I realised that drivers had the bigger picture to worry about. I needed the others to play their parts. If they weren't there, weren't ready or didn't have everything required then we'd be delayed – and that would reflect on me. I willed the others along as I swung myself up into the driving seat. Not one of them let me down. We were ready in seconds. The appliance-room doors opened. I fired up the engine, turned on the blue flashing lights. I released the handbrake. We were off. This really was it.

John clicked the siren on as we left the yard. In response the car approaching from my right slowed down and flashed his lights to let me out. We dipped over the slope in the main road and powered up and on towards the first T-junction fifty yards up the road. How many times had I been through that junction? Hundreds of times? More than a thousand? It was impossible to say. But this time it was different. Because this time people were relying on me. Today everything I did or didn't do would matter.

The fire had been reported in Wenlock Road – and my breathing sped up because that meant I had an early decision to make. There were two ways of getting to the incident – and they both began right here at this junction. So which route should I choose? I knew it was six of one, half a dozen of the other. There was no way of knowing in advance if there would be worse traffic or extra hazards one way rather than the other. But I was the one who had to decide on the day. I looked into the mirrors. The second appliance was on my tail. And I was right there at the junction. It was decision time.

I went for it. I opted for the right turn. I picked up my first piece of speed and headed down St Michael's Street towards the town centre. That was when I noticed it. My right foot, on the accelerator, was starting to shake. I managed to stop it affecting the way I drove, but I couldn't stop my leg from moving. It was pumping up and down like some kind of sewing machine. This had never happened to me in training. It had never happened when I brought the engine back after a shout or took it to the supermarket or on a school visit. There was traffic ahead and I had to slow down. The car at the front of the pack pulled over and made room for me to get by. I picked up the pace – and my leg started to shake again. Can anyone see it? I asked myself. Please God, don't let anyone see it.

I swung us round into Dogpole and through Shrewsbury. The second appliance was still on my tail. It was being driven by George, one of our most experienced old-timers. More questions raced through my mind. Why was he so close to me? Wasn't I going fast enough? Was that what he was trying to tell me? Were they all ripping me apart in the engine behind? Gripping the steering wheel tightly and flushing all doubts from my head, I powered ahead. I remembered my training and I knew I was good at this. Concentrating on where I was going, I pressed on.

I got us to the outskirts of town. On the back seat of the engine I could sense the others getting rigged and ready into their BA sets as they'd be the first into the fire. A hundred thoughts raced through my mind as I powered down on the accelerator. I thought about fire, smoke and people trapped inside their own home. I thought about neighbours trying to help and getting in trouble themselves. I came up with any number of reasons why we had to get there fast. We had so few facts at this part of a shout. Just the bare bones of information – the where and the very vague what.

I saw the usual traffic build up ahead of me in the narrow, twisting streets of Shrewsbury. Most drivers did everything they could to let me through – and it wasn't always easy. The streets weren't designed for the normal day-to-day traffic they got in the early 1980s. They certainly weren't designed for the sudden arrival of a sixteen-ton fire engine that must have loomed up on your average Mini Metro driver like a creature from the deep. Country drivers dealt with the situation well. They edged up on kerbs, dipped into side roads and did anything they could to move out of the way. Shoppers and passers-by tried to help as well. Old men were always the best

– the most unlikely of them could come alive when we hit trouble. They'd guide cars into the tightest of spots to give us the space we needed. Then they'd wave us through. On that first live drive, one old man all but saluted me. I wish I'd had the time to salute him back. And on the main roads on the other side of town the feeling of power was even more pronounced. It truly was the parting of the Red Sea. It was tangible. The whole road opened up before me. I owned it. It was mine and I took full advantage. I swept through every gap. I powered down every clear stretch. I didn't flinch as the sirens went on to see us through any hairy patches. The sense of urgency was intoxicating. At one point I was so wrapped up in the moment I felt detached from it. The two tones of the siren, the roar of the engine, the rasping sounds from the radio, it all merged and blurred and folded over in my head as the adrenalin flooded through my veins.

The fire had been reported in a house on Wenlock Road. I thanked all my lucky stars that I knew exactly where that was. I could get there without asking for help. Seeing that street sign, spotting the crowds outside and identifying the correct house gave me a huge sense of relief. Pulling up right there and knowing I'd done my first live job was the single most thrilling moment of my life. A new wave of adrenalin surged through me. And of course the job itself was only just beginning. From now on we had to do what we really trained for. We had to start fighting a fire.

I parked the engine in the fend-off position and yanked on the brakes. I'd only turn the engine off if we were part of a really big shout with several engines and I'd been told my equipment wasn't going to get used. On a shout like this we needed everything to be ready, so it was better to leave the engine running and waste a bit of fuel than risk flattening the battery supplying power to all the lights and the radio. John jumped to the ground. My focus shifted. I looked up at the house and got ready for action. It was obvious we had work to do. Smoke was pouring out of a broken bedroom window up on the first floor at the front of the house. A family of five, two adults and three young, school-age kids were standing on the front drive, hugging each other and crying. Caddie, Pete and Charlie jumped off the engine, the first two of them grabbing the hose-reel and running off towards the house with it. Charlie helped pull it off the drum in the rear nearside locker. Just before I jumped off the engine myself I engaged the pump by pulling the power take-off button out. That done, I hit the ground and ran to the pump bay at the back of the engine and pulled up the roller shutter. I dropped the tank, opening the tank valve to allow the water on the onboard tank to come into the pump. Then I turned up the pump's speed to increase the pressure of the water in the hose-reel. First job done. The BA team now had water. My task now was to make sure they didn't lose that precious water when they were inside fighting the fire.

'What's happening? What are they doing in there? What are you doing? Is the house going to burn down? Will we lose it? Can you help us? Is it going to be OK?'

A barrage of questions hit me from the cluster of figures on the drive. This, I realised, was another part of the engine driver's job. At this point in the shout the public wanted information. Only two firemen were likely to be beside each of the fire engines – the driver and the man in charge of the BA board who recorded who went in and out of the property and calculated when they'd run out of air. Whenever I did the BA board I thought I was fielding all the questions. Now I realised they came from all sides.

'We're doing everything we can. We're putting the fire out right now. There's nothing to worry about,' I heard myself say. I was trying to be helpful. I wanted to be kind. But really they were empty words. The major part of my brain was firmly focusing on what I had to do next.

I headed round to the back of the pump and took a look at the gauges. I needed to ensure there was no break in the water supply. I couldn't have Caddie and Pete left in a burning room with no water.

'Windsor, get on to control at Shrewsbury. Send an informative message from me at this address, two BA, one hose-reel in use, no persons trapped, OK?' John had appeared from the front of the house. He barked out the message then turned on his tail and headed round the side of the house to check on the rear. I swung myself into the cab and grabbed the radio, desperately trying to remember every word that John had said. No one ever wrote instructions like these down. No matter how much pressure you were under it was part of the job to remember instructions.

'What does two BA mean? Why did he say that? What was all that about?' It was the dad. Clearly he'd heard John's message. I tried desperately to tune him out and to focus on John's words.

I think I managed to be word perfect getting the message across.

'Roger M2YU out,' Control replied curtly. I looked for John so I could pass that short message on. He was nowhere to be seen.

'Will we be able to go back in as soon as the fire is out? Will there be a lot of damage? Can we go in and get some of our clothes out?' The family began firing more questions at me as I re-checked the main gauge. The dial was reading twenty bars – perfect!

'I live next door. I was the one who called. Will we need to get out of our house as well? Could the flames jump across the fence to us? My mother's in her eighties. She's not well and she'll need time to move. Am I going to have to move her?' Someone else had joined the throng and had chosen me as the font of all knowledge. John appeared as I began to tell the man that his mother would be a lot safer staying where she was. I broke off. 'Boss, two BA, one hose-reel, no persons trapped. Message sent,' I fired out, word perfect – to my huge relief.

John gave me more information to pass on to Control as Caddie and Pete came out of the house. 'Fire's out,' Caddie said, answering my unspoken question. As a long-standing driver himself he must have known how isolating it can be for anyone stuck by the appliance – and how desperate the driver will always be for information. He and Pete were taking off their face masks and BA sets. The BA board operator gave them their tallies back, then they set about cleaning their sets and attaching new air cylinders to them, so they'd be ready if we had another emergency call. John had earlier given the instruction to ventilate the property. We only open windows when we're as certain as we can be that the fire is out and won't jump back to life once we give it lots of lovely fresh oxygen to feed upon. Caddie headed back into the house to continue that process. Soon after that they moved on to our next stage – salvage.

Caddie and Pete began throwing burned items out of the bedroom window, knocking off plaster and taking up floorboards to make sure the fire hadn't spread and wasn't smouldering somewhere. The family didn't like the look of this and started firing a new set of questions at me when the first of their ruined possessions began to fly out of the window. I tried to answer as I wound the hose back on to the drum, cleaning and checking it as I did so. It was only when I knew the appliance was ready for another emergency shout that John released me from my post and told me to join the others inside the house. At this point my job was to start a very basic clean-up job. There was no law saying we had to sort things out like this after a fire. But back then it did feel like part of the job. It was all about goodwill and going the extra mile. We'd normally do as much as we could.

After an hour, John gave the command to pack up and leave. We were on quite a narrow residential close with a fair few parked cars on both sides, but I got us out with Caddie and Pete watching me turn round and soon we were headed back to base. I didn't need to worry about my speed on the return journey. The second appliance was on my tail, but it wasn't right up my arse. Cars carried on moving out of my way. I had one hairy moment when a wide-load tractor came down the road towards me as we left Sutton Farm Estate and joined the Wenlock Road, but there was just enough room for the two of us so any crisis was averted. My right foot was still pumping up and down like the pistons on a steam train but it seemed to be calming down, and it didn't bother me as much now. I thanked my lucky stars that no one had noticed it – and it hadn't affected the way I'd driven. I pulled into the station yard and drove us into the appliance room. I turned the engine off, opened the door and jumped down on to the tiled floor alongside all the others. As I plugged the engine in to keep its batteries and equipment charged, Pete was continuing with a long-running grumble about the cost of his car insurance while Caddie and Charlie had begun discussing a new hiking trail that had been opened up across the Stiperstones. I did a quick walk around the engine and soaked in the atmosphere. Everything was completely normal. No one commented on my first live drive. And all of a sudden I realised that was exactly how I'd wanted it to be. If I'd screwed up in some major way and delayed our arrival at the fire it would have been a disaster. If I'd messed up in a more minor way the mickey-taking would have been intense. No one would have cared about car insurance or hikers if I'd knocked off someone's wing mirror or carved up a grass verge when I'd been taking a corner. I smiled, hung up my tunic and joined the others upstairs for a cup of tea while Mabel and Betty finished getting our lunch ready. That's when it happened. I was shovelling in the sugar when the tannoy came to life. Looking back it was a good job that I'd spent the last five months desperate to drive the fire engine on a live shout. Because I was about to do it again.

15

We were on our way to another house fire. This time it was in Pitchford, over by Acton Burnell. Like my first shout it was a persons reported call so the pressure was on from the start. But my second drive of the day would end very differently. Though I had no way of knowing it at the time, I was about to get a short, sharp shock to my system.

Icy rain was sweeping across the windscreen as I drove us out of Shrewsbury, over the English Bridge and off across the county towards Pitchford. There seemed to be hazards at every turn on a day that was becoming increasingly wintery. We had long since left the wide smooth main roads. Now we were on a maze of narrow lanes, with a never-ending series of tight bends and barely visible driveways, exits and junctions. Cars pulled out in front of us then struggled to find room to let us pass. Rickety old tractors and low loaders blocked the road as they tried to make right-hand turns into unexpected farm tracks. And things weren't much easier when the roads did widen out. I was picking up speed on one broad, straight stretch when a bus approached from the opposite direction. The road was wide, but it certainly didn't look wide enough for the both of us. Getting past it was a test of nerves and I was proud to pass. But once I'd done so I noticed my right leg had started to shake again. I looked into the rear-view mirror and saw the other engine right on my tail. I held the steering wheel tightly as we hit another roller-coaster of a camber and the road dipped down into a deep hollow, then disappeared round yet another blind bend.

'Drive to arrive,' I told myself as we thundered over a cattle grid, the motion and the teeth-grating noise sending shock-waves through all of us. 'Drive to arrive' was one of the mantras Keith had drummed into me back in training. There was no point going so darn fast in the first part of the journey that you crashed and didn't make it to the end. Speed was important, but so was safety. That came home to me again a few moments later when I spotted a five-bar gate that had come off its hinges and was lying halfway across the lane. 'Hold on!' I yelled as I swerved around it. There weren't any seat belts for the three men in the back of the engine. As we never wore the ones in the front, sudden manoeuvres like this were a real test of everyone's balance. Shame there was no time to radio the guys in the engine behind to warn them. In the mirror I saw them swerve even later than I'd done. But they too got past the hurdle unscathed.

In the back of my engine two of them were in their BA sets by the time the roads cleared and we drew near to the call-out address. If all went well, I estimated that we would be there in no more than a couple of minutes. My leg was still pumping away like crazy but my mind had begun to move on to the next phase of the shout. I reckoned I'd done OK over at Sutton Farm Estate that morning. I reckoned I'd run the pumps and the radio as well as any of the old-timers. This time, however, I was sure I could do even better. I'd be faster, smoother, more assured. The adrenalin was packing out my system, racing through my veins and powering everything I did. I was your classic coiled spring, ready for action, ready to fight fire, itching to be released.

'OK, this is it. That's number eleven so number fifteen will be the house with the For Sale sign down there,' John said.

I parked us outside as the second engine drew up behind. John jumped out of the cab and ran towards the house to investigate. The rain and the wind were heavier there. Big raindrops were thrown against the windscreen. The cab echoed to the soft rattle on our roof. There was a real sense of drama about the situation. But there didn't seem to be any sign of a fire.

'It's a false alarm. There's nothing doing. The house looks empty. No sign of a break-in, no obvious damage anywhere and nobody around.' John was back. His cheeks were slightly red as he spoke. I'd worked with him long enough to know why. He was angry. So was I. I felt my own breathing pick up as I looked at the silent, empty house alongside us. Dealing with malicious false alarms was an occupational hazard in the Fire Service. We got one every so often. Sometimes when you're at the back of the engine they are irritating and annoying. Sometimes they don't feel as bad – you have all the fun and excitement of the call-out drive but no one's hurt or upset and you get to go straight back to base for an early cup of tea. That day, as the driver, I was in the first category. I was starving and we were in the middle of nowhere after a tough, challenging drive. I was furious.

'You know what I'd do with them if I met them?' I said under my breath. 'I'd swing for them. If I saw one of them now, sniggering out from behind some net curtain I'd have a blinkin' word.'

'Hey, steady on, Windsor, calm down. It's only kids,' said Caddie.

'That's why I'm so hacked off. How can kids do this? How can their parents let them? What's going through their thick, useless skulls?' I didn't stop there. I kept muttering away for ages because I had a lot of questions for my sneaky, hidden tormenters. I wanted to know why they'd done it. I wanted to know who they thought would help with a genuine fire on the other side of the county after we'd been called out there as a prank. I wanted to know how the toe-rags would feel if they needed us one day and some snotty-nosed kid had called us out to a false alarm half an hour away. All of a sudden I realised I was breathing fast as well as talking fast. I could sense my chest rising, falling and straining through my shirt. Up ahead of us, on the same side of the road, was a red phone box. That would be where they'd made the call, I thought. Shouldn't we call the police and get them to fingerprint it? I looked around at all the local houses again. The useless, stupid idiots. Were they looking at us now? Were they smirking? Did they really, truly think this was funny?

'Windsor, forget it. It's not worth it. You know this kind of thing happens. It's just one of those things we have to put up with,' Caddie said, having a second go at calming me down.

The rest of the guys were looking at me in shock, and I suppose I could understand why. I was competitive and I got hot under the collar on the volleyball pitch. I didn't suffer fools and I always fought my own corner. But I was still a lifelong joker. I rarely let the stress show or took things personally. I doubt any of the lads had ever seen me get this wound up.

'Yeah, well,' I said, struggling to think of a way to conclude my little rant.

'At least if we head back now lunch won't be totally ruined. Mabel will have put it all in the hot box for us. We'll even give you first dibs on seconds,' Caddie said.

'Is it shepherd's pie?'

'Yes, it is.'

'Plenty of cheese on the crust?'

'Probably.'

'Then that's a deal.' I calmed down and cooled off fast. I cracked a few more weak jokes about lunch to prove I was in a better mood. It was important. I was number two on the board. I was taking the engine home. I'd never have allowed John to judge me unfit to drive.

'By the way, Windsor, when we get out of the village can you try not to swerve around any five-bar gates this time?' Pete asked from the back seat when we were on our way back to base. 'I nearly had Charlie in my lap on the way out – and that's not something either of us wants to repeat in a hurry.'

'If I see a gate in the road now I'll just floor it and ram it, OK? I'll imagine the toe-rag who called us out here is hiding underneath it. That OK, boss?'

'Permission granted.'

Funnily enough, the gate was still lying halfway across the road when we retraced our steps on the way home. 'Excellent! Eyes locked on target. Hold tight and prepare for warp speed!' I yelled when I saw it. Then I put my foot on the brake and stopped the engine so we could get out and drag the gate off the road and out of everyone else's way. Not quite as much fun as ramming it into oblivion. But we were the Fire Brigade. We were supposed to make things safe.

For the next six days until my next shift I relived those first two drives endlessly in my mind. It didn't matter that the second of them had been a false alarm. I still thought about them all day and I dreamed about them all night. I talked of nothing else. Poor Alice must have been bored rigid as I described every bend in the road, every vehicle that had strayed into my path, every old lady who had chosen exactly the wrong moment to start crossing the road in front of me. I told my mum and dad every detail over Sunday lunch at theirs. I told my hang-gliding mates, the guys I went rock climbing with – pretty much everyone I knew or had ever known got to hear the story.

I suppose I had always known that driving for real would feel different. I just hadn't been prepared for how different. I had really, really liked it. I also realised that it had woken up another ambition in me. I'd always lived by the motto: 'If you're going to be a bear, be a grizzly.' That was how I saw my latest challenge. It wouldn't be enough for me to be a driver. I had to be a good one. I had to be one of the best. In the meantime, I carried on reliving those first two drives. I smiled so much I very nearly hurt my face!

It carried on raining cats and dogs through the first couple of weeks of December, but it was yet another sheep that needed our help as we started our next set of day shifts. I was back in the rear of the engine, positioned in the number three slot and sitting alongside Caddie and Woody. We got the call-out at ten in the morning – not bad timing as the shout would probably take us right through the time John and Joe had put aside for our daily drills.

Even better news came through as John unfolded the big OS map and plotted our route. 'You know what, lads, I think this could be our lucky day. I've been up here before. It was for a barn fire back in the spring of last year, I think. They'd been doing some welding and sparks had set it off. The farmer and his family put most of it out. We were there for a watching brief. You were on the shout, weren't you, Caddie? And you, Windsor. Remember?'

I certainly did. A broad smile began to spread over my face. Like Pavlov's dog, I think I may well have started licking my lips too. It had been a pretty decent spring day. The fire had been well on its way to burning itself out by the time we arrived. But because it had been pretty ferocious for a while and had threatened a line of barns, sheds and assorted outbuildings, we'd kept an eye on it from midday till knocking-off time at six p.m. In that six-hour stretch we'd been all but adopted by the farmer's wife. She'd not only made us feel like part of the family, she'd fed us accordingly.

'She had the kettle on and the teapot out before we'd got off the appliances,' said Caddie dreamily.

'Yeah, and the teapot and a couple of plates of home-made biscuits were just the starters. They were oatmeal, if I remember rightly. Huge, the size of saucers. They were the best biscuits we had all year.'

'Then when she found out we were there for the duration, she got really busy. When we came back from our first patrol she was there offering tea and flapjacks. An hour or so later we had a spread fit for a king. Bowls of home-made tomato soup. Huge doorstops of crusty white bread, thick slices of ham and the tangiest, tastiest mustard I'd had in ages.'

That hadn't been all. The lady had disappeared for a while after that – giving us a chance to congratulate the farmer on his wonderful wife. 'Don't you worry yourselves, she'll be back,' he told us. A couple of hours later she had proved him right. She'd been in the kitchen, baking cakes. For tea we had steaming-hot rock cakes and a thick ginger cake topped with cream, everything made with farm-fresh ingredients and eggs that had been collected that morning.

'As long as she's still around, it's fair to say that Christmas has come early for us this year,' John said as we made our final approach to the farm. 'I only hope everyone's hungry.'

All of us were. So all of us were in a very good mood as the appliance climbed up the hill towards Much Wenlock. The fields were smaller up there, most of them bordered with grey, drystone walls, making the traditional patchwork of squares and shapes. It was a harsh landscape, but even on a lousy wet day like this it had a touch of grandeur to it. If I were an artist, I'd have painted it.

'So you said you got a choice of grub? Decent sandwiches? And two different types of cake, right?' Woody asked, still thinking about the food.

'Yes – and I reckon she'd have baked more, if we'd only asked. As long as we can spin this shout out past a couple of hours, I reckon she'll cook us something to take back to the station as well.'

We were busily arguing what we should ask for when John cut us short and spoiled everything.

'Sorry, lads, I've got bad news,' he said from the front seat. 'It's not the same farmer.'

Caddie stopped the engine. As the officer in charge, John would ordinarily have jumped down to speak to the member of the public who had called us. That day he simply rolled down his window and shouted through it. Maybe, he must have been thinking, this man had flagged us down for some other reason. Maybe the shout really was at lady bountiful's farm up the road.

'Did you call us, sir?' he asked.

'What's that you say?'

'Did you call us?'

'Call you? Of course I called you. But you took a fine old time getting here. I've been standing here half the day already.'

With a deep sigh John rolled up his window, opened his cab door and jumped down to speak to the farmer properly. With heavy hearts the rest of us joined him.

'If this guy's got a beautiful, hospitable wife back home then I'm a Dutchman,' Caddie muttered.

I gave a rueful smile. Last year's farmer had been middle-aged, friendly and very clearly prosperous. His neighbour was none of these things. He'd used bailer twine to tie a floppy, black oilskin hat on to his head. His waterproof jacket looked as old as he did – and he looked as old as the Mendip Hills. His trousers were firmly tucked into a pair of well-patched wellington boots. He was leaning on a stick and chewing on something as we approached him and appeared to be gazing morosely down the valley at nothing in particular. He certainly didn't seem to be noticing the rain.

'This is your farm? You've got a problem with one of your sheep?'

'Aye, this is the edge of my farm, right enough. Sheep's got tangled up. She's over there,' he said laconically. We followed his disinterested gaze. 'Tangled up' was an understatement. The sheep had got herself snagged in a mass of barbed wire rolled around a small mountain of manure. As she had thrashed around, a fair few rotten posts must have broken, giving her even more wire to wind around herself. And a lot more manure to roll in.

'So we're here to get her free,' Woody said, with a clear lack of enthusiasm.

As he spoke, the sheep pulled herself to her feet and started to thrash around again, dragging and jerking the barbed wire in all directions. She looked as if she would kick the heck out of anyone who came near her. What we really needed was a vet to sedate the animal and let us get closer to her, but vets cost money. The farmer would have had to pay a chunk of cash to get one of those out here in the rain. We, on the other hand, had come out for free. We were the good old Fire Brigade. So we had to get as up close and personal with the sheep as we could – without being kicked somewhere very personal and even more painful in the process.

'Well, I reckon she's hurting enough already. Sooner we start, the sooner she's free,' said John. 'Get your gloves on, grab some wire cutters and let's have the leather sheet out.'

'A clothes peg on the nose might help as well, boss. That manure stinks to high heaven,' said Woody.

'Rain's getting worse as well. When we get the blighter free, I reckon we'll have to build her an ark,' Caddie added.

Equipment in hand, we moved in on our prey. There's no point in trying to creep up on a sheep. These skittish creatures can sense a threat from any and all directions. So we simply went for it. We held out the leather sheet – the thick blanket we normally put on the floor to protect people's carpets in chimney fires – then Woody and I moved in on the sheep and bundled it. Our aim was to keep it as still as possible and cover up as much of the barbed wire as we could. Woody had certainly been right about the manure heap: it really did reek. Caddie, who was wearing the thick leather Thermalite gloves we normally used to pull hot metal parts out of fireplaces, started to tug the barbed wire away from the animal's body. The sheep was clearly exhausted after thrashing around so much trying to get free on her own, but as we worked she found a new lease of energy – and this made matters even more tricky.

'Watch out for the end of that wire!' I shouted after one snip as the newly free wire flew through the air in a very dangerous arc. 'Watch out for that one!' I called again after another quick snip. The wind on the moors picked up and the rain became almost horizontal as we reached in to try and twist out the tangles. And still the sheep fought on. It had a stab at kung fu at one point, its legs lashing out, the hooves as sharp as dirty diamonds.

'We're trying to help you, you testy little bugger,' Woody told it after yet another near miss.

A couple more cuts of the wire and a few more tangles untwisted, and we were all but done.

'Hold the wire tight up there. I reckon I can pull her leg out from this side,' Caddie told us. 'As long as the little bugger doesn't—'

It did. It went for a black-belt move and Caddie took a savage blow right in his stomach and ended up falling on to his knees in the manure patch. The rest of us tried not to laugh as we took over from him, grabbed and pulled the leg he'd been aiming for and got the animal free.

For a split second the sheep stood still as a statue. It looked – and smelled – as if it had suffered a very bad haircut and then been in a plane crash on the edge of a sewage works. Fortunately, sheep don't really care much about appearance or personal hygiene. The moment its initial shock had passed it moved, skittering off across the field at a cracking pace. We didn't get so much as a single 'baa' of thanks. All we were left with was a mass of rusty barbed wire, and half a dozen tufts of filthy, blood-stained wool.

'I suppose you got the job done in the end. But that's a lot of damage you've done to my fence, you know. There's no chance you'll repair my fence for me?' was all our unfriendly farmer could say. He had his hands on his hips and appeared to be distinctly unimpressed with the service we'd provided. The service we'd provided entirely free of charge.

'There's no chance of an invite back to your farm for a

Christmas drink or a bite to eat?' Woody fired back cheekily as we packed our wire cutters away and tried to wipe the worst of the mud and manure off our uniforms. 'Your lady wife's not spent the day baking, I don't suppose?'

The farmer's selective deafness came to the fore and he didn't even bother with a reply.

'Tight sod,' said Caddie. 'We've got more chance getting a mince pie from the blinkin' sheep.'

The rain had turned to sleet as we gave up on our departing farmer, squelched through the mud and jumped back on to the engine. 'Someone's going to have fun cleaning all this up later,' I said, looking at the appliance as well as at our kit. I brightened up as I thought this through. For years that someone would always have been me. But now I'd become a qualified driver, I reckoned I could pull rank. Unless the other appliance was on a call, Dodger and Des would be waiting in the warm, dry station back in Shrewsbury. This was very much a job for them.

16

Christmas came early to our fire station – and because of the way our shift patterns worked, it lasted quite a long time. Every year each watch, Green Watch, Blue Watch, White Watch and us, Red Watch, had a big Christmas lunch. It was held on a weekday when the relevant watch was on days in the run-up to Christmas itself. This year Green Watch was first out of the trap. They were holding theirs two and a half weeks before the big day. White Watch had theirs three days later and ours came the following week.

Each watch probably did things differently, the way every family builds up different traditions over the years, but two factors were always the same. The first was that the meal was the only one of the year that was cooked by the officers on the respective watch. The officer in charge, Sub-O and leading firemen weren't on the usual meal roster, so they got to sit back and eat our food all year – and to criticise it at will. Each December their penance was to cook a vast turkey and to produce a mountain of roast potatoes, a couple of bucketfuls of sprouts, parsnips and other vegetables, a selection of extras like bacon, sausages and stuffing, plus of course a swimming pool of gravy and a lake of bread sauce.

The second common factor for our Christmas blowouts was that Babs and Maggie, our early morning cleaners, were invited to all four of them. 'It's a dangerous time of year for me. All this eating. I could lose my slim, girlish figure,' Maggie said in the run-up to the food fest. She was the first to admit she had lost her slim, girlish figure a long, long time ago.

Of course each of our Christmas lunches could have been shot to heck by a badly timed call-out. A big shout in the morning would ruin the officers' preparations and put our turkey in jeopardy. A shout at lunchtime when the meal was on the hatch would have been the ultimate disaster. Though sometimes I swear Babs and Maggie would have welcomed it as they could have tucked into all the best meat and trimmings while we were gone.

This year all was quiet from parade time onwards. We didn't do any of our usual drills in the morning. Instead we found lots of excuses to sneak upstairs and take a look at the work that was being done in the kitchen. That seemed to involve an inordinate amount of swearing and banging of pans. But as midday approached we were all doing our impression of a Bisto advert – sniffing the air, smiling broadly in anticipation and saying: 'Ahhh!' as the cooking smells wafted round the station.

Babs and Maggie arrived bang on schedule at half past twelve. We all did a double take when we saw them. They were dressed up to the nines in honour of the occasion. Babs was wearing a long, swirly skirt and a tight pale-blue top. Maggie was wearing a much shorter skirt and an equally tight fluffy jumper. Both of them had big earrings on, lots of necklaces and a lot of make-up.

'Scrub up well, don't we?' Maggie trilled coquettishly. 'We don't spend all our lives wearing overalls and smelling of bleach. I'll have you know this is Chanel No. 5 I've got on today.'

'Canal number five – bought from some dodgy bloke with a suitcase at the back of the arcade, more like,' Arfer said as Maggie threatened him with a sprig of mistletoe she'd brought in her bag.

'Babs, Maggie, let me get you both a drink,' I said, keeping a wary eye on the mistletoe myself as I led the pair to the bar. We'd dipped into the mess fund we used for our food to buy a load of wine and brandy, and as long as the cash didn't run out we'd have free beer as well for a while yet.

'So how's the cooking going?' Babs asked, taking a hefty slug of her red wine.

'We've not been allowed anywhere near the kitchen since we had a brew at eleven. Smells good, though. Nothing burning, which is always a good sign.'

'God knows who would be able to help if we had a fire up here. Maybe we could call old Mr Thom to come over with a bucket of water. I don't see anyone else who looks halfway handy in an emergency,' Maggie declared.

All the usual insults were flying happily when John, Joe and the others officers rapped on the side of the serving hatch. 'Gentlemen – and ladies!' John shouted. 'Take your seats. Lunch is served!'

Babs and Maggie had been found space at the top of our long table, between the officers. The rest of us were bunched up further down the room, but all in our usual seats. We pulled our crackers, put on our paper hats and hooted with laughter at the worst of the cracker jokes. Pretty soon we were tanked up on wine and brandy. The officers' cooking had been pretty good. Taking the view that quantity could be as useful as quality they'd made a truly mountainous amount of grub. We could have built a rockery with the pile of roast potatoes they produced. They'd done huge saucepans of veg and twice as much of everything else as any normal group of men would eat. There was nothing left by the time we'd finished.

'John, you cook a better turkey than my mum. Though to be fair, my mum has been dead for twenty years,' Charlie said as we sat back and waited for a couple of bucket-sized trifles to be carried across to the main table. The officers were happy to laugh along at all of it. Though as usual there was a touch of healthy competition in the air.

'Babs, Maggie, come over here. How did Blue Watch get on this year?' John asked when we'd all left the table and were lounging on the comfier chairs round the telly. 'We heard they had a problem with the turkey. They didn't weigh it properly or time it right or something. And we heard White Watch forgot to do bread sauce and gravy.' We'd heard nothing of the sort, of course, as Babs and Maggie well knew.

'I don't know about bread sauce or gravy, but White Watch's turkey was cooked to perfection,' teased Babs. 'They must have timed it to the very minute. Soft and moist and crumbled in your mouth like a dream, it did.'

'What? More than mine? Was it better than mine? Are you trying to say that there was something wrong with my turkey? You're joking, right? Come on, Babs, tell me you're joking.'

The Christmas spirit lasted right through to the end of the shift at six. The ladies had hung around and played a few games of 'Killer' in the afternoon, but they left at four, still joking with the officers about the quality of their cooking and terrorising the rest of us with their sprig of mistletoe. We kept the Christmas music blaring out – and headed downstairs to build a sleigh.

The sleigh was to be the centrepiece of the kids' Christmas party the station was holding a week before Christmas. All the different watches were getting together to host the event. Any fireman could invite his kids or grandkids. Every watch was making a different contribution. Some were going to help with the entertainment and the food and drink on the day. Others were going to decorate the station the night before. We were charged with giving Santa an entrance to remember.

Simon was in charge: not least because he had been a pattern maker in a component factory before joining the Fire Brigade. But as we had some of the most practical men in Shropshire on the watch there was no shortage of other talent. Nor did we have any problem finding raw materials. With so many spiv jobs in the building, painting and decorating trade between us we could all pitch in with something. That afternoon we set to work on sheets of plywood. Simon got them cut into an elaborate sleigh shape and we worked out how to fix it to the stores trolley so Santa could be transported down the top-floor corridor. The decorators among us began to paint and by the time Green Watch arrived for the night shift we had something Santa would be proud of.

The kids certainly went wild when they saw it on the Saturday. Red Watch had drawn the short straw so we were on duty in the station that day. It meant that however hard I tried I couldn't escape the ensuing bunfight. 'They're like locusts,' I said to Mabel from the relative safety of the kitchen as we watched the party through the hatch. Dozens of kids were swarming round the room, grabbing paper plates full of jam sandwiches, sausages on sticks and hefty lumps of cheese. They'd already munched their way through huge bowls of crisps, nuts and Twiglets.

'Don't they remind you of anyone?' Mabel asked.

'Who?'

'You! All of you. I'll have you know this is just a child-sized version of what Betty and I have to look at every day at lunchtime,' she told me triumphantly. 'Now bring that jelly and ice cream out of the fridge while I go and check my grandchildren haven't fallen down the pole hatch.'

Ten minutes later Mabel got me to take the jelly and ice cream into the mess room and I narrowly escaped with my life. The station did look pretty good, I thought, as I headed back to the relative safety of the kitchen. We'd opened up the doors to the dormitory and pulled the beds to one side to make the most of the space. One of the other watches had put up a load of decorations and even created a grotto that could have put a department store to shame.

But where, amidst all this, was Santa?

The wives and mums were given the nod and heralded his arrival while I was sent out to clear up the latest wave of discarded paper bowls.

'I can hear sleigh bells! I can hear reindeer hooves! Let's look out the window and see who's coming to join us!' one of the mums cried.

A sort of thunderclap broke as dozens of tiny feet charged towards the windows. Mabel's got a point, I thought as I heard it. That's pretty much the same noise we make when we run up to the hatch at feeding time. I joined the kids and looked over their shoulders. Babs and Maggie will have their work cut out cleaning up after all these runny noses have been pushed against the glass, I thought as I looked around me. That's payback for them getting to eat four Christmas dinners in a row.

The scene out in the street was good enough to make Scrooge smile. Dylan, one of the old-hands on Green Watch, had elected to be Santa – he had curly white hair, silver-rimmed glasses and a bit of a belly so he could have walked right out of central casting. With a red sack on his back, a fluffy white fake beard on his face and all decked out in a bright red outfit, he looked the business. Best of all was his transport – the turntable ladder. Bang on cue, they drove it into the station yard, Dylan standing on top of it waving and smiling. The kids loved it and I headed back into the kitchen so I wouldn't get trampled underfoot when Santa came upstairs and started doling out the presents.

'It would be a laugh if we got a call-out now,' I told the mums. Although, as Dylan wasn't on duty, he could have stuck around to keep the kids happy on his own.

'Well, remember the call we got that New Year when we were having the Incredible Hulk party?' Charlie said. 'A dozen men with green painted faces turned up at the Royal Shrewsbury and tramped through the maternity ward to find out what had triggered the automatic alarm. I'm amazed most of those women didn't give birth on the spot.'

I passed around a big bag of crisps I'd hidden away earlier on. It was always nice talking shop at a party when you were being paid to be there. I chewed the cud with Dodger, Des and Woody, the only others who didn't have kids, grandkids or assorted relatives' kids at the party. 'Did you see the card we got from Jennifer, by the way? The sunbather who got her finger trapped in the garden fence?' I asked. It had come in earlier that morning. It was dedicated to: 'Everyone at Shrewsbury fire station' and she'd signed it with three kisses. 'That's one each for the three of us,' Dodger decided.

Overall the watch had done pretty well out of the ladies that year. We'd already got a card and big box of Milk Tray from Barbara, the flirty girl we'd cut out of her dad's Fiesta back in the early summer. She'd put a load of kisses on her card, as well as yet another invitation to visit her at work in her solicitors' office. We'd also got a huge tin of Quality Street from Mad Pam from the animal charity. She'd taped a note to the lid. The first part said how grateful she was for all the times we'd helped her animals over the course of the year. When we read that I think we all felt a bit guilty for calling her Mad Pam. Then we read the next part: 'I know in my heart that each and every one of the animals and all of the birds send their love and thanks to you as well,' she had written, amidst a flurry of capital letters and underlined words. So Mad Pam it was.

'Funny how we never get any presents from the farmers. Deep pockets they've got, as well as the shortest arms in the country. Too busy buying new Land Rovers to remember all the good turns we did them earlier in the year,' Caddie moaned, striding into the kitchen, muscling in on our conversation and rummaging around the Quality Street tin in search of his favourites.

When the party and our latest two-day shifts were over I made a bit of cash helping Arfer and George with a couple of pre-Christmas removals jobs they had on. We had a relatively quiet tour of night shifts where I mostly sat around watching TV and struggling to dunk the latest packet of broken biscuits we'd been given by the Thoms.

We didn't see action again until Christmas Day itself. As it was a bank holiday we were on 'stand down' – which meant that, after turning up, getting into our uniforms and doing all the standard checks on the operational equipment we weren't required to do any other Fire Brigade-related work unless it was to go to a shout. Even in the cold that tended to mean hours of volleyball out in the yard. Some stand-down days we'd have a cup of tea at nine, play straight through till our second brew of the day at eleven. Then we'd play again. On Christmas Day we all went our separate ways after eleven. A few of the lads went to wash their cars, others lounged around reading yesterday's papers or watching TV. The canasta school began early and a re-match of 'Killer' got going round the dartboard. As I didn't have kids at that point I wasn't too bothered about working over Christmas. So as far as I was concerned, getting paid to loaf around like this was terrific. I wasn't even that bothered that I was on kitchen duty. I liked cooking. I'd have been happy to do a Sunday roast, but as we'd all been stuffing our faces lately we'd voted on a more relaxed meal so we could all get in front of the telly for the afternoon. Des and I just needed to prepare soup and lay out a pile of do-it-yourself rolls and sandwiches. We were nearly done when we got the call. 'Attention,' then those three warning chimes sounded out. The soup stayed in the saucepans, the newspapers were thrown on the floor, the cards got laid on the table and the darts were left in the board. We headed for the pole. The call was to a house fire with persons reported. So much for a calm, relaxed day. Instead it looked set to be business as usual.

Pete got us there fast with Joe on his tail in the other appliance. Somewhere, possibly from a different direction, a police car and an ambulance would be on their way. Fortunately the roads were almost empty. A few cars were heading for hotels in Shrewsbury and some of the pub car parks further afield were pretty busy. But everyone else in Shropshire must have been at home with the family or sat in front of the telly.

'At least it's daylight and at least someone looks to have spotted it early,' Charlie said grimly as we pulled on our BA sets on the back seat of the engine. I knew exactly what he meant. Christmases past were littered with families whose tree lights had sparked in the small hours and poisoned them with smoke while they slept. Stockings put in front of the fire for Santa had done just as much damage. Some people didn't wake up at all on Christmas morning. Or if they did it was to a scene of horror, not delight. I checked my torch and axe were in position on my body straps. I wanted this story to have a happier ending.

The engine clattered round one corner. I got my familiar wave of travel sickness as Pete steered us round another. We were aiming for a housing estate on the far edge of town. Houses were crammed into a maze of curves and cul-de-sacs. Parked cars on either side of the roads added extra obstacles. It was never that easy to drive through areas like this at speed. All the same, I wished I was in the driving seat that day. The back seats in these new appliances faced forward but it was hot and airless with the windows shut tight. As we were hemmed in on all sides by houses there was no far horizon to gaze at to try and settle my stomach. Instead I closed my eyes for a moment and focused on the task ahead.

'That's got to be the house. Isn't that smoke?' Pete shouted from the front. I leaned forward so I could see. We were aiming for the second of a pair of semi-detached houses up on the right. Smoke was coming out of the kitchen window at the front of the house. We screeched to a halt right in front of the address with Joe and the others directly behind us. All told, we'd taken less than five minutes to get from mess room to destination.

Joe jumped out of the cab. All of us did. When you can see smoke the moment you arrive, you have to move fast. You don't wait for the boss to suss out the lie of the land or find out what's what. You just prepare yourself to get in there. So Charlie and I lifted the hose-reel off the appliance, Pete dropped the tank and

Caddie set up the BA board. The ambulance and the police car arrived, blue lights flashing, as Charlie and I rushed towards the front door of the house with the hose. As we did so the door was yanked open. I was expecting to see one or more people run out, fleeing the fire, desperate to be saved. This was the moment I loved most about the job. Saving lives, being a hero, scooping up those beautiful damsels in distress. I pulled myself up short, with Charlie all but crashing into me from behind. For this wasn't quite what we had been expecting.

Instead of a family fleeing a Christmas Day fire there was one lone figure at the door. It was a woman of about thirty. She wasn't running anywhere. Nor was she pleased to see us. She was wearing a dirty apron and her hair was sticking out in all directions. She stood there, hands on hips, a look that was half anger, half horror on her face. I'm no trained lip-reader, but when she did start to speak she was clearly repeating the same short phrase again and again. 'What the @$%*? What the @$%*?'

'What's on fire? Is there anyone else in there?' John yelled, brushing past me and striding across the front garden towards the woman.

She said nothing for a moment. Then she took a very deep breath and began to shout right back. 'I'll tell you what's on fire. The effing turkey is on fire and no, there's no one in there yet but there are fourteen people coming in twenty minutes, so unless you've got a cooked turkey on one of your fire engines you can all just eff off and let me get on with sorting it all out!'

With that she took another huge gulp of air, gave us the finger, the evil eye and slammed the door in our faces. We all stood there like naughty schoolboys for a second or two. Did we take the lady's word for it and head back to base? Or did we force our way in to check it out for ourselves? John made the executive decision to take the lady's word for it. Technically speaking, we've got the right to enter almost any premises where we think there is a risk to persons or property. But in reality we're guided by good old-fashioned common sense. John went over to speak to Joe in the second appliance and to have a quick word with the other emergency services. We re-stowed the hose-reels. Then, as we all started to fall about laughing, he climbed back into our engine and told us to follow suit. That's when we had our second unexpected event of the day.

Pete was on the point of driving away when there was a very faint tapping on the driver's door.

'What the heck is that?' he said, pulling on the brake.

We looked out of the window but there was no one there. Then the tapping began again. We looked down, rather than straight out. And then we saw her.

'It was my fault, I'm afraid,' a voice piped up.

We all leaned over and looked down. A rather short lady with concerned eyes and a royal-blue housecoat was standing in the street. She could barely have been taller than five foot two and she was blinking at us through a pair of very thick spectacles.

'My name is Kate Measures. I live just across the way. I saw the smoke coming from the window. She's not the nicest neighbour I've ever had, but I didn't want her house to burn down at Christmas. So it was me who dialled 999. I'm sorry for calling you out on Christmas Day. I'm sorry if she was rude to you.'

'My dear lady, we've heard a good deal worse,' John said, leaning across Pete and taking control of the situation as usual. 'And this is just an ordinary day for us. We're on duty whether we get a call or not. All you have done is give us something to do. That's no bad thing, bearing in mind all the good food we've eaten of late.'

'Well, if you're sure.'

'I am sure. I'm also sure that your neighbour would have thanked you if it had been a real fire.'

'She didn't thank me when I started to feed her cat in the summer,' the lady began, doubtfully. Charlie caught my eye and

I looked away, hoping I wouldn't laugh. John, though, was still very serious.

'Mrs Measures, do you have somewhere to go for Christmas yourself?' he asked. I wondered, suddenly, if he was going to bring her back to the station with us. She was probably small enough to fit in one of the lockers, but I wasn't sure if that was allowed.

'I have a friend over in Telford and I shall be joining her later on for my evening meal,' we were told.

'Well, let one of my fine gentlemen walk you back to your door,' said John. 'Windsor, you're the nearest. You go.'

17

It was our first night shift of the New Year. The party period had carried on way past Christmas and was only now starting to calm down. Green Watch had changed into their civvies and headed off. In an hour or two's time a lot of them would be partying at home or off for a good night down the pub. We'd be sitting upstairs trying to relax – and that was never easy when you knew a lot of drivers would be having one too many and then playing dodgems on the roads when the pubs closed.

In the calm before the expected storm we played as many pranks on each other as we could think of. First up we put black boot polish on the inner headband of Woody's helmet before sending him across to the Thoms' shop to buy milk. He spent about twenty minutes chatting to them before heading back across the road. Bless them, neither Mr nor Mrs Thom had the heart to tell him he had a huge black mark running right across his forehead. Later on, Des took a battering when we played spoons. A couple of weeks before we had tried but failed to get Dodger to go to the storeroom and ask for 'a long weight'. 'I'm too smart to fall for that one. I've seen the "Fork Handles" joke on the *Two Ronnies*, I know this is a piss-take', he'd said, smugly. But he did head off to stores on the following tour when John sent him to ask for an 'extended stand'. A good ten minutes later, having had one, he was back to face a wave of laughter from the rest of us.

The last person to be pranked was me. It was a standing joke on the watch how much I liked hot food and chilli. So one of them injected the hottest chilli sauce they could find into the 'last' mince pie that they left on a plate in the mess room. They'd correctly predicted that I would nab it the minute I walked into the room. I did just that, grabbing the pie and stuffing it in my mouth. After a couple of chews I did a fire-eating impression as the sauce kicked in.

'That'll teach you some table manners, Windsor,' Arfer crowed as the rest of the gang jumped out from behind the dormitory doors.

We had a decent dinner and got a bit of a party going as the evening wore on. But all along we knew we'd probably get some early hours shouts. We did – and we were over the moon over the first of them. It was our favourite place, the Radbrook Nurses' Home! The call had come almost exactly on the stroke of midnight. We were expecting the usual false alarm, which was exactly what we got. Better still, we got to have a laugh when we discovered how it had come about.

'It was me. I set off one of those party poppers at midnight – we were working on New Year's Eve, so we're having our party late,' said a nurse about my age, who was blushing royally and looking as if she might never stop. 'It said on the back "Don't aim at your face" so I didn't. I aimed it at the ceiling.'

'She only went and hit the smoke alarm,' her colleague butted in.

'And I've got the worst aim in the world. I couldn't do that again if I tried. I thought we could somehow cancel the alarm, but we couldn't. I'm so sorry for having disturbed you.'

She and her colleagues made amends by offering us a big plate of mince pies and a generous measure of whisky. 'What are you doing with a bottle of whisky in a hospital? You're supposed to be healthy, aren't you?' Woody protested, taking a hefty slug.

'We're not in a hospital now, love, we're in a nurses' home. Drinking is something we're very good at. That's why this bottle of whisky isn't the only one we've got stashed away to see us through the wee small hours,' he was told by one of the prettiest faces.

Much as we wanted to stay, John got us back on the engines fast. The weather had changed. Rain was lashing down as we returned to the station. Visibility was terrible. So it came as no surprise when we had an emergency call within the hour. And a bad one.

We approached the scene from the south – we'd beaten both the police and the ambulance, but at first it wasn't easy to see why the other services might be needed. There was no evidence of a car crash. All we could see was an articulated lorry parked right across the road, blocking both lanes. The worst that seemed to have happened was that it had got stuck trying to pull into a farmyard.

'I was driving the lorry, it's mine,' a squat, swarthy man said as the rain blew almost horizontally across at us.

'My farm's just up the lane,' said a second man from under cover of a thick, black sou'wester. He was pumped up with self-importance, determined to star in the show. 'I heard the crash from my house. Hell of a crash. Thought it was a plane coming down, a light aircraft or something. You hear of that sort of thing happening. Happened to a friend of a cousin of mine out in Herefordshire. Plane came down on his land. Set off a hell of a fire. Three people on the plane. All of them dead. I called the police and I called the Fire Brigade because I thought there could be a second explosion. The driver, here, came up my lane. Said there'd been an accident. Said the road was blocked. So I got a torch and we came down here to stop any traffic. You're the first to have come along.'

'So what was it that happened here?' John interrupted.

'I'd taken a wrong turn. I was going the wrong way. So I tried to turn in the drive right there.' The driver looked ashen-faced in the night. Even in the shadows it was clear that his eyes were red and his face was drawn and tight. If we'd paid much attention to things like shock back then we'd have had him treated for it.

I looked down towards the lorry. The headlights from our engines were shining on the cab. Further along, in the middle of the left lane of the road, there appeared to be some debris. I squinted through the rain. A lot of debris.

'The car came out of nowhere. It was going like the clappers. I never saw it till it was too late and it hit me. I couldn't have moved fast enough even if I'd seen it. They can't have seen me. They wouldn't have known what happened to them.'

'Where's the car now?' John asked sharply.

'It's under the trailer section. It's jammed under there. Whoever was in it is dead. They can't have survived. They hit me like a bomb going off. They must have been doing sixty, maybe more. I just ran in to the farmhouse to call the police. I can't go back to the lorry. There's no way I can face it.'

John gave me the nod. I began to run towards the main body of the truck.

Everything became clear as I approached. The signs of impact were obvious. A car must have hit the trailer square on. As it had been reversing across the road, they'd not have seen it in time. There'd have been no lights on the side. The car would have slammed right into and under the trailer's chassis. That was where it remained.

'Blinkin' heck,' I muttered to myself as I re-enacted the scene in my mind and ducked under the trailer's chassis. The car was right there, exactly as the lorry driver had said. Or at least the remains of it were. Before the impact it must have been a perfectly ordinary Nissan Bluebird. Now it was a hellishly designed sports car. Its roof had been sliced off the way you slice the top off a boiled egg. Everything above windscreen-wiper level was gone. The twisted metal was piled up and squashed down on top of the boot.

'Blinkin' heck,' I kept repeating under my breath as I ran round the back of the lorry so I could check the car from the other side. I jumped over the ditch and squeezed past the hedgerow to get there. The lorry driver had been right. No one in the car could have survived this. I was steeling myself for the inevitable. It had to be a decapitation. Possibly more than one. This was going to be so, so terrible.

'Blinkin' heck,' I mumbled when I got to the side of the car. It was pitch-black round there. We were so far from civilisation. The last street lights were miles away. There were no houses to shine any light on the scene. Even the moon was hiding behind deep, thick rain clouds. If I wanted to see what was in the car I'd have to use my torch. And I needed to see what was there. On the other side of the lorry the others were preparing equipment and lights to sort the situation out.

I unclipped the torch from my belt and aimed it at the broken, twisted interior of the car. After taking a deep breath, I turned it on.

'Blinkin' heck!' This time I shouted the words. I was looking at the passenger's head. It was a woman, aged about forty. And her head was still very much attached to her body. Two eyes blinked at me, dazzled by the torchlight. Two hands lifted up to shield the eyes.

'Are you all right?' was all I could think of to ask.

'I'm fine,' she told me.

'How's the driver?' I asked apprehensively.

I steeled myself again and moved the beam of the torch across the car. I found another head. It too was attached to a body.

'I'm fine too. But we're trapped. We can't get out.'

I took a gulp of air. And I said one of the most stupid things I've ever said in my life.

'Stay where you are.'

*

'You're kidding me,' John said when I'd run round the back of the lorry to pass on the news.

'I'm not. Couldn't you hear them?'

'I don't believe you. If anyone's in that car then they're dead.'

'Well, they're not. They're fine. I've never seen anything like it.' There was a split-second delay while everyone calculated whether this was a wind-up. When they realised that it wasn't, we all sprang into action. We radioed to find out what had happened to the ambulance and told the operator it should approach from the east to be closer to the patients. The rest of us raced round the back of the lorry to check on the car.

'Hello,' the driver said when we got there. He couldn't have sounded more normal if he'd been greeting a few old pals in the street.

'Hello,' repeated John, in an equally everyday fashion. 'Are both of you all right?'

'We're both fine. But like I told your colleague, we're stuck.'

'No injuries? There's an ambulance on the way.'

'I hit my head and I've bashed up my hand, but it's not too bad. My wife is fine, though, aren't you? We can both move, can't we?'

'We can wiggle our fingers and toes, which is important, isn't it? I don't think I got even as much as a scratch. It's a miracle,' his wife agreed.

I crouched by the car while John and Caddie went back to the engine to get lights.

'You're the luckiest people in the world,' I said. 'You didn't get hit at all?'

'Nothing. I've never had a shock like it. I nearly had a heart attack. I was doing about fifty, there was nothing on the road and we were nearly home. We came round the corner and there was nothing ahead of us – nothing I could see, at any rate. Then bang. Bang. It was like an explosion. It was like something off a film. It's a lorry, isn't it? An artic or something? I'm guessing it was right across the road for some reason? I never saw any lights. We slammed into it at fifty. It was like nothing on earth.'

'I was asleep,' said his wife. 'I'd reclined my seat. I was leaning right back. That was what saved me.' For the first time there was a tremble in her voice. After holding it together for so long, waiting in shock for someone to find and rescue them on this dark, rainy night, she was finally about to cry.

'It's OK, pet. These lads will get us out of here any minute now. We've had a very, very lucky escape.'

'And you, sir? You didn't get hit? The top of your car has been sliced off. I don't want to say it, but I was expecting the worst when I approached you. The lorry driver thought you were dead from the very start. I agreed with him. I didn't think anyone could have survived this.'

'I think I moved my head to one side at the last second. It must have been sheer instinct. But my seat was already a bit reclined,' the driver said. 'It shouldn't be, but it's broken. It drives me mad. I can pull it upright when I get into the car but within a few minutes it starts to slide back. If we had the money and we could be bothered, I'd take it to the garage to get it fixed. It really does drive me mad. It means I get a crick in my neck when I drive. It's uncomfortable. It's not good for my back.'

'But it saved your life.'

The man's eyes, bright in the torchlight, filled with tears. 'It saved my life.'

We stood back and gave the situation the usual couple of coats of looking at as we worked out what to do. We confirmed that the couple had no spinal injuries for us to worry about. They weren't impaled on anything or twisted up in compressed metal. All they needed was the space to get free of the lorry.

'You know what, I don't think we need to get too fancy about this,' John said after a short pause. 'Let's just jack up the trailer, let the air out of the car tyres and see what happens.'

We did it. The lorry went up an inch or so and the remains of the car sank three or four.

'OK, lads, let's give it a pull,' Caddie instructed.

We gave it everything we had, but the car remained wedged in place. Cursing, John moved us on to Plan B. We got the powered winch from the Emergency Tender and attached it to the car's chassis. It made a savage noise, but all four wheels on the Bluebird turned relatively easily so with the extra power from the winch the vehicle was free within a few seconds. We eased it out into the circle of light from our floodlamps. 'Right, we'll hold everything nice and steady and help both of you climb out. Ladies first?' John asked.

'Yes, please, ladies first,' the driver said.

Caddie kept the car steady, I held out my arm and supported the man's wife as she squeezed her way out of the passenger seat. She twisted herself around a little, stepped on to the ripped-off side of the car, then jumped down on to the roadside. John helped the driver do the same on his side. The pair of them stood there, faces bleached of colour in our lights, trembling and swaying slightly as they looked at the remains of their car.

'It's impossible to believe,' the driver began. He stopped. There was a moment when I thought he, and his wife, were going to burst into tears. Instead they did something else. They started to laugh. Thrilled, euphoric, stunned at their good fortune, they started off with a few slightly embarrassed chuckles of shock and surprise. Within minutes the chuckles had turned into full-blown gasps of laughter. Soon the pair of them had almost collapsed with relief as the hysterics continued. Tears of laughter were streaming down their faces as they walked round the front of the car and examined what was left of it. They clutched each other and all but danced in the road. It was infectious, unexpected and strangely wonderful. In the middle of a stormy night, on a distant country lane where we could have seen a terrible tragedy, we were all caught up in their extraordinary good fortune. The lorry driver, a tough man made sheepish by the horror of what might have been, had edged his way round his lorry towards them. They welcomed him to their circle of light with open arms. They could have blamed him. There could have been recriminations, anger or even violence. There was none. At some point in the coming days the police might charge the man for dangerous driving. Maybe they'd charge the Nissan driver for something similar. Or they might agree that this was merely a freak accident. None of us knew, or really cared in this heady, crazy celebration of life. No party anywhere in Shropshire over the last few weeks could have been as happy. No joy could have been as intense.

By the time the ambulance arrived we had learned a little more about how the accident had happened. We'd also learned that the car driver had taken a few more blows than he had thought. His right knuckle was pretty badly bashed in and his shoulder looked to have taken a knock. 'We'll get you to Shrewsbury Hospital to see if it's broken, and sort out your hand and face, but none of this should take very long. We'll check you over properly as well, madam, but I don't think you'll be detained for long,' the pair were told by the ambulance crew after a quick initial examination.

We were putting the winch and our lights away when the ambulance got ready to leave. 'Thank you again,' the couple shouted to us as the doors closed. 'And Happy New Year!'

18

My ski trip to Austria was fantastic. I should have taken up the sport years ago. My mates and I threw ourselves down the mountains as fast as we could. We tried to drink the bars dry every night. We did every après ski activity on offer – from bowling nights and tobogganing to fondue evenings and ice skating. Back in Britain every part of my body ached and I could have done with another holiday to recover. I didn't get one. Shropshire was a bit like Austria that month, hunkering down in one of its coldest winters in years. At one point the thermometer at the station dropped to minus twenty-one degrees. Trains stopped running as the points froze. Buses struggled to get kids to school and anyone else into town. When we headed across country it was into a treacherous world of white. The fields had been flattened and made anonymous by snow and ice. The branches on the trees were silver fingers reaching out into the icy air. So no surprise that we were busy. Country roads are particularly dangerous. Cars skid off all over the place so we were always being called out to make something safe or drag someone out of a ditch.

Less predictable, though, was the fact that in the heart of a bleak winter, and amidst such an extreme of cold, we were about to fight the biggest, hottest fire I'd ever experienced.

The station got the call around six o'clock in the morning. Green Watch were on nights and they powered through the early morning streets to the heart of medieval Shrewsbury. The fire was in a terrace called Talbot Chambers. The building comprised a row of five shops at street level with three floors of offices above. Weeks later, when all the investigations had been done, we learned that in the early hours a faulty heating system had set off sparks in one of the offices, starting a small fire. And as the building's fire alarms had unaccountably failed to ring, this small fire had grown dangerously large before anything could be done. By the time Green Watch got the call, the flames had taken a firm hold. The officer in charge on Green Watch called for back-up and three crews of firemen in BA sets had stormed into the building. They'd been beaten back almost immediately by the intense flames. The fire had already spread too far, making it impossible to get close enough to tackle it at the heart. Plus it had been pretty clear that the building was in a bad way. The fire had eaten its way up towards the roof and crept down into all five units on the ground floor as well. The OIC's view was that the entire structure was well on its way to becoming dangerously unsafe. The more time the fire had and the more damage it did, the closer the terrace would come to collapse.

We knew something big was afoot when we arrived for our day shift at nine. Green Watch weren't there and neither were our two fire engines or our turntable ladder. The retained crew from Baschurch had been mobilised at seven to replace the others. They had headed over in their own engine and were holding the fort, ready to cover any call-outs that came in. They were also able to fill us in with the news they'd heard over the radio: 'There's six engines at the fire, plus the turntable ladder from here. A couple of senior officers have gone by car as well. That's three dozen firemen, three dozen who've been there for a full three hours and it sounds like it's still going well,' we were told.

'Persons reported?' I asked.

'No. It's all shops and offices and it kicked off in the middle of the night. There's hardly any flats round there and it was too early for cleaners or the like.'

We paraded in a hurry. As it was set to be a long, cold day we grabbed as much extra clothing as we could – thermals, hats, extra socks, thin under-gloves to go beneath our fire gloves and as many T-shirts, long-sleeved shirts and jumpers as we could lay hands on. Everyone except me got their fire kit on as well so they would be rigged and ready to go the moment they got to the fire. Then, twice their normal size due to all the layers and taking up far too much room, they piled into the station mini-bus so we could relieve Green Watch and take over their job.

It was the first of our latest tour of days and I was number two again so I got to drive. It was my first time taking the minivan out on a live shout – and it was frustrating to face the remnants of Shrewsbury's rush-hour traffic without lights or a siren. I'd already got used to the Red Sea effect you get driving the fire engine, when traffic fades away and roads open up ahead of you. In the unmarked van we were just another vehicle on the road. We could have been a bunch of farm workers, builders, anybody. I wasn't racing against any clock because a relief-duty drive isn't as important as the first drive to a live shout. Nevertheless I wanted to get us there as soon as I could. Apart from anything else, I was excited. Big town-centre fires don't come round all that often. Complicated jobs with half a dozen or more appliances and several teams of firemen are rare too. They're what we spend hour after hour training for – and as long as no one gets hurt, you can get a real buzz out of them. I couldn't wait to get to grips with this one.

The lights changed just past the railway station, and I sped forward. I hit the horn and edged past a couple of cars at the next junction – a couple of angry faces turned to us as we passed, but the drivers' expressions changed when they saw our uniforms. The police had closed a lot of roads in the centre of town and it felt even more exciting to be waved through to cover the last few hundred yards. I slowed down and made the final turn towards Talbot Chambers.

'Blimey O'Riley,' I said under my breath. Up ahead of us were all the engines and appliances you might expect to see at a major incident in an American film – all squeezed into the narrowest streets of one of England's most beautiful historic towns. The half-dozen fire engines, the turntable ladder, the support vehicles, the police cars and the ambulances were parked alongside and around a row of buildings that were very much in the wars. There weren't any visible flames, but the fire was making a lot of noise and the smoke was intense. It was billowing out of all the upper-storey windows and was pumping out from what was left of the building's roof.

'No one's going to be getting their keys cut there any time soon,' Des murmured when a shop sign fell to the ground as one of the other crews directed a stream of water against it.

'That was a greasy spoon café next to it, wasn't it?' Woody asked. 'It was a good place. They're going to get a fright when they turn up for work. A lot of people are.'

John and Joe headed off to be briefed by the officers-in-charge of the other watches and the retained crews, while I pulled off my shoes and put on my fire boots. I placed my shoes in the off-side middle locker of the fire engine Green Watch had brought out three hours earlier. This was our engine now. It was mine.

'Looks like you've had a tough morning,' I said as the Green Watch number two approached to get the minibus keys from me. He'd been sweating and had taken a bit of a soaking from the hoses. The water in his hair and on his jacket was already turning to ice. Little crystals were glistening in the morning light.

'Aye, and it's gonna be a tough day. This fire's gonna get a lot worse before it gets better. You'll still be here at six, I reckon. So we'll be seeing you again then.'

He got into the minibus and I stood alongside the rest of Red Watch as we awaited our instructions. We all drank in the scene, trying to work out what the others had already done and what was left for us. A heck of a lot, was the only possible conclusion.

John came back to us. His face was serious, his voice curt.

'OK, chaps, gather round. As you may already know, the fire began on the top floor. The first crews here took the decision to fight it from the outside after going in and seeing how much damage had been done to the internal structure. We have two main jobs to do. The first is to keep playing water on to the building from all angles to damp it down as fast as we can. The second is to stop the fire spreading to any of the neighbouring properties. As you can see, the old Music Hall is right next door over there. It's got heritage value, so it's something we want to protect at all costs.'

We nodded. John pointed towards the turntable ladder. It was now a water tower. It had been extended to its full 115 foot height and someone from Green Watch was up at the top, directing the stream of water into Talbot Chambers from above. 'Arfer and Charlie, you're taking over from Green Watch on that. Move fast, because it'll be cold as hell up there and they'll want to get down and get out of here as soon as possible. Clive, I want you to do the retained crews a favour. They're staying around a while, so radio the station and get the lazy buggers on the Emergency Tender to fill an urn with hot water and bring it down here with a load of tea and coffee. Tell the retainers that drinks are on the way. Woody, you go with Ben and relieve the Wem crew on the jet round the back. Andy and Howard, you do the same with the Baschurch crew by the Music Hall. And remember, chaps, once you've got water in the hoses keep it flowing else it will freeze and you'll be stuffed.'

'Yes, boss,' we chorused.

'Now get to work. Windsor, Dodger, Des and George – come with me.' He led us along the front of the building to the junction with Swan Hill. As we passed, some of the retained guys came out of neighbouring shops and business premises where they'd been turning off gas and electricity supplies. In Talbot

Chambers itself one of the crews was smashing windows on the ground and upper floors so they could fire jets of water even deeper into the heart of the fire. All around crews were pummelling the area with water. The trick was to cool as many adjoining walls as possible so the fire wouldn't jump or be spread by radiated heat. We wanted as many firebreaks as possible.

'There,' John said, pointing up to the top of the TSB branch on the corner ahead of us. 'That's where we need to be. It's not as high as the turntable ladder, but it will do. We can aim the water on to the roof from there. It'll have a parapet roof, I bet, so you'll have somewhere to stand. Get the 13.5 metre ladder and get up there.'

The four of us raced back to our engine and lugged the 13.5 metre ladder from it. This was our longest, heaviest ladder. This was the second time I'd used it on a live shout this year, I thought as I got into position. Even with two of us at the head and two at the heel it was a bugger to move, especially on icy roads.

'OK, let's go.' The four of us began the walk towards the bank. We were in the middle of the road, walking right alongside the burning building, when it happened. There was a deafening crack. It was like a gunshot, a sudden whiplash of a sound. The earth didn't move beneath our feet or anything like that, but it was clear that something had collapsed inside the building. A split-second later we found out what it had been. There was another loud crack. Then came a rumbling, crunching noise that started low and soon got a lot louder. Then a fourteen-foot wooden beam, some sixteen inches in diameter, fell out of the side of the building and thumped down right across the street, landing on the pavement where we had been carrying the ladder a matter of seconds earlier. The four of us stood rooted to the spot less than six feet away. That timber had slammed into the pavement with the force of a truck, throwing up a mass of sparks, splintered wood and broken glass like a mini explosion.

'Bloody hell! We were right there. That would have killed us,' Des said in a low voice.

'We wouldn't have stood a chance. Two seconds earlier and we wouldn't have stood a chance,' said Dodger.

No one spoke. What else can you say after something like that? What else can you think? In my four years in the Fire Brigade that was the closest I'd come, thus far, to being killed. And it had felt very, very close indeed.

'Our time wasn't up,' George said firmly.

I remember looking at that fallen beam for a second or two. Then we all got moving again. We had this monster of a ladder to move and we had a job to do. We didn't look back.

'Here – we can wedge it here,' I said as we positioned the ladder outside the bank's front door and began to extend it towards the roof. When we were done, I was first to monkey up to check out the lie of the land. John had been right about the parapet roof. There was a flat space around a foot and a half deep where we could perch. It wasn't a lot, but it was enough. Now all we needed was the water. Dodger joined me and we dragged the empty lengths of the 70 mm hose up the outside of the building, tied off the hauling line so it would take the weight of the hose once it was full of water, then got ready to work. We kicked our heels into the ice and snow on the roof to give us some purchase. This wouldn't be the time or the place to stumble or fall. Then we gave the command. 'Water on!' Within moments the hose came alive. It pulsed and filled with water and gave us power. We directed the stream in a wide arc over the road and into the broken heart of Talbot Chambers.

It was clear straight away that this was going to be one of those fires where you don't get the satisfaction of seeing your efforts make a difference. We were sending hundreds of gallons of water a minute into that fire. It didn't feel that way. The stream simply disappeared into the thick black smoke that was mushrooming up into the sky. We aimed the water at the very centre of the building for a while, then we spread the stream out towards the edges before moving it back to the middle. The smoke didn't let up for a single moment. The building was starting to implode and the fire still had enough strength to shrug us all off. It could swat us away almost as if it was swatting away a fly.

Down below we watched the Emergency Tender arrive and drop off the tea urn for the retained crews. 'Lucky sods,' was all we said. Our first long, frozen hour passed. The smoke continued to billow out of the building into the cold, cloudless sky. Shrewsbury was built to be defended. It sits atop a hill about one hundred feet above the curves of the River Severn. People must have seen this smoke from halfway across the county. They must have thought their beautiful, precious county town was under attack.

'Keep moving, Malcolm. If you stand still, your boot freezes to the roof. Try it,' Dodger said at one point as we tried to pass the time. He was right. We were standing on a good inch of ice and it really was possible to get frozen to the spot. It was blinkin' painful as well. Our boots had metal plates in them. The idea was that they'd protect us from getting rusty nails through our feet in house fires or other dangerous incidents. Standing on freezing metal wasn't much fun, however. 'These boots conduct the heat when we walk on fire embers and they conduct the cold when we're up here on the ice. They're a nightmare. We'd be better off in our bedroom slippers,' Dodger decided as we shuffled from foot to foot to try and relieve the pain.

Ahead of us we watched as the guys on the turntable ladder changed the direction of their stream of water. Instead of directing it to the closest point of the building, they aimed it at the far wall. They changed the bore of the branch as well so as to make a fine spray – and that was all it took for the water to turn briefly to snow. With a mischievous look at each other, Dodger and I redirected our hose for a few seconds to produce the same snow shower.

'It looks like a Christmas card. But it's not good. If this gets any colder we're going to be in real trouble,' I said when we got serious again. All the science and invention in the world couldn't alter the fact that water was our primary tool in a big fire. John had made the point at the start: if a hose froze solid and got taken out of commission, we would be well and truly snookered. The good news was that all our hoses were connected to nearby hydrants so they were drawing water into our pumps, straight off the mains. Underground, and flowing fast, it should stay running. But other parts of our operation were more vulnerable. The water in the tanks in our unused engines was still, for example, and it wasn't lagged against the cold. It wouldn't be useable for long. Any water standing still in dormant pumps would be just as much of a problem.

Down below they were clearly thinking exactly the same thing. Caddie had acquired a blowtorch from a nearby house and was running it along the locking devices on either side of the extended turntable ladders to prevent them from freezing solid. Up in our frozen eyrie, our hand-held radio came to life as we watched the activity on the ground. It was John.

'Windsor, I'm swapping you over with George. Get down here right away.' I headed down the ladder to where John was waiting for me. 'The water in the pump of that appliance has frozen,' he said, pointing towards the end of a line of fire appliances. 'I want you to take it back to the station. Get it into the workshop, get the space heater on the pump and thaw it out. Then get back here as fast as you can and take the next engine. We're going to have to do this like a relay for as long as it takes.'

Our workshop manager, Archie, was there when I arrived with the first appliance. He had a cigar in his mouth, the way he always did. He helped with the heater while I filled him in with the news from the fire. When we'd thawed it out I headed back into town and on towards Talbot Chambers. Driving wasn't that easy. With so many roads closed, traffic was backed up all over. Several of the roads that were open were icing up fast. I switched appliances and headed back to the station to do a second warming job. The moment I parked up in the workshop Mabel rushed across the yard for a word.

'Mabel, you'll freeze, you shouldn't be out here in this,' I said.

'I'm perfectly fine. I just wanted you to tell the others that Betty and I have got lunch in hand. We guessed you didn't have time to get your mess money to Pete and do a supermarket run before heading out this morning, so we've been across to Mr Thom's and we've bought a few things. He says we can sort out the money another time.'

'Mabel, you're a superstar. I'd forgotten it was mess day. I'd forgotten about lunch altogether.'

'Well, you'll remember soon enough when you get hungry. It won't be a fancy meal. There wasn't much to choose from, to be honest. Horrible frozen food, all pre-prepared, covered in cardboard and plastic and nothing remotely fresh. But we'll cook it up all the same. We'll plate it up and put it in a hot box for you. Just tell everyone that you've not been forgotten.'

I passed the message on to John and Pete when I got back to town. Even as we stood in the street talking it was clear that the temperature had dropped still further. The wind had picked up. It was now bone-shatteringly cold. But the fire continued to burn. Smoke was rolling out of the roof in huge black clouds. And despite our best efforts we'd lost one of our weapons. A length of hose had been left, full of water, on the ground while the crew got ready to move it across to the far side of the building. By the time they got back to lift it, the water had frozen. That hose was now like a solid, concrete snake. And about as useful.

'How's it been?' I asked Pete.

'Boring as anything, to be honest,' he said. I looked around and I could see what he meant. After the excitement of turning up and seeing all the action, we had long since passed the point where there was any urgency or real excitement in the situation. It was going to be a long, hard slog from now on. A long, hard and very cold slog.

'A few more beams have fallen inside the building, by the sound of it,' Pete continued. 'Apart from that, it's nothing but a waiting game.'

'We just have to keep piling on the pressure,' said John. 'You go and relieve Dodger up on the roof. Tell him to join Caddie and the others over on Market Street.'

I climbed the ladder and tried to see through the smoke and work out if anything had changed. Every now and then, as the wind blew a clearing in the smoke clouds ahead of us, I could see a gaping hole in the roof. There were no visible flames. But we kept on aiming the water at the roof, regardless.

One more long, cold and boring hour passed before I saw our Emergency Tender come back down the street towards us. The cavalry, I thought. With lunch. A couple of the guys stepped out of the cab to talk to John. Over the next hour or so we all got the call in turn. A handful of men at a time got a ten-minute break from the cold to sit in the warm cab and wolf down our grub. It wasn't half bad. Mabel and Betty had made us fish and chips with peas and sweetcorn, followed by a thick slice of apple pie. They and the Thoms had thrown in cans of Coke and a few packets of chocolate biscuits for good measure.

Other crews came and went throughout the afternoon. It got dark at around five o'clock, and while we'd seen a lot of progress the job wasn't over. Soon after six p.m. we were stood down when Green Watch turned up in the minivan.

'You were right, it was a long day,' I said as the driver and I swapped keys again. Then I drove my crew back to the station. We'd find out the next day that Green Watch had stayed for another five freezing hours.

For us, it was one of the rare nights that a fair few of us hung around the station in our off-duty hours. Mostly we rushed home like greyhounds out of traps at knocking-off time. That night the warmth of the bar was too tempting. Even in the cold you sweat a lot, lugging ladders and hoses around, so it felt good to have a pint or two to replenish fluids. Plus, of course, we wanted to talk about what we'd all done and compete over who had been the coldest, the wettest, the most useful, the most heroic or the best in any other category we could imagine.

The following morning the conversations carried on as if they'd never stopped. The fire had been on the news and we were waiting for the local paper to come in to see if any of us were famous. Better still, seeing as we'd lugged the 13.5 metre ladder around on a genuine shout, we were told to take a break when we would normally have been using it in our drills. We had an extra hour of volleyball instead. At one p.m., hungry as anything, we thundered up the steps to the mess room.

'After feeding you horrible frozen food yesterday we thought we should put on a better show today,' Betty said as I grabbed my plate from the hatch.

They'd certainly pulled out all the stops. Everyone had different favourites, but today's would have been close to the top of most of our lists. We devoured a huge beef pie with a crust as thick as your arm. Then we practically fought over bowls of rice pudding and strawberry jam Betty had brought in from home.

'Mabel, Betty, come out here. You've done us proud!' Charlie yelled when we were finally done.

But neither Mabel nor Betty appeared.

'Have you got lost? Come and take a bow!' Charlie urged.

The pair remained firmly behind the hatch.

'Anything wrong back there? Cat got your tongues? Fallen down a well? Do you need a hand?' Caddie asked after a few more seconds.

Still nothing. We sat there like lemons, unsure what was

happening until John stood up at the head of the table. He banged a spoon against his water glass to ensure everyone was paying attention. All of us were. He wasn't looking very happy. My first thought was that someone must have died. When he spoke, I had a horrible feeling that I might be right.

'Gentlemen,' he said, 'I've got some very sad news.'

19

'**D**on't worry, no one's being made redundant and it's nothing to do with Talbot Chambers or the work we did there yesterday,' John said. A ripple of relief went round the mess table as John paused and looked at the floor.

'He must be resigning. Oh, no, that would be good news,' Charlie whispered next to me. John silenced him with a glare.

'I'll keep this short. The sad news is that Mabel has decided to leave us in the middle of next month. She's been making her marvellous meals, watching our table manners and keeping us all in line for more years than it would be polite to count. She's decided she deserves a break and nothing Betty or I could say to her this morning would change her mind.'

All eyes shot towards the hatch to the kitchen. Mabel had finally appeared. She was standing there, staring at the floor and looking uncharacteristically glum.

'Come round and join us in here, Mabel,' said John.

She did so. She'd dressed up for the occasion, I noticed. Instead of her usual dark blue skirt and high-necked blouse she was wearing a smart olive-green dress. She had also taken off her apron. Mabel never took off her apron. That alone seemed to make this moment special.

'So none of us can change your mind either?' Arfer asked. 'We can't beg you to stay? Can we persuade John to prise open his wallet for a change and pay you double? I reckon Pete's been fiddling the mess money for years now. Can't he cough up and buy you a car?'

'The doctors say I need to start taking it easy. It's the cold, you know. I made my mind up a while ago. But these last few weeks of freezing weather have been too much for me. Yesterday and today have been quite horrible. I get the bus in, you know. Betty drives me home, but I make my own way in every morning. I can't keep on. I'm no spring chicken any more.'

She and Betty took the chairs John pulled over for them at the mess-room table. A group of us headed into the kitchen to do the clearing up while they chatted to the others. There was a lot of laughter, but Mabel couldn't fully hide her sadness. We headed over to the comfy chairs by the telly and she and Betty got into a long conversation about all the different firemen who'd worked in our station and all the changes that had happened over the years. Most of the time the conversation was full of laughs, but every now and then Mabel's face would crack.

'You do know that my leaving has nothing to do with the chip-pan fire I had last year, mind you,' she said several times. 'That could have happened to someone half my age. I could have done that when I was twenty. That had nothing to do with my age. That was because old Mrs Hawthorne won't stop talking when she comes round. It wasn't my fault. You agreed it wasn't my fault.'

We had agreed, many times. Six months on and it was clear that Mabel was still very sensitive about it.

'No one else will ever make liver and bacon quite like you do,' Woody said at one point to bring her good mood back.

'No one else will make quite as much of anything either,' Charlie said. 'If we get some penny pincher in to replace you, we'll all starve. I'm wasting away just thinking about it.'

The conversation moved back to the olden days. I stayed apart from it for a while, sitting back and listening. I couldn't believe how uncharacteristically emotional it was getting up in our mess room. If we don't all calm down soon, someone's going to start to cry, I thought. And it might not be Mabel.

As usual we were saved by the bell. We didn't get an urgent

call-out to a fire that would have transformed us instantly from girls' blouses into fire-fighting heroes. But we got the next best thing. Somewhere, out there in the frozen Shropshire country-side, a dog was in trouble. Yelling some macho 'see you laters' to Mabel and Betty, we headed off to rescue it.

'You ready for this, Windsor? It's tough out there. It's going to be the hardest drive you've done so far. You sure you're up for it?'

I didn't even reply to John's question. A tough drive? Whatever it was, I was up for it. I swung myself into the driver's seat. Joe was at my side. Caddie, Arfer and Ben were in the back. We were a good gang. I wasn't going to let anyone down. Plus, of course, I wanted to help the dog. I like dogs. And it was blinkin' cold out there!

We crunched over the dirty snow on the roads round the station and I squeezed us through the sporadic afternoon traf-fic. No surprise that the further from town we got, the worse the conditions became – and the faster they changed. Light snow became heavy – and it looked to have been falling for quite a while. I snatched a quick look at some of the side roads we passed as we headed south towards Condover. Pretty soon they'd be impassable. A couple of years ago, in my first winter on the watch, we'd had a call to a farm fire in conditions like this. We'd made it off the main road, got halfway up a narrow lane then ground to a halt in a massive drift. Four of us had to carry every piece of equipment we thought we'd need on to the farmer's tractor on the other side of the drift. When we got there all the grumpy farmer had done was moan about how long we'd taken to reach him.

I wasn't taking any risks with my driving that freezing late January afternoon. We gained altitude as we drove through Berriewood. After a few more miles the weather changed yet again. The skies were clearer on the higher ground but the con-ditions were no less treacherous. My big problem was that up there the snow had been replaced by something far more dangerous: ice.

'Take it easy,' Joe murmured as the roads got narrower and the margin for error became increasingly small. 'If this thing starts to slide there'll be no stopping it. It's a sixteen-ton weapon. It'll take anything out in its way and there's no knowing where it'll end up.'

Joe wasn't wrong. Driving the engine was hard enough in these conditions. Stopping it when we got to our destination would be even worse. The long, straight lane we were driving along was like an ice rink. At some point over the past few days water must have coursed across the road from the swollen river alongside it. Now it was a potentially lethal mass of solid sheet ice.

'Think it through, Malcolm,' I told myself as I looked ahead and sized up the problem. Over the years I'd heard enough stories about fire engines heading to road traffic accidents and crashing into the cars they were aiming to help. Legend had it that one driver over in Cumbria had shunted a police car when he overshot his arrival in bad weather. The police car had then ended up bashing into the side of an ambulance. The story was that, until the fire engine arrived, the two crash victims had only needed a cup of tea for the shock. After falling off the bed in the back of the ambulance when the police car hit it, they had both needed stitches.

I kept my eyes firmly on the road. I certainly didn't want to end up in a hedge, a field or, worse, the river. Fortunately, I was already driving slowly when the black ice got even more treacherous. 'Just touch the brake like a feather. Let the gears help you. Get ready to steer out of it,' I said under my breath. I inched forward then came to a stop almost in the middle of the road, right by the man we'd been sent to help. I'd originally been aiming for a lay-by further ahead, but I decided to stay where I was. I couldn't imagine many other cars would be coming by in the next half-hour or so. If they did, the hedges were so low and the road so exposed that they'd be able to see us a mile off.

'Hello, sir,' Joe said to the smartly dressed elderly man who had been waiting for us on the grass verge. He looked to be wearing a shirt and tie under his thick woollen overcoat. He had a deerstalker hat on his head and was twisting his hands together in brown leather gloves. His face was craggy but clean-shaven. His eyes were red. Red and desperately worried.

'Hello, officer, thank you so very much for coming,' the man replied as Joe opened his door, stepped off the fire engine – and fell straight on to his arse.

None of us could stop ourselves from laughing. Ben, I think, was probably laughing the loudest as he climbed down in Joe's wake. He too landed on his arse. I don't think I've ever laughed as much. Mainly because I'd probably get to stay toasty and warm in my nice safe cab for the duration of the shout. The driver's job wasn't so bad after all, I thought as I settled back to watch the action.

'Your dog's in trouble? What's the problem?' Joe asked, holding on to the running board to keep himself upright and trying to pretend nothing had happened.

'Yes, it's Lady, just over there,' said the elderly gentleman from the relative safety of the frozen grass verge. He turned and pointed. 'It's hard to see it with all the snow and ice, but there's a pond there. The flood's made it much, much bigger. Lady must have walked on to it without realising what she was doing. Her feet must have been frozen. She wouldn't have known she was on the ice till it was too late.'

'And she won't come back to you?'

'She's half deaf. She can barely hear me. She's a bit short-sighted as well. I'm not sure if she can see us from so far away. She'll be so scared. She's such a good dog. She'd never want to cause this much trouble. I tried to get to her myself. I got nearly halfway there, but I could hear the ice cracking underneath me.

I was worried because I didn't know how deep the water might be. The flood means I couldn't tell where the old bank used to be. The ice cracked again and I'm ashamed to say I got really concerned. When Lady wouldn't come towards me I had to creep back to solid ground. A car went by down there on the main road and I managed to flag them down. They said they'd call you from the first house they got to. Ever since they left I've been trying to coax Lady back to me, but she won't move. I'm worried she might be injured. I don't know what to do any more.'

The old guy looked close to tears after his monologue. His dog looked a sorry sight as well. She was a hefty-looking golden retriever with a shaggy, long coat, stuck some forty yards away from us in the middle of a wide expanse of ice. Looking through the open window of the cab it was hard to tell if she was lying down on the ice or simply crouching, cowering low upon it. Either way, she must have been freezing. Even over the noise of the engine I could hear a cross between a whimper and a howl when the cold wind blew in our direction.

'It's been over an hour,' her owner said, reading my mind and answering my question.

'Then let's get her back,' said Joe.

Caddie stepped gingerly out across the road and on to the grass verge. He had a chat with Joe, and I watched him do a walk-round of the field, adding his usual 'couple of coats of looking at' to the problem. Then he rejoined the dog owner. 'Does Lady have a favourite toy or ball?' he asked.

'Yes, I've got her ball right here.'

Caddie took hold of it. 'Are you OK if I try something out, boss?' he asked Joe.

'Be my guest.'

'Ben and Woody – take the owner and stand right over there by that patch of reeds. Make sure you're positioned right in front of the dog so she can see you. I'll be going round the other side of the water. I'll throw the ball from there. I'll throw it right past the dog's nose. She'll start to chase it, and as soon as she does she'll look up and see her owner and all of you as well. She'll carry on running right towards you till she's safely on the bank. Trust me, it can't fail.'

Famous last words. The initial plan did fail, though not through any fault in Caddie's aim. I had a perfect, ringside view from the height of the cab. When everyone was in position I watched him stand back, survey the scene one last time, test his arm then throw the ball right in front of Lady's frozen nose. It had perfect pace and near military accuracy. Lady ignored it completely.

'Right,' Caddie called out from his side of the pond as Ben picked up the ball. 'Let's try that again.'

Ben lobbed the ball back over to Caddie. Caddie measured out the scene in his mind again and threw it past Lady's nose. This time it went closer than ever. I swear it couldn't have been more than a matter of inches in front of her. Once again there was no reaction. 'She's a bit short-sighted, did you say?' came Caddie's incredulous call from the other side of the pond. 'Like Hitler was a little bit bad? She's blind as a bat, isn't she?'

'She doesn't see as well as she did. She's nearly twelve,' Lady's owner admitted weakly.

'Well, let's try it one more time before we think of something else. Ben, throw me the damn ball.'

Ben did so. He sent it in an arc, high over the centre of the pond. In this gloomy afternoon the ball must have gone twenty feet in the air at its highest point. But this time Lady saw it. She gave an excited yelp. She staggered up on her old legs as quickly as she could. Her head twisted around as she followed the ball's progression. Then, leaping almost like a puppy, she set off to chase it. Her legs skidded and slipped on the ice like Bambi. But there was no stopping Lady this time. She fell twice, each time picking herself up to carry on careering over the last few yards of the pond. Finally she jumped on to the ice-hard dry land and ended up in a furry heap at Caddie's feet. 'You crazy old fool!' he shouted, bending down, giving her the ball and wrapping his arms around her.

She was happily licking his face as he led her round the edge of the pond towards her owner. Caddie deposited the dog at her delighted owner's feet. She certainly recognised him. The whimpering we'd heard when she was on the ice was replaced by half-human moans and groans – moans and groans of sheer happiness as she was reunited with her master. Lady's tail was wagging so hard she could have taken off. She ran round and round her owner's legs, pushing and nuzzling up against him. He was on his knees to pet her and for about five minutes the pair of them seemed almost fused as one. 'Thank you,' he kept saying. 'Thank you so much. I know you'd rather be fighting fires, but thank you. Just thank you for this.'

We looked away discreetly as the old codger wiped tears from his eyes.

'Where do you live? Can we give you a lift home?' Joe asked when the moment seemed right. The man shook his head.

'Thank you so much, but I need to walk her home,' he said, putting Lady on the lead and tucking her tennis ball safely in his pocket. 'If I put her in the fire engine she'll think she's going to the vet's, the poor, dear thing. She's had a bad enough day without thinking that.' He thanked us yet again and gave a cheery wave as he skirted the frozen pond and the pair headed back across the fields.

I left my perch on the running board and climbed back into the driver's seat as the others took the last few steps back towards the engine.

'Good trip? Go anywhere nice?' Caddie called out as Ben did yet another slip on the ice and began to swear loudly and imaginatively at all and sundry. I didn't laugh quite as loud as the others as they climbed up into the engine. After all, their challenge ended when they got back into their seats. Mine was only just beginning. I had to get us out of there.

'This might take a bit of time,' I said as I checked the mirrors and released the brakes.

'Take as long as you need. I could use the overtime,' Caddie said. I had a feeling we might all get it. I started off with as few revs as possible. There was nothing doing. The wheels didn't grip for a single moment.

'I suppose the ground is too solid to dig out any soil?' I asked after a few more equally unsuccessful tries. If we got trapped in ice or mud we often dug up grass verges or took a few shovelfuls out of someone's front garden to put something solid under and in front of our tyres.

'It's as hard as an effing rock. We'll have to try the bags and hope for the best,' Ben said. He got some empty hessian sand-bags from one of the lockers and laid them out in front of the wheels. If I could move the engine as much as a couple of inches they'd be dragged under our tyres and hopefully give us the friction we needed to get moving. If that failed, we could try getting the Tirfor winch out of the front nearside locker. Its maximum horizontal pull was only five tons, but with luck that could still do the trick. Fortunately, we didn't need it. My next low rev attempt rocked us towards the hessian bags. Inch by inch, try by try I got us enough traction to move off the ice rink. There was an inch or so of fresh snow on the rest of the lane, but that wasn't going to cause us any problems. Ten minutes later I gave a massive sigh of relief as we got on to the wider, clearer Much Wenlock road. We were well on our way back to civilisation.

'If you don't like the weather, just wait a minute,' Joe muttered as we drove through Cross Houses. We'd had clear skies and ice when we'd been at the rescue. Then there had been sleet as we dipped through Cressage. Now we were passing through our third climate zone in as many miles – a sudden flurry of heavy snowflakes.

'There's no other traffic around. Put the blue lights on for a moment, Windsor,' Caddie called from the back seat. I did it, just for a few moments. It produced a little bit of magic. All the thick, white, snowflakes were instantly bathed in blue. They seemed to crowd in on the cab. We were surrounded by them, encased in them. They were mesmerising, strangely beautiful and utterly captivating. I smiled, yelled, 'Show's over', clicked off the lights then took us back to base.

'Windsor, you want some good news?' John asked when I'd got us there.

'I always want good news. What is it?'

'How do you feel about riding the Emergency Tender?'

I was over the moon, of course. The Emergency Tender was the two-man vehicle that went to road-traffic accidents and the like. We covered roughly 1,500 square miles of rural Shropshire. If we got a shout with a retained crew, they could take a while to get to their stations and then on the road, so the ET would normally be first on the scene. So before you got allocated an ET job the boss had to be sure that you could drive it – and that you could handle yourself properly when you arrived. You wouldn't get on an Emergency Tender if the boss didn't think you had the experience or the wherewithal to cope. 'You can't blend into the background when there's just the two of you on the ET,' we had been told from training school onwards. That's why being offered the chance to be part of the crew left me walking ten feet tall for the rest of the day. It was unspoken feedback that I was doing OK, a vote of confidence in my ability. I remember Alice laughing when I told her that. At university, tutors gave their students feedback every step of the way. She thought it was hilarious that things were done so differently in my world.

'So no one would think to say well done if you did a particularly difficult drive one day?' she would ask.

'Not really, no.'

'And you'd not think to say well done if anyone else did a good drive?'

'No, not really.'

'And if someone messed up?'

'It would be hilarious. We'd never let them forget it. We'd laugh about it for years.'

'And you don't think that's odd?'

'No, not really. It's the Fire Brigade.'

20

A month later, when the time came for Mabel's last lunch at the station, everyone made an effort to be on time, smartly dressed and ready for a great meal and a pleasant afternoon. What we didn't want was to turn up horribly late, soaking wet and smelling of, well, birdshit.

Each of the watches was doing something different as a good-bye bash. We'd had a whip round and bought her a watercolour of Shrewsbury. The Chief Fire Officer had got a bunch of flowers to hand over as well. It was sitting in a fire bucket in the appliance room when the call came in.

As usual we only got the bare bones of information in the original call. Two animals were fighting at a golf club out towards Whitchurch. 'Animals? I think we need a bit more detail than that,' John said as we got ready to mobilise and head out the door. 'My mate runs the bar there. Let me give him a ring and find out more.' He disappeared into his office. When he came back he had a big, wide smile on his face. I think we all knew straight away that this was very bad news. 'Five men on the first appliance should be more than enough, so I shall leave you five to it and remain here,' he said, pointing to my squad.

'So what have you found out?' asked Arfer.

'Oh, didn't I say?' John's smile was broader and even more ominous. 'The animals are swans. They're fighting in the middle of a very large pond. A vet has been called, but he was in the middle of an operation so he's been delayed. Best of all, though, Mad Pam is waiting for you at the scene. Good luck, gentlemen. I fear you may be needing it.'

We spent a riotous journey talking about fictional fights between a variety of animals. Spring had certainly sprung and the fields of Shropshire were beginning to be touched by the softest of greens. It had been raining solidly for days so the earth was rich and dark. When the clouds had finally cleared that morning, the sky was the pale blue of duck eggs. Pete pulled his window down and there was a hint of warmth on the wind. Everything smelled moist, mossy and fresh. Nature was coming alive across the county. Growth and birth were in the air. This, rather than the start of January, felt like the real New Year. Life felt optimistic, exciting and full of promise.

'Mad Pam and a pair of fighting swans. What exactly have we done to deserve this?' Arfer asked.

'Well, you cut the legs off Dodger's trousers on the night shift last week. Left him pulling on a pair of shorts when he got up for breakfast.'

'Oh, he thought it was funny. In the end. And every newbie has to get their trousers cut at least once. It was long overdue.'

'I still reckon it means you're the one who holds Mad Pam by the hand while we sort out the swans. It's the least you can do.'

'Sitting in the nice warm cab is the least I can do. I think dear Pamela deserves the attention of our younger firemen. Windsor – you get a choice. Mad Pam or mad swan.'

'Mad swan.'

'Woody?'

'Mad swan.'

'Well, Pete, that leaves you to look after the dear lady. And we're almost there. No sniggering, anyone. Golf clubs are serious places. The CFO is probably a member. And besides' – he looked at his watch – 'we do want to be back in time for Mabel's lunch. Whatever it is that's going on here, let's try and sort it out as quick as we can.'

The gravel drive of the club ended outside a relatively modern and modest-looking clubhouse. The car park was bumper to bumper Rovers and Jags and we took the last available space, right alongside a canary yellow Renault. I had no idea, but I'd have bet my house on it belonging to Pam.

The club manager greeted us in the car park. 'It's this way, gentlemen,' he said. 'The members and I are very grateful to you for coming out here this morning. It may sound trivial, but it has been a very distressing few hours while we waited for the vet and then called yourselves for help. You will soon see why.' He led us round the side of the clubhouse – the big double doors at the front were clearly off-limits to the likes of us. Having edged past the dustbins and an old cold store, we went through a second garden gate and arrived on the club's lawn. The grass was lush and green in the spring air. A few sets of wooden chairs and tables were scattered around, most of them offering good views of the big, oval pond. 'It's not a pretty sight,' the manager said quietly. It wasn't. Two huge swans were lying low in the reed-beds a dozen or so feet from the edge. Clumps of white feathers were floating on the water and stuck in the reeds all around them. To be precise, clumps of mostly white feathers. Whatever the swans had been doing they'd drawn a lot of blood. Dark red, almost purple streaks covered most of their bodies. As we got closer you could see patches of flesh, like a raw chicken, where beakfuls of feathers had been plucked away.

Pam was standing at the water's edge. She was wrapped in a multicoloured, check cloak and her hair was tucked under a bright green bobble hat. In her hands she had a four-foot fishing net.

'I'm so glad you are here. Not a moment too soon. Thank you, thank you,' she said, gazing at us and correctly identifying Joe as our officer in charge. 'It's very hard to work out precisely what's been going on. They're quiet now, as you can see. But every few minutes something happens.'

It did, just as she spoke. The swans came together and feathers flew in a flurry of sweeping wings, pecking beaks and loud, strangulated cries.

'One of them seems to have some sort of a weapon,' said Pam.

'A weapon?'

'It does sound odd, I admit. But the blood must be coming from somewhere.'

'I think actually it's a fishing line from somewhere that's the problem,' the club manager interrupted. 'If you look closely you might be able to see it. I think they've got tangled up in it. That's why they won't fully separate and why they can't fly away. I think their wings are damaged as well. The wing on the one that's closest to us, its right-hand wing, it's broken, I'm sure. They're both in a bad way.'

Squinting across the pond we tried to see the fishing wire but failed, not least because the swans were still kicking up a storm in the water and bashing merry hell out of each other. It was time for us to act.

'How deep is the pond? Any hazards in there?' Joe asked the manager.

'Two feet deep, not much more. And I don't think any of my members would throw a Tesco trolley in there.'

'Windsor, you and Woody volunteered for this. I suggest we cut the fishing line if it's there. Then we'll use a couple of tarpaulins to cover the birds up, separate them and bring them to shore.'

We headed back to the engine to collect our kit. Arfer, who'd come along for a quick look, was smirking away.

'A weapon. A swan with a backin' weapon. What does she think – it's got an AK-47 under its wing? It bought a knuckleduster off of some other low-life swan down the pub? Mad as a box of frogs, bless her. But rather you than me, separating those two. Are you absolutely sure they're fighting, by the way? You get in the middle if they're mating and I'll laugh my head off.

I know you like animals, Windsor, but there's laws against that sort of thing.'

Woody and I ignored him and started talking about the old urban myth that a swan can break your arm. 'How does that actually happen?' Woody asked, looking worried. 'Does it nut you? Is it a head butt? It whacks you in the arm with its beak or something?'

'It's the wings, not the beak that breaks your bones, you backin' idiot,' roared Arfer. 'There's a hell of a lot of power when a swan flaps its wings. If it catches you, it'll break your leg, not just your arm.'

'Terrific,' we both said, heading back to the pond.

'Do take care of them. Please don't scare the poor little mites,' Pam said as we stepped into the water. Two feet deep, my eye. Our boots sank way down into the mud and the water was up to my thigh straight away. The pond, presumably very beautiful from the safety of the clubhouse, stank to high heaven. The more mud, water and reeds we disturbed as we waded towards the birds, the more awful the stench became. Worse still, it wasn't only feathers on the surface of the water.

'They've crapped all over the place. This is disgusting. I didn't sign up for this,' Woody moaned.

'Well, I don't think we can catch them anyway. Not while they're like this.'

The swans had been calm when we first got in the water. Now they had reared up and were flapping their wings and squawking like crazy. Our plan had been to rugby tackle them with the tarpaulins when they were still. We could damage their wings even more if we tried to do it while they were in action.

'You're going to have to wait till they settle. Can you see what they're caught up in?' Pete yelled from the grass.

We could. 'It is a fishing line. Really thick stuff. There's a lot of it.' We moved in as close as we could and began to snip away at the line. It was impossible to be sure if we'd done enough, but the swans did seem to be able to pull further away from each other, which was a start. I cut a couple more strands then I spotted something. The line itself wasn't the only thing cutting into the swans' flesh. 'There's a hook, a fishing hook, on the end there,' I said.

Woody looked across. 'Blow me if Mad Pam wasn't right,' he said in a low voice. 'The swan has got a weapon. Who'd have thought?'

We stayed low in the water in the hope that the animals might get used to our presence and calm down. It wasn't much fun. A couple of cold, smelly minutes later we had our moment. Or we did, until Pam yelled, 'The vet is here!' from the bank and set them off all over again.

Five more minutes passed. The swan closest to me was first to settle down and tuck its wings into its sides. It drifted towards me, so I guessed it was no longer connected to its buddy. I couldn't tell which way it was looking, but I took a chance that it wasn't at me and I went for it. Lunging at the swan, I managed to wrap both arms round it and began to lift it out of the water. There was no resistance from the fishing line so we must have cut it. But there was one other slight problem to deal with. Swans, I found out, have particularly flexible necks. This one was whipping around in all directions. I wasn't sure if Woody hadn't been right about the beak breaking your arm after all. This one looked capable of cracking a skull.

'I've got it, Windsor!' Woody yelled. He'd left his swan alone and grabbed the neck of mine. He looked like he was trying to wring it. 'Let's get it on to the side.' We bundled it the few feet towards the grass and deposited it at Pam and the vet's feet. No surprise that the second swan was going wild by this time. It was flapping its broken wings like it was possessed. We went for it anyway. We didn't so much grab it as push it bodily towards the edge of the pond. We got our heads down, tucked our shoulders underneath the wings and drove it through the reedbed to the shore.

The vet opened up his box of tricks and set to work injecting and patching up the first of the swans as Pam held the other one down and cluttered and clucked away at as if it was a giant, fluffy house-pet. The club manager offered us a hot drink, but Joe said we were needed back at the station so we had to leave. 'Windsor, Woody, I've got two words for the pair of you,' he said as we got ready to board the appliance.

'Thank you?' suggested Woody.

'Good job?' I offered.

'No,' said Joe. 'You stink.'

John was waiting for us in the appliance room when we got back from the job. He'd heard from his friend at the golf club so he knew what we'd done. But he didn't look particularly impressed. 'This is Mabel's big day. All of you are late. And the least you two can do is shower.'

I looked over at Woody. Showering in the station was never a great idea.

'I don't want everyone turning the all hot taps on when I'm in there. It was freezing enough in the pond. And I don't want some joke call-out coming over the tannoy either. Is that a deal?'

'Maybe it is,' Joe said. 'Maybe it's not.'

Fortunately we managed to get cleaned up unscathed and took the stairs two at a time to join the rest of the crew in the mess room. The others had all eaten, but Mabel had kept our plates warm and piled them up with food. 'Sorry we're late. We had a fight with a couple of swans,' I said.

'I'm just glad you're here. And you barely smell at all,' Mabel said, to hoots of laughter from all the others.

John stood up, made a speech and handed over the painting and the flowers while we ate. Mabel, dressed in her Sunday-best green dress again, accepted them to a round of applause but said she'd burst into tears if she said anything herself. We were still yelling 'speech, speech' when the first of her guests arrived and everyone got a bit distracted. Betty was there, of course, and Maggie, who was the new assistant cook, had come along as well to say goodbye to her predecessor. The Thoms had turned up and given Mabel a matching scarf and gloves, and then a group of Fire Brigade old-timers arrived. Most of them had left the watch long before I'd joined – or before I'd been born, judging by the look of some of them. 'Look at those old guys. Can you imagine working alongside them?' Dodger whispered to me as we looked across the room at a pair of real classics. They were the generation of firemen that used to be called smoke-eaters. Back in the day they had grown long, thick beards – and when they strode into bad fires they stuffed the beards into their mouths to protect themselves from the smoke. It didn't work, of course. It was one of the most stupid theories you could think of. But the smoke-eaters had stuck with it. They'd held out against a lot of other things as well. I remembered Caddie telling me about the trouble they'd had on the watch when the first face masks and breathing apparatus sets were introduced. The smoke-eaters had refused to use them. They were far too hard, too macho for gimmicks like that. They'd stick with their beards, thank you very much. No wonder they all looked so rough today.

'How old do you reckon he is?' I whispered.

'A hundred and fifty. Maybe more. I think he might be a wizard.'

I opened the bar and the drinks began to flow.

'You know, you all need to enjoy that while you can,' one of the smoke-eaters bellowed as I pulled the first pints.

'What do you mean?'

'There's been talks in HQ in London about whether fire stations should have bars any more. There's talk of shutting them down. The job's going to go dry. That's what they're saying in the boardroom.'

A massive discussion began as a couple of dozen men faced up to the horror of night shifts without an open bar. I didn't say anything; I was too busy looking at the smoke-eater. How could someone who looked like Worzel Gummidge have any possible connection with Fire Brigade headquarters in London? He didn't look the type to know what a boardroom was, let alone be privy to what went on inside of one.

'You know there's something else you boys need to worry about,' Maggie shouted when there was a brief lull in the arguments.

'What's that, love? Your steak-and-kidney pudding?'

'No – women, that's what. My husband says there's supposed to be a woman signing up to the Fire Brigade in London this year. She won't be the last. We've got Maggie in Downing Street after all, and she's just won us a war. If women can do that, they can work in this place.'

'Over my dead body!' one of the Green Watch guys shouted out to a roar of laughter.

'That can be arranged when I start cooking for you tomorrow,' Maggie fired back, to even more laughs.

'A bit of a madhouse, this place,' Mabel said quietly to me. She was sitting on one of the stools on the opposite side of the bar. I couldn't tell from her face if she was happy or sad.

'Are you going to miss it?' I asked.

'I'll miss it every day. But I've made my decision now, so I'm going to stick to it. Maggie will be a breath of fresh air. She'll keep you all in line.'

'You'll have to come back and see us. Come and have lunch some days.'

'I'd like that. I might just do it. And you, Malcolm,' she looked right at me, her soft, blue eyes looking tired but clear. 'You should stop those silly hobbies of yours. I worry about you. I don't like to think of you throwing yourself off the top of a mountain or climbing some cliff edge. It's not natural. You want to go back to fishing. Caddie would like that too.' We both looked across the crowded, smoke-filled room. Caddie was in a deep conversation with a couple of the old-timers. He held his hands out in front of him to emphasise his latest point. It looked as if he might actually have been talking about fishing.

'Well, I have got one other hobby you might prefer,' I said, lowering my voice because I knew if anyone else heard they would take the piss for the next twenty years. 'I'm thinking of joining a drama group. I always liked putting on plays at school and one of Alice's friends has told me about a group she's part of.'

'You're going to be busy,' Mabel said. I thought about it. A full-time fireman, running a building business, going rock climbing and hang-gliding, seeing Alice, my family and all my mates. Yeah, I was busy. But I reckoned I could fit drama on to the list as well.

'You'll be starting riding the Emergency Tender as well, won't you, son?' Mabel asked.

'You really do hear everything that's going on, don't you?'

Mabel stood up. 'Malcolm, I think you'll be fine. But remember what I said about cliffs and hurling yourself off the top of mountains. It's not good for you. You'll end up having to get one of this lot to rescue you. And they won't let you forget that in a hurry.'

She walked across the room and sat and talked to almost all of us for a few moments at a time. I knocked back a drink and got involved in a long, complicated conversation about the pros and cons of fishing with Caddie and Dodger. Across the mess room I saw Mabel step towards John and have a few final words with him. He stood up and banged on the table to shut us all up for a while. Mabel wanted to say goodbye to her 'boys'. She got a round of applause, then made sure she had the last word as usual.

'I don't want any of you forgetting your manners when I'm

not here, I don't want you making any trouble for Maggie either. I'm only a few minutes away, remember. I'll be coming back to check you're all behaving.'

At which point two and a half dozen burly firemen stood up straight and said the only thing we could.

'Yes, Mabel!'